SHADOW
BOX

SHADOW BOX

GEORGE PLIMPTON

Lyons & Burford, Publishers

Printed in the United States of America

10 9 8 7 6 5 4 3 2 1

Portions of this book have previously
appeared in a different form in
Harper's, *Sports Illustrated*, and
The New York Review of Books

Library of Congress Cataloging-in-
Publication Data

Plimpton, George.
Shadow box : amateur in the ring /
George Plimpton.
p.   cm.
Reprint: Originally published: New York :
Putnam, c1977.
ISBN 1-55821-276-0
1. Boxing. 2. Plimpton, George.
I. Title.
GV1133.P56   1993
796.6'3—dc20
93-31710
CIP

ACKNOWLEDGEMENTS

It is odd to thank an index list, but since the publishers have included one, it is not inappropriate: those listed have all had a hand in my education, such as it is, in matters pugilistic. Particular gratitude should be expressed to Archie Moore, Muhammad Ali, Roger Donoghue, Angelo Dundee, Bundini Brown, and George Brown (from the boxing profession); to John L. Heinz, who was so helpful with the history of amateurs in the ring (Chapter 5); to Joanie Hitzig, for providing the information about Albert Payne Terhune in that same chapter; to Jim Jacobs, who helped with the photo section, and provided much of the material for it; to my literary friends who helped me through my boxing experience (especially Blair Fuller); to Edward T. Chase, Gail Hochman, and Frank Kurtz, of Putnam's; and to Fayette Hickox, of *The Paris Review*. I am especially grateful to those friends who contributed fantasies to Chapter 21.

To Pat Ryan

INTRODUCTION TO THE 1993 EDITION

I suppose one should not be predisposed in this matter, especially an author, but I am inordinately fond of *Shadow Box*—very likely because Muhammad Ali, the most colorful athlete of our times, dominates its pages. It was very hard to write about him without a book coming alive. After *Shadow Box* was published, Norman Mailer—I believe I must have written him for a blurb—asked me to have lunch with him. He wanted to discuss the book. He had many nice things to say about it, but he felt I had not put enough of myself in its pages. I remember saying that I wasn't much good at introspective, self-analytical prose—perhaps my New England background was to blame—and besides, the cast of characters was rich enough to carry everything along quite nicely.

The focal scene in *Shadow Box* is the great Ali-Foreman fight in Zaire, Africa. Norman was there. He wrote a fine book about it called *The Fight*, so anyone interested can see how he went about it. There is a lot of him in it.

Muhammad Ali quit the ring in 1981, far too late for his health, as everyone knows. I covered some of the later fights—exulting when he won, though sportswriters are not supposed to be as biased, and in despair when he lost. Three years after he retired, out in Los Angeles to cover the Olympics, I paid him a visit in his home there. I regretted it. He was a shadow of his former self—his voice slow and slurred, his step a shuffle. He was gracious, of course. He showed me some magic tricks—not only performing them but then explaining how they worked, very much against the magician's code! He said that his Muslim teachings didn't allow him to hoodwink anyone. All of this, though, was carried on at a pace I found despairing, remembering how quick of mind and body he had been in his great years.

After that visit I quit covering the fights for good, much less going to them for pleasure. Every time I saw Ali on television, usually sitting silently ringside at a championship bout, I was reminded that Oscar Wilde truly had it wrong: you don't kill the thing you love (which is what he said), but rather what you love kills you.

In early 1993 Ali turned up in New York to introduce a new line of clothes at Macy's. His photographer friend, Howard Bingham, came around to see me and to talk about old times. He said, "Hey, you ought to come down and see the champ this afternoon at the store. He'd like to see you."

I shook my head. "He wouldn't remember," I said. "It's been too long a time. He's forgotten."

"Oh no," Bingham said. "He'll remember. He called you 'Kennedy' 'cause he thought you looked like one."

I laughed and said that sometimes he called me 'the author.' He'd say 'put the author in the front seat of the car' and we'd drive off somewhere."

I had lunch with friends in midtown that day, and afterwards I changed my mind and dropped into Macy's . . . just for a glimpse. Outside, a thousand people by my estimate were waiting for him to come out of the store. The word had swept through the neighborhood that he was in the vicinity. Inside, the fashion show was over and Ali was leaving, which on such occasions is a lengthy process since he slowly moves through the crowds, signing autographs, passing out his picture and tracts promoting Islam. It's a wonder he ever gets out at all.

I stood at the outer edge of a ring of people, perhaps twenty deep, Ali in the middle, slowly working his way toward the exit. On the far side of the crowd I spotted Bingham, cameras dangling from his neck. He grinned and waved.

Just then, Ali caught sight of me and began pushing through the crowd. At first, I thought he was heading for someone else, but then a few feet away he put out his arms and pulled me to him. He whispered in my ear, "Hey, hey, Kennedy." I was enormously touched; indeed, I am not ashamed to say my eyes filled with tears.

So that's that. I suspect that Bingham told him I was coming and prepared him, reminding him of the old days. No matter. It was a memorable moment. And then there's always *Shadow Box* on hand to refresh my mind on how vital and rare he was . . .

—George Plimpton
August, 1993

He was not born in the woods to be scared by an owl.

never understood boxing. When I was a boy, I think if my family had pointed out a famous prizefighter in the same restaurant, I would have stared at him, but out of curiosity, not admiration. Certainly I never liked the art itself. At school, once a month, we were required to box down in the gym—paired off, with enormous gloves tied to our pipestem arms. When the master blew his whistle, we strained and lifted up these monstrous pillows to push and flail them at each other. It was the worst time of the month. Sometimes you could make an arrangement with your opponent. "Let's pretend," you could whisper nervously, and if he nodded wide-eyed at the temerity of the suggestion, you could have a reasonably good time. You could throw a tremendous stiff-armed haymaker, miss and fall down on the wood floor. But there were always many in the class—just about everyone, it occurs to me—from whom you could never hope for any such accommodation. You could see it in their eyes. The thought of trying "let's pretend" would linger, but only until the master's whistle would blow.

These, who liked to sock and who listened carefully to the

master's instructions as to how to do it better, went on to be admirable people, I suppose: abstract expressionists, scratch golfers, bond salesmen, police chiefs, bagpipe players, defensive tackles, most members of the New York Yacht Club, taxicab drivers, military men, of course; and they married young, and a lot of them were politicians, contractors, deep-sea fishermen, insurance salesmen, certain types of tennis players who play doubles very close to the net, daily columnists, duck hunters, citizens'-band users, Little League coaches, just about everyone in the repair business, short-order cooks, and goat ranchers. There are many others.

The other category—the nonpunching types—is large, too. I am not good at lists of this sort, but I do know that the latter category includes all apartment-house doormen, a group who have agreed very early to accommodation, to "let's pretend." They are supposed to be custodians, the grandest of them in brown greatcoats with gold buttons in a long row down the front, and occasionally they help unload a taxi. They rock back and forth on their heels. Everyone who lives in the apartment house must pass by. But, in fact, in the cells of the high rises that rear up behind them a huge range of activity—some of it splendid, much of it humdrum, some of it traumatic—goes on over which the doormen have no control. Like deaf zoo-keepers they stand at the entryway to all this. "Yes, madam, the Zuckermans live on the fifth floor." They are custodians, but they are not committed, which is why on occasion in New York City doormen submit with great ease to having adhesive tape pasted over their mouths by armed robbers with satchels going up to fleece the Zuckermans. The doormen are quite docile about it. Later, they are discovered seated, tied to the finely polished oak benches in the lobby. Their eyes roll above the tape.

As a youngster I came home past a doorman. He was very large and important-looking, but even at a young age I knew that he was a nonbelligerent. He was a polite Englishman. When he blew a whistle for a taxi, he never gave it a furious blast the way a policeman would—or an abstract expressionist, or a goat rancher. His name was John.

"John, we boxed today," I told him.

"I see you are unscathed," he said. "You are either very nimble, or the other poor chap is a ruin."

He said that every month.

Outside of those gym sessions at school, I never hit anyone when I was growing up. Once, down on Lexington Avenue and Ninety-sixth Street, my younger brother and I were accosted by a pair of kids a couple of years older, perhaps eleven or twelve. They were nervous about what they were going to do. We were coming back from Sunday School. They demanded our money, backing us against a wall, and my brother shot his fists up—they were about the size of plums—in a classic old-time-fighter's stance, like a miniature Jem Mace in the boxing prints, but I said, No, no, no, and I forked over the twenty cents that was left over from busfare. The shame of it lasts to this day. My brother and I never talked about it. I didn't say anything to John, the doorman, when we went up to the apartment. I told Mother. I told her that I had tried to trick the thieves by handing over what I thought was an empty fake-leather change purse, thinking that the twenty cents was in my other pocket, but I heard the coins click inside when I gave it to them, and they turned and ran. So they got everything.

"It wasn't very good thinking in the first place," my mother had said, "since the purse was worth a dollar." She got a detective up to the apartment from the local precinct station and suggested, as he was writing up his report, that he hang around the local cigar stores where these sorts of kids lounged around, to see if he could, as she put it, "hear anything."

I could have gone peaceably enough through life without taking a poke at anyone or being poked at, but then, when I became a writer for *Sports Illustrated,* in the late fifties, and got involved in "participatory journalism"—that ugly descriptive—friends would say, "Well, now that you've played professional baseball and are writing a book about it, and you're thinking of basketball and football and playing the tambourine in some music group, and all those things, when are you going to fight a professional fighter? When are you going to fight Sonny Liston?"

"Well, I'm not going to fight anyone," I said. "I am going to play tennis. Perhaps I am going to sing. Would it not be interesting to sing in the Metropolitan Opera?"

It was not that my friends turned away and shamed me, or kept badgering me, but finally that I realized that boxing *was* perhaps the ultimate confrontation, certainly the most time-honored one—one man versus another in the most basic terms—and that I could hardly go on as a participatory journalist without investigating the sport.

I began considering how to go about it. My notion became to persuade a champion fighter to box a three-round exhibition for which I would train extensively, learning as much as I could about the profession and its practitioners as I went along. I decided to write a letter. Floyd Patterson was the heavyweight champion then, just a few pounds over my weight. He might have been a better fighter to contact for what I wanted to do, since, as Red Smith once wrote about him, he looked like a man who wanted to carry an opponent and didn't know how. He could have practiced on me. But a friend pointed out that things were going to be difficult enough without my trying to fight out of my class, especially up in a heavier division. "If you're going to box someone in another division," he said, "pick the bantam-weights."

So I sat down and wrote an extremely polite letter to Archie Moore, who was in the proper weight classification and was then the light-heavyweight champion of the world. The little I had read or heard about him suggested that he was exactly right for my purposes. Quite unlike the withdrawn Patterson, Moore was a flamboyant and gregarious champion; he was a favorite of journalists for his liveliness of mind; he was certainly a dis-tinguished figure in his profession, being a sly craftsman (one of his monikers was The Mongoose) who had knocked out more people than anyone else in ring history. Everything I read and heard about him (except perhaps the latter) I liked. I had seen him fight Rocky Marciano in the Polo Grounds—the only prizefight I had attended. Moore suckered the champion into the wrong moves, but he didn't (though he knocked the champion down once) have the power to capitalize on them. By the eighth round, he was in awful trouble. The reports were that the ring physician, Dr. Nardiello, came and looked at him in his corner; he found him battered, one eye nearly closed; he leaned forward to look at matters more closely, and he heard Moore whispering, "Don't stop it, Doc; let me try once more with a desperado," and the doctor let him.

In my letter I asked Moore if in the cause of literature—a phrase I underlined once or twice—he would be willing to come to New York to fight a three-round exhibition. He wrote back promptly on a letterhead which included a head portrait of himself, a montage reproduction of a few representative newspaper clippings extolling his virtues, and an embossed announcement down one side of the stationery that the missive was from the "Offices of the Light-Heavyweight Champion." He told me that he would be delighted to participate. There was barely enough room left on the letterhead for him to say this.

My feelings on receipt of his letter were mixed: one, a fine sense of anticipation, of curiosity; the other, a foreboding, a vision of opening a door and stepping across the sill into a terrifying place, a Bedlam, not unlike what years later Muhammad Ali described so brilliantly as the "Near Room," a place to which, when he got into trouble in the ring, he imagined the door swung half open and inside he could see neon, orange and green lights blinking, and bats blowing trumpets and alligators playing trombones, and where he could hear snakes screaming. Weird masks and actors' clothes hung on the wall, and if he stepped across the sill and reached for them, he knew that he was committing himself to his own destruction. As for me, I had indeed stepped across the sill. It had been done. I had no illusions about what happens when a professional boxer, with his mind on his job, finds an amateur in the ring with him. The professional is invariably in complete control, and only his temper and his state of mind dictate what he is going to do to

the fellow pawing nervously at him ... the latter's status just a
jot or so above that of a mouse being cuffed around by a finely
conditioned cat.

But with all of it so far away I allowed myself the luxury of
imagining that somehow I was going to ... well, startle my
opponent. Mark Twain once wrote, "The best swordsman in the
world doesn't need to fear the second-best swordsman in the
world; no, the person for him to be afraid of is some ignorant
antagonist who has never had a sword in his hand before; he
doesn't do the thing he ought to do, and so the expert isn't
prepared for him; he does the thing he ought not to do, and
often it catches the expert out and ends him on the spot."

John, my old doorman, would have understood that. Even if
he had been rocking back and forth on his heels in front of a
place as mysterious and sinister as the Near Room, he would
have bowed slightly and smiled, and if I told him I was going in
there to fight against the light-heavyweight champion of the
world, he would have declared, with his gentle optimism, "Oh
yes, how nice, how very nice.... The other poor chap will be a
ruin."

2

had two months in which to get a quite questionable apparatus ready for the confrontation with Archie Moore. I am not properly constituted to fight. I am built rather like a bird of the stiltlike, wader variety—the avocets, limpkins, and herons. Since boyhood my arms have remained sticklike: I can slide my watch up my arm almost to the elbow. I have a thin, somewhat fragile nose which bleeds easily. Once, in my military days, I brought up my hand in a smart salute which banged the tip of my nostrils and started a slight nosebleed there in ranks, a bead of blood quivering at the end of my nose, like a drop at a shot bird's beak, before it fell to the dust of the parade ground. A lieutenant colonel stared at me solemnly. He sighed slightly and went on down the line.

Also, I suffer from a condition which the medical profession refers to as "sympathetic response," which means that when I am hit or cuffed around, I weep. It is an involuntary reaction: the tears come and there is nothing I can do except dab at them with a fist.

Charley Goldman, Rocky Marciano's famous, gnomelike trainer, once said of fighters built along my lines, "You know them fighters with long necks and them long, pointy chins. They cost you more for smellin' salts than they do for food."

Yet, I knew the first step in getting ready for Moore was to find a trainer like Charley Goldman willing to take me on. I reached a man named George Brown. I had been introduced to him by Ernest Hemingway, who always spoke of him with highest regard—as a boxer who could have been a champion fighter if he had been able to accept the idea that he was going to be hit once in a while. But having classic features better suited, perhaps, to an Irish dandy sitting astride a hunter, he stayed on the periphery of boxing, as the proprietor of a famous gymnasium on Fifty-seventh Street, where he sparred with a fancy New York clientele, if they were of a mind to try it, and where he taught boxing. Hemingway spoke of his skills with awe, saying that he could never remember having landed a good punch during a sparring session with Brown.

So I telephoned Brown. After I had explained what I wished of him, he said no, he was taking a job on the Isle of Pines, off Cuba, and wouldn't be able to help me train for the fight. He admitted that the idea of preparing a "tiger" to go against the light-heavyweight champion intrigued him, but frankly, and he hoped I didn't mind his saying so, he felt that in his future he'd be better off in Cuba—despite the fact that Fidel Castro's forces were beginning to work down from the Sierra Maestra and the place was in a political uproar. He was very polite about it and jocular at the same time.

"Well, what am I going to do, George?" I asked. I told him I had been advised by Martin Kane, of *Sports Illustrated,* to go down to Stillman's Gym, on Eighth Avenue, and get myself a trainer—I mentioned Charley Goldman and Joe Fariello—and work out in that crowd for at least a month.

Brown was appalled. "Stay out of Stillman's," he said. "You'll get some awful disease fooling around there. Stillman and his people don't know what a *mop* looks like, much less how to push such a thing through the crud in that place. . . ."

"How about the trainers?" I asked.

Brown sounded very concerned on the other end of the phone. "Listen," he said, "most of the trainers you'll find in Stillman's don't have the brains God gave a goat. Maybe they'll give you one lesson—how to lace on the gloves—but then they'll get you up there in the ring for their bums to maul you around so you 'learn experience.' You'll get ruined. Listen," Brown said, "if you have to go to Stillman's, go and work on the light bag, the heavy bag, but don't get yourself pushed into the ring if anyone else is fooling around in there. Go into the ring when it's empty—*alone*—shadowbox, get the feeling of the canvas, and *get out* if anyone starts climbing through the ropes. I don't care if it's Lou Stillman himself, or someone who looks like your grandmother . . . get out!"

"They'd really tee off on me?" I asked.

"In the ring with those guys you're fair game," Brown said. "Those guys'll hit anything moving—the timekeeper, if he got in there; a handyman sent in to check the ring posts; anybody. And as for a writer, those guys'd smack a writer on the beak just to see what would happen."

Brown heard me whistle softly over the phone; he said, "Don't forget, in the ring friendship ceases; and as for fooling around with Stillman's crowd, you'd be better off jumping into a bear pit. Wouldn't smell as bad."

With George Brown warning me sternly away from physical contact with the trainers in New York's gyms, I fell back on the theory that I could teach myself what to do from books and a self-imposed training program. I paid a visit to the library of the Racquet Club, on Park Avenue, where a small section of the shelves was devoted to boxing. I looked through the titles for a manual and arbitrarily selected one of a number—a thin volume which produced a fine aroma of mold when removed from the shelf. *The Art and Practice of English Boxing,* the volume was called, first published in 1807. I took it off to one of the library's large leather chairs, settled myself down, arranged a wooden footrest under my feet, reached up then and switched on a reading lamp—all this with a genuine sense of accomplishment, of getting underway. Around me, unaware that a fellow member was starting his preparations to fight the light-heavyweight champion of the world, quite a few members dozed in their chairs. One of them, in an adjoining chair, slept with a thin page of the *Wall Street Journal* over his face, the paper rising and falling barely perceptibly to his gentle snores. The library is used for sleeping as much as for reading. But it was peaceful that afternoon, some of the leather chairs occupied but quiescent, a fire murmuring in the grate the loudest sound in the room, and so I opened up *The Art and Practice of English Boxing* and began.

The first paragraph, devoted to some general remarks, included a reassuring sentence: "Both parties," the line read, referring to contestants in the ring, "should keep in the best humours possible." How this was to be done was not specified, but at least the inference was that George Brown's dictum that friendship ceases in the ring was not inflexible. I shifted comfortably in my chair and read on:

"One of the chief studies of a pugilist of character is to know where he can most successfully plant his blows. The parts of the body in which a blow is struck with the greatest probability of terminating the battle, are on the eye, between the eyebrows, on the bridge of the nose, or the temporal artery, beneath the left ear, under the short ribs, and in the pit of the stomach . . . a blow under the left ear forces back the blood which proceeds from the head to the heart [I shifted uneasily in my chair] . . . so that the vessels and sinews of the brain are overcharged, particularly the smaller ones, which being of too delicate a texture to resist so great a change of blood, *burst* . . . and an effusion of blood succeeding from the aperatures of the head completes his business. . . ."

My footrest fell over with a crash. In the next chair the member under his *Wall Street Journal* gasped and came awake; panic seized him under the pale sheet of the paper and he fought for air, batting feebly at the *Journal* with his hands; a foot flew up and *his* footrest toppled over. The library stirred and heads came up over the backs of those deep chairs and revolved suspiciously, bridling and haughty, before sinking again from view. Some throats were cleared. I heard the click of a pocket watch being snapped shut. The library began to settle down. My neighbor and I reached for our footrests; I returned somewhat gloomily to my reading.

But I kept to it, afternoons on end. I read everything I could find—manuals, histories, autobiographies. Sometimes in my reading—to my relief—I turned up chronicles which made me feel much more comfortable about the world I was entering; for one thing, it was not entirely occupied by killers: there was "Fainting Phil" Scott, an English heavyweight who survived a twelve-year career in the ring (1919–1931) with very little ability. He was actually the heavyweight champion of England for a while, but writers referred to him as the " 'so-called' heavyweight," very often as the "Horizontal Heavyweight," and on occasion as the "Swooning Swan of the Soho." His particular maneuver was to sink to the canvas at the first suggestion of a low blow and cry, "Foul!"—hoping that the referee would award him the fight on a technical ruling. He tried this for nine fights in a row; the referees finally caught on, and after the Jack Sharkey fight in 1930, in which Scott, as usual, claimed from the canvas that he had been hit in the groin, the referee announced, "Scott is the yellowest bum I ever saw. For 10 cents I'd take him into any cellar and give him a licking myself."

Even after Scott left the ring he continued to elicit waggish comments. One writer said that the common practice of setting a retired boxer up in his own pub would not have worked with "Fainting Phil," since every time Scott heard the bell on the cash register he would have doubled over and stretched out on the bar. In one of the books I found a picture of him in boxing togs—a thinnish fighter . . . with a build not unlike mine . . . with rather elegant, slightly startled features who looked as if he were sniffing something as he peered out over his upraised fists.

There were a few others like him. I kept notes on them, as if they could keep me company. One of my favorites was Jack Doyle, who was known as the Irish Thrush for his habit of singing in his corner before a bout. He was an awful fighter. Once, while he was singing "Mother Machree," a friend sighed, "Ah, if he could only *fight* her instead of sing her."

Naturally, the books I concentrated on were the manuals, trying to imagine as I sat in the deep leather chairs how I could transpose what I read to my solitary exercises in the club gym. The most arresting of the books was one by Jack Dempsey; its first words were as follows: "What would happen if a year-old baby fell from a fourth-floor apartment onto the head of a burly truckdriver standing on the sidewalk?" As if this stunning opening were not enough, it was accompanied by an illustration: it showed a truckman in uniform, wearing a cloth hat, and striding purposefully along, his features suggesting a personable fellow lost in thought—perhaps what he was going to have for supper that night—thoughts that could not have included an awareness of his imminent and peculiar doom. Two or three feet above his head was the baby, diapered, its mouth ajar, descending from an upstairs fourth-floor apartment at a sharp speed indicated by a broken black arrow pointed violently downward and labeled "gravity."

I cannot recall *any* book I have read which started off with such panache. I hurried on. "It's practically certain," I read, "that the truckman would be knocked unconscious. He might die of brain concussion or a broken neck. Even an innocent little baby can become a dangerous missile *when its body weight is set into fast motion.*"

The italicized part of the sentence turned out to be Dempsey's secret of success—to get power behind such an ineffective missile as a fist (or a baby). I looked back at the illustration. The baby's expression was hard to decipher; it was not clear whether it *wanted* its body weight set in fast motion. The text had nothing further to divulge about the young innocent, not even its fate after conking the trucker, though it turned up in the next sentence of the book, used rather brutally as a bridge to Dempsey's next thought: ". . . mention of the baby reminds me of what happened at Toledo. Standing there under that blazing Ohio sun I felt like a *baby* as I glanced across the ring . . ."

From such books I took notes when they seemed pertinent. I prepared a file. I supplemented my reading with more contemporary material. When I left the library in the evening, I bought boxing magazines at the newsstands. The inside covers invariably carried the same Charles Atlas advertisement ("Don't Be Half a Man!") that I remembered from the scrawniest days of my youth . . . the same picture of the "World's Number 1 Body

Builder" poised in a leopard loincloth, the identical typography and layout that I remembered ... indeed such a strong tug from the past that I turned to the cover to assure myself that I had bought a current issue. The dialogue was certainly the same: the couple under the beach umbrella and the bully running past ("Hey! Quit kicking that sand in our faces!" and the girl commenting, "That man is the worst nuisance on the beach"), with the bully in the next panel returning with his insulting, "I'd smash your face ... only you're so skinny you might dry up and blow away," leading on to the humiliation in the next panel—the girl looking over her shoulder and saying scornfully to Mac (the strip was entitled "The Insult That Made a Man Out of Mac"), "Oh, don't let it bother you, little boy," a devastating zinger, that "little boy" business, which quite predictably drove Mac in the next panel to kick over the furniture and a lamp in frustration ("I'm sick and tired of being a scarecrow ... Charles Atlas says he can give me a real body ... I'll gamble a stamp"), and then the denouement on the beach as, transformed by the Atlas Method into Herculean stature, Mac beats up the bully ("Now it's *your* turn to dry up and blow away"), the fine spectacle of his revenge being witnessed by *three* girls now, sitting demurely on the sand, one of them saying, "Oh, Mac! You are a real man after all!"

In my preparation for Archie Moore, I passed up sending for the Charles Atlas material. I recalled it had not wrought any discernible changes in my eleven-year-old body. Besides, there were other advertisements in the boxing magazine which seemed more suitable. I was especially drawn to one which showed an item referred to as the Killer Karate Krusher. It seemed to be some sort of leather gripper (the illustrations were always very dim in advertisements of this sort, as if the picture of the device had been taken through a keyhole by a spy on the run). The hyperbolic come-on for the Krusher was in the best tradition of such notices: MAYBE YOU DON'T WANT TO BREAK A BRICK IN TWO WITH YOUR BARE FISTS OR RIP A PHONE BOOK IN HALF—BUT WOULDN'T IT BE GREAT IF YOU COULD! The text went on to say that the exercises with the Krusher had been developed from the centuries-old secrets of Japanese Killer Cults and were quite capable of turning the user into a "two-fisted tank of power." I ordered the Krusher; I also ordered what showed on the opposite page: the 007 "Twister"—a piece of steel tubing, ribbed like a length of vacuum-cleaner hose, which was being bent double in the hands of a broad-chested blond youth with two girls leaning in on him from either side, their heads resting on the slopes of his shoulders. The "Twister" came ready made—it could be used "right out of the box for musclebuilding fun"— and it gave its user after almost no time at all "the power to lift girls over your head with one arm." The headline at the top of the page read MUSCLE UP AND MAKE OUT!

Very heady stuff. I also ordered a nutritional "wildcat" drink named Crashweight Formula #7 that was guaranteed in vibrant prose "to put an end to your hungry-looking muscle-poor body." There were before-and-after photographs showing what happened to somebody who had quaffed the Formula #7—in the "before" picture a thinnish fellow standing almost hidden in the shadows with his hands on his waist, holding up a pair of oversize boxer trunks, with the "after" picture showing a cataclysmic change to someone of such muscled proportions that his arm could hardly hang naturally at his side.

Odd. I cannot remember the 007 Twister's arriving, or the Krusher's, but I recall the Crashweight Formula #7's arriving. I certainly do not remember drinking the stuff. I suppose it arrived and sat on a shelf somewhere. What took my mind off these devices was that the phone rang one morning and it was George Brown on the other end. He said that the job on the Isle of Pines had not worked out, and that as long as he was back in New York, he was willing to take me on. What had I been doing to get ready, he wanted to know.

Well, I had ordered some equipment, I had been doing a lot of reading. Not much else. I heard him grunt. Reading!

I told him that some of it had been interesting. I wanted to tell him about ordering the Killer Karate Krusher and the 007 Twister and about Dempsey's baby and the trucker striding along under it, but I thought I'd wait.

3

George Brown went to work. The reading tapered off. He got me to stop smoking—from two or three packs to nothing, cold turkey, pointing out that it was not likely that I would ever find a better reason for quitting (short of a lung disease) than having to get into condition to fight the light-heavyweight champion. In the Racquet Club gymnasium he began showing me the boxing fundamentals themselves—how to throw the jab and duck slightly behind the right to protect oneself from the counterpunch. Though he taught me one or two combinations, and we worked on the heavy bag, he said we would "rely" mostly on the jab. "No man, I don't care who he is," Brown explained, "likes to have a glove flicking around his eyes. It's like a fly up there. So we're going to stick him—peck, peck, peck; just keep that glove floating in his face."

He worked me hard. I learned what an extraordinary length of time three minutes of effort in a ring is; that even holding one's arms extended, especially with the gloves on, requires considerable stamina and strength. I could understand the extensive exercises Albert Speer reported Hitler went through to hold the fascist salute while reviewing the long columns of troops. Much of the work was simply conditioning—working with weights, strengthening the stomach muscles so I wouldn't get "sick," as George Brown put it, when I was hit there. At the end of the workout I would work at the heavy bag, circling it, peppering it for three-minute stretches, and finally, to conclude things, I would face the light bag that hung from its swivel under the bangboard. Along with skipping rope, it was the traditional boxer's exercise—the *rat-a-tat-tat* you could hear out in the street from the innards of Gleason's or Stillman's. It seemed symbolic in my case; though the bag was easy enough to hit four or five times, it then escaped the rhythm and slued violently around on its swivel, as independent as a balloon losing its air.

Brown arranged things for me to do outside the gym. He ordered me out into Central Park to run in the early morning. I hated getting up to do it. It was certainly one of the burdens of a fighter's life. In my Racquet Club reading I had read that Willie Pep once caught Jake LaMotta spiking his premorning-run orange juice with a jigger of brandy to make the exercise more palatable. "Hell, Willie," La Motta explained, "I don't run good, but I'm the happiest guy in the world."

Once out there, though, I enjoyed it. I told Brown how lovely it was in the Park, with the light of the sun coming up, making the facades of the buildings on the West Side shine like a theater curtain in the footlights; and if one ran down by the zoo, the lions were grunting and the keepers were getting ready for the morning feedings. The seal pond was very lively at that hour.

Brown made a face and said I was not tending to business. Always I had to remember why I was out there—and that I should try to work up a controlled rage against Archie Moore, seeing him always in my mind's eye, shadowboxing as if his presence were just beyond reach, and to hell with what was going on in the seal pond. He told me that when Gene Tunney was training for Dempsey, he would take off time to play golf, but even on the course he would tag after his drive, shuffling and feinting and shadowboxing, and his caddy, hurrying after him, could hear him muttering between his teeth, "Dempsey . . . Dempsey . . . Dempsey."

So I tried it while running through Central Park on those cold mornings, whispering between my teeth, "Moore . . . Moore . . .

Moore," but the picture that hastened into my mind was not a reassuring one at all: a mental vision of Archie Moore glowering down over his gloves, and *enormous,* dwarfing the ring as if he had been pumped up with helium and steadied in his corner of the ring with guy ropes. He swayed and looked down at me. "Moore . . . Moore . . . Moore!" No, I could not cook up much rage against him. It was best to let the mind go blank and run mindlessly past the tree trunks and under the footbridges, where the echo of my sneakers against the vaulted ceilings was sharp.

We began sparring sessions with a friend, Peter Gimbel, who had been coached for the Golden Gloves by George Brown when Gimbel was an undergraduate at Yale. Peter was a stockbroker (he left the brokerage business not long after to pursue his great love, which was ocean diving, and to make films about it, most notably one on his search for the great white shark), and he would arrive at the Yale Club with his attaché case to meet me and George Brown. We would change and spar in the gym, a high-ceilinged room which was being used as a temporary storage area for scores of stuffed-animal heads from the walls of the bar and lounge—an antlered spectator row of moose, elk and deer under whose dull agate stares Peter and I shoved and belted each other around. The room seemed very crowded. Sometimes members came in and exercised in the rowing machines in the corner, and one afternoon, glimpsed over Peter's shoulder during a clinch, I saw an elderly man in a gym suit lying on his back and straining to lift a tiny barbell—it didn't seem much bigger than two golf balls impaled on the opposite ends of a cane.

Peter and I sparred on a large blue wrestling mat—Brown off to one side, watching, calling out "peck! peck! peck! come on now! come on now!" keeping us at it for three minutes at a time, sometimes more if he felt I could take it, until finally the breath whistled out of me with calliope shrillness, the arms and body sagging, and Brown would say, "twenty more seconds, come on now! peck! peck! peck!" as the knees would begin to flutter, and Peter's face blur behind his gloves, and then Brown would stop it. I would stumble off the wrestling mat to crouch down among the moose heads; he'd call out, "No, no, on your feet, take big breaths, fill your lungs ... only forty-five seconds to get your breath back," and I would stand ashen-faced and gulp in sweat-tainted draughts of gymnasium air.

There seemed no respite. Once, just as the rest time was expiring, two men in Yale-blue sweatsuits strode in and threw themselves down on our mat, where they began to wrestle—furiously and with long sad gasps of exertion. I was relieved. There wasn't enough room on the mat for the four of us to compete; the wrestlers' innocent usurpation of our mat meant a halt. But Brown led us quickly into an empty squash court just off the gymnasium and set us at it again—our gym shoes shuffling across the tiles—and I remember the sharp echoes in that white chamber, and how the walls seemed to perspire in the heat.

We usually spent an hour in the gym, and then, after showering and having a drink in the dressing room, the three of us would ride uptown in a taxi—Peter with his attaché case at his feet, Brown holding the equipment bag with the boxing paraphernalia on his knees—and the two of them would argue about boxers, most often about the relative merits of Joe Louis versus Jack Dempsey. George Brown said that Dempsey could have licked anybody in the modern era easy as pie; he was just the greatest tiger there had been, "except for this tiger we got sitting here in the cab," and he would laugh and dig me in the ribs. "Why, this tiger could take Dempsey and Louis in one afternoon and chew up Gene Tunney in the evening time," and I would look out the window at Third Avenue in the rain and think how much I enjoyed being called "Tiger."

Once, George Brown motioned out into the street and he told me that I now knew enough to take on just about 95% of the people out there—wouldn't have no trouble with them at all—and I looked out at the pedestrians, innocently hurrying along in the rain with their shopping bags, and I thought, "Fancy that." I felt like a substantial piece of weaponry being transported in the back of the cab. I hoped they'd refer to me as a "Tiger" again. There wasn't a more satisfactory word.

4

The fight, or exhibition, or what people later called "that time when you..." took place in Stillman's Gym, which was a famous and rickety boxers' establishment on Eighth Avenue just down from Columbus Circle. A dark stairway led up into a gloomy vaultlike room, rather like the hold of an old galleon. One heard the sound before one's eyes acclimatized: the *slap-slap* of the ropes being skipped, the thud of leather into the big heavy bags that squeaked from their chains as they swung, the rattle of the speed bags, the muffled sounds of gym shoes on the canvas of the rings (there were two rings), the snuffle of the fighters breathing out through their noses, and, every three minutes, the sharp clang of the ring bell. The atmosphere was of a fetid jungle twilight. When Gene Tunney trained at Stillman's, he wanted to open the windows, which were so caked that it was hard to pick out where they were in the wall. "Let's clear this place out with some fresh air," he had said, and everybody there had looked at him astonished. Johnny Dundee, the feather-weight champion at the time, made an oft-quoted remark: "Fresh air? Why, that stuff is likely to kill us!"

The proprietor was Lou Stillman himself. His real name was Lou Ingber, but he had managed Stillman's so long—it was originally opened by a pair of philanthropist millionaires as a charity mission to bring in kids off the street—that he found himself named for the gym that he made famous. His attitude about his place was as follows: "The way these guys like it, the filthier it is, the better. Maybe it makes them feel more at home." He announced this in what Budd Schulberg had once described as a "garbage-disposal voice." He sat up on a high stool under the automatic timer that set off the ring bell.

I remember him for leaning forward off the stool and delivering himself of a succession of tiny spits—oh, the size of BB shots—and though there were signs nailed up everywhere that read NO RUBBISH OR SPITTING ON THE FLOOR, UNDER PENALTY OF THE LAW, Stillman himself expectorated at almost every breath. Perhaps he felt that he was exonerated by the infinitesimal size of his offerings.

I had gone in there to ask him if we could take over the premises for an hour or so; I told him about Archie Moore and what we hoped to do. *Sports Illustrated* would pay him a small sum for the inconvenience. He did not seem especially surprised. An eyebrow might have been raised. It turned out that he condoned almost anything that would break the dreary tedium of the workouts—the never-ending three-minute doomsday clang of the ring bell, the mind-stupefying slamming of the punching-bag equipment—and that in the grim steerage-hold atmosphere much more hanky-panky and joking went on, perhaps as a sort of therapy, than one might have expected. For years the fall guy for practical jokes had been a huge scar-faced black fighter known as Battling Norfolk, employed by Stillman as a rubdown man, who became such a target for a hotfoot, or a bucket of water on the nape of the neck, that as he moved around the gym he *revolved,* turning to make sure no one was coming up on him from behind. They never let up on him. When he answered the phone, an explosive charge would go off; a skeleton was set up in the little cubicle in the back reaches of the gym where he gave his rubdowns, and when he saw it there, glistening in the dull light, he gave a scream and was said to have fainted, crashing up against the wood partition.

Perhaps Stillman saw me as another in the line of Battling Norfolks. He agreed to turn over his premises, though he told me what a businesslike establishment he was running there, and what a considerable inconvenience it was going to be to stop operations for the hour or so of the exhibition. Couldn't *Sports Illustrated* come up with more scratch? I said that I would see what I could do. I told him that, frankly, it was the least of my worries.

As the day of the fight approached, I began to get notes in the mail. I don't know who sent them. Most of them were signed with fighters' names—aphorisms, properly terse, and almost all somewhat violent in tone. I suspected Peter Gimbel, my sparring partner, but he would not fess up.

One of them read, "If you get belted and see three fighters through a haze, go after the one in the middle. That's what ruined me—going after the other two guys."—MAX BAER.

Another, on the back of a postcard that had a cat sitting next to a vase of roses on the front, announced succinctly, "Go on in there, he can't hurt us."—LEO P. FLYNN, FIGHT MANAGER.

Another had the curious words Eddie Simms murmured when Art Donovan, the referee, went over to his corner to see how clear-headed he was after being pole-axed by Joe Louis in their Cleveland fight: "Come on, let's take a walk on the roof. I want some fresh air."

Joe Louis' famous remark about Billy Conn turned up one morning: "He can run, but he can't hide." So did James Braddock's description of what it was like to be hit by a Joe Louis jab: "... like someone jammed an electric bulb in your face and busted it."

One of the lengthier messages was a parody of a type of column Jimmy Cannon occasionally wrote for the New York *Journal-American* in which he utilized the second-person form for immediacy and dramatic effect. "Your name is Joe Louis," a column might start. "You are in the twilight of your career..."

The one I received read as follows: "Your name is George Plimpton. You have had an appointment with Archie Moore. Your head is now a concert hall where Chinese music will never stop playing."

The last one I received was a short description of a fighter named Joe Dunphy, from Syracuse, a fair middleweight, who became so paralyzed considering his prospects against a top middleweight Australian named Dan Creedon that he stood motionless in his corner at the opening bell, his eyes popping, until finally Creedon, carefully, because he was looking for some kind of trick, went up and knocked him down, much as one might push over a storefront mannequin.

Occasionally, someone of a more practical mind than the mysterious message-sender would call up with a positive word of advice. One of the stranger suggestions was that I avail myself of the services of a spellcaster named Evil Eye Finkel. He possessed what he called the "Slobodka Stare," which he boasted was what had finally finished off Adolf Hitler.

"Think of that," I said.

"Evil Eye's got a manager," I was told. "Name of Mumbles Sober. The pair of them can be hired for fifty dollars to five hundred dollars depending—so it says in the brochure—on the 'wealth of the employer and the difficulty of the job.' "

I wondered aloud what the price difference would be between saving my skin in the ring against Archie Moore and what it had cost to preserve the Western democracies from fascism.

"I don't know," I was told. "You'll have to ask Mumbles."

As it was, I picked corner men who were literary rather than evil-eyed, or even pugilistic—composed of the sort of friends one might have as ushers at a wedding (or perhaps, more appropriately, as someone pointed out, as bearers at a funeral) rather than at a boxing showdown in a gymnasium. They were Peter Matthiessen, the novelist and explorer (he appeared on the day of the fight and gave me the tibia of an Arctic hare as a good-luck token—the biggest rabbit's foot I had ever seen); Tom Guinzburg, of the Viking Press; Blair Fuller, the novelist; Bob Silvers, then an editor of *Harpers;* and, of course, George

Brown, the only professional among us, who of course had literary connections because of his friendship with Ernest Hemingway. None of them, except Brown, had anything to do, really. I asked them if they would have lunch with me the day of the fight. They could steady me through the meal and get me to eat something. They could distract me with funny stories.

On the morning of the fight, to get a flavor of what the boxer goes through on the day of his bout, I turned up at the offices of the Boxing Commission, just uptown from Madison Square Garden, to get weighed in with the rest of the boxers scheduled to fight on various cards that evening around the City. John Conden, of the Garden, who was in charge of the proceedings, had said he would see to it that I got weighed in along with everyone else. The room was crowded with fighters, their managers, and more press than usual—a boxer-policeman from New Jersey named Dixon had raised considerable public interest.

I got in line. The fighters who were scheduled to fight in the Garden that evening and were staying in local fleabag hotels came ready for quick disrobing—overcoats over a pair of underwear shorts. One or two of them were wearing shoes with the laces already untied, so that all they had to do was shuck their overcoats and step up out of the shoes onto the scales. The official at the scales jiggled the weights and announced the figures. We shuffled forward. I had my overcoat on my arm. I was wearing a Brooks Brothers suit, a vestcoat that I was affecting at the time, a button-down-collared shirt with a striped regimental tie, and a pair of dark scuffed shoes over long calf-length socks.

When I was within eight boxers of the scale I began to take off my clothes. I removed my suit-coat, tossing it and my overcoat on a chair as I passed, and I started taking off my tie, just picking at the knot. But then I saw someone staring at me—one of the journalists, probably—nudging the man next to him to attract *his* attention, the two of them staring at me as surprised as if the boxing commissioner himself had decided to step out of his trousers. That was enough. I could not go through with it. My fingers slipped off the tie, and I rolled my eyes ceilingward to suggest how stifling I felt the room was.

I did not tell my corner men at lunch about my experience that morning at the commissioner's office. It was not appropriate to the temper of the day to dwell on bungles of any sort. We had the lunch at the Racquet Club. My friends stared at me with odd smiles. We ordered the meal out of stiff large menus that crackled sharply when opened. I ordered eggs benedict, a steak diane, and a chocolate-ice-cream compote. Someone said that it was not the sort of place, or meal, one would relate to someone going up against the light-heavyweight champion of the world, but I said I was having the meal to quiet my nerves; the elegance of the place, and the food, arriving at the table in silver serving dishes, helped me forget where I was going to be at five that afternoon.

I took out Matthiessen's enormous rabbit-foot. "How can I lose with this thing?" I said. We talked about good-luck charms and I said that in the library down the hall I had read that when Tom Sharkey was preparing for a fight against Gus Ruhlin, he was sent a pair of peacocks by Bob Fitzsimmons, the former heavyweight champion. Sharkey was somewhat shaken by the gift, because he said he had heard from an old Irishwoman that an owner of a peacock never had any good luck. But Fitzsimmons was such a good friend that Sharkey didn't want to insult him by sending the birds back. So Sharkey kept them around, walking past their pens rather hurriedly, and indeed when he lost his fight to Ruhlin in the eleventh round, he blamed it on what he called his "Jonah birds."

"You trying to tell me you feel awkward about that hare's foot?" Matthiessen asked.

I had the sense that he had been reluctant to give it up in the first place. It was a *huge* foot, and it probably meant a lot to him.

"Perhaps you could hold it for me," I said.

"You better keep it," he said.

During lunch I kept wondering what Archie Moore was up to. I knew that he was in town, not far away. I thought of him coming closer all the time, physically moving toward our confrontation, perhaps a quarter of a mile away at the moment, in some restaurant, ordering a big steak with honey on it for energy, everybody in the place craning around to stare at him, and a lot of smiles because a month before he had won an extraordinary fight against Yvon Durrelle, a strong pole-axer French Canadian, in which he had pulled himself up off the canvas five times, eventually to win, so that the applause would ripple up from among the tables as he left the restaurant; then he would turn uptown feeling good about things, people nodding to him on the avenues, and smiling, and then he might duck into a Fifth Avenue shop to buy a hat, and afterward perhaps he'd wander up by the Plaza and into the Park where he might take a look at the yak over there in the zoo. Then he'd glance at his watch. That might get him upset. It disturbed the equanimity of the day. Who *was* this guy? The nerve! This creep who had written him a letter. So the distance would be shortened; he was coming crosstown now, then up the stairs of Stillman's, just yards away from me in the labyrinthine gloom of the dressing lockers, and then finally in the ring, just a few feet away, seeing me for the first time, looking at me speculatively, and then when he put a fist in my stomach, there wouldn't be any distance between us at all!

Later I discovered what he *was* doing. At the same time I was having lunch with my entourage, he was sitting in a restaurant with Peter Maas, a journalist friend of mine. Over dessert, Archie Moore asked Peter who I was—this fellow he had agreed to go three rounds with later that afternoon. Maas, who knew about the arrangements—I had invited him to Stillman's—could not resist it: he found himself, somewhat to his surprise, describing me to Moore as an "intercollegiate boxing champion."

Once Peter had got that out, he began to warm to his subject: "He's a gawky sort of guy, but don't let that fool you, Arch. He's got a left jab that sticks, he's fast, and he's got a pole-ax left hook that he can really throw. He's a barnburner of a fighter, and the *big* thing about him is that he wants to be the light-heavyweight champion of the world. Very ambitious. And confident. He doesn't see why he should work his way up through all the preliminaries in the tank towns: he reckons he's ready *now.*"

Moore arched his eyebrows at this.

"He's invited all his friends," Maas went on gaily, "a few members of the press, a couple of guys who are going to be at the McNeil Boxing Award dinner tonight"—which was the real reason Moore was in town—"and in front of all these people he's going to waltz into the ring and *take* you. What he's done is to sucker you into the ring."

Maas told me all of this later. He said he had not suspected himself of such satanic capacities; it all came out quite easily.

Moore finally had a comment to offer. "If that guy lays a hand on me I'm going to coldcock him." He cracked his knuckles alarmingly at the table.

At this, Peter Maas realized that not unlike Dr. Frankenstein he had created a monster, and after a somewhat hollow laugh, he tried to undo matters: "Oh, Arch, he's a friend of mine." He tried to say that he had been carrying on in jest. But this served to make Moore even more suspicious—the notion that Maas and the mysterious man with the "pole-ax left hook" he was describing were in cahoots of some sort.

At the time, of course, I knew none of this. I dawdled away the afternoon and arrived early at Stillman's. George Brown was with me, carrying his little leather case with the gloves, and some "equipment" he felt he might have to use if things got "difficult" for me up in the ring.

We went up the steps of the building at Eighth Avenue, through the turnstile, and Lou Stillman led us through the back area of his place into an arrangement of dressing cubicles as helter-skelter as a Tangier slum, with George Brown's nose wrinkled up as we were shown back into the gloom and a stall was found. George sat me down in a corner, and, snapping open his kit bag, he got ready to tape my hands. I worried aloud that Archie Moore might not show up, and both George and I laughed at the concern in my voice, as if a condemned prisoner were fretting that the fellow in charge of the dawn proceedings might have overslept. We began to hear people arriving outside, the hum of voices beginning to rise. I had let a number of people know; the word of the strange cocktail-hour exhibition had spread. Blair Fuller arrived. He was the only one of my seconds who seemed willing to identify himself with what was going to go on. The rest said they were going to sit in the back. Fuller was wearing a T-shirt with THE PARIS REVIEW across the front.

Suddenly, Archie Moore himself appeared at the door of my cubicle. He was in his streetclothes. He was carrying a kit bag and a pair of boxing gloves; the long white laces hung down loose. There was a crowd of people behind him, peering in over his shoulders—Miles Davis, the trumpet player, one of them; and I thought I recognized Doc Kearns, Moore's legendary manager, with his great ears soaring up the sides of his head and the slight tang of toilet water sweetening the air of the cubicle (he was known for the aroma of his colognes). But all of this was a swift impression, because I was staring up at Moore from my stool. He looked down and said as follows: *"Hmm."* There were no greetings. He began undressing. He stepped out of his pants and shorts; over his hips he began drawing up a large harnesslike foul-protector. I stared at it in awe. I had not thought to buy one myself; the notion of the champion's throwing a low blow had not occurred to me. Indeed, I was upset to realize he thought *I* was capable of doing such a thing. "I don't have one of those," I murmured. I don't think he heard me. The man I took to be Doc Kearns was saying, "Arch, let's get on out of here. It's a freak show." Beyond the cubicle we could hear the rising murmur of the crowd.

"No, no, no," I said. "It's all very serious."

Moore looked at me speculatively. "Go out there and do your best," he said. He settled the cup around his hips and flicked its surface with a fingernail; it gave off a dull, tinny sound. He drew on his trunks. He began taping his hands—the shriek of the adhesive drawn in bursts off its spool, the flurry of his fists as he spun the tape around them. During this, he offered us a curious monologue, apparently about a series of victories back in his welterweight days: "I put that guy in the hospital, didn't I? Yeah, banged him around the eyes so it was a question about could he ever *see* again." He looked at me again. "You do your best, hear?" I nodded vaguely. He went back to his litany. "Hey, Doc, you remember the guy who couldn't remember his name after we finished with him ... just plumb banged that guy's name right out of his skull?" He smoothed the tape over his hands and slid on the boxing gloves. Then he turned and swung a punch at the wall of the cubicle with a force that bounced a wooden medicine cabinet off its peg; it fell to the floor and exploded in a shower of rickety slats. "These gloves are tight," he said as he walked out. A roll of athletic tape fell out of the ruin of the cabinet and unraveled across the floor. Beyond the cubicle wall I heard a voice cut through the babble: "Whatever he was, Arch, he was not an elephant."

Could that have been Kearns? An assessment of the opposition? Of course, at the time I had no idea that Peter Maas had built me up into a demonic contender whom they had good reason to check.

"What the hell was that?" I said. I looked at George Brown beseechingly. He shrugged. "Don't let it bother you. Just remember what we've been doing all this time," he said, smoothing the tape on my hands. "Move, and peck at him."

"At least he didn't find out about the sympathetic response," I said.

"What's that?" Brown asked.

"Well, it's that weeping you've noticed when I get cuffed around."

"Maybe he'll think it's sweat," Brown said cheerfully.

After a while he reached for the gloves and said it was time we went out.

The place was packed; the seats stretching back from the ring (a utility from the days when the great fighters sparred at Stillman's) were full, and behind them people were standing back along the wall. Archie Moore was waiting up in the ring, wearing a white T-shirt and a pair of knit boxing trunks like a 1920s bathing suit. As I climbed into the ring he had his back to me, leaning over the ropes and shouting at someone in the crowd. I saw him club at the ring ropes with a gloved fist, and I could feel the structure of the ring shudder. Ezra Bowen, a *Sports Illustrated* editor, jumped up into the ring to act as referee. He provided some florid instructions, and then waved the two of us together. Moore turned and began shuffling quickly toward me.

I had read somewhere that if one were doomed to suffer in the ring, it would be best to have Archie Moore as the bestower. His face was peaceful, with a kind of comforting mien to it—people doubtless fell easily into conversation with him on buses and planes—and to be put away by him in the ring would not be unlike being tucked in by a Haitian mammy.

I do not remember any such thoughts at the time. He came at me quite briskly, and as I poked at him tentatively, his left reached out and thumped me alarmingly. As he moved around the ring he made a curious humming sound in his throat, a sort of peaceful aimless sound one might make pruning a flower bed, except that from time to time the hum would rise quite abruptly, and *bang!* he would cuff me alongside the head. I would sense the leaden feeling of being hit, the almost acrid whiff of leather off his gloves, and I would blink through the sympathetic response and try to focus on his face, which looked slightly startled, as if he could scarcely believe he had done such a thing. Then I'd hear the humming again, barely distinguishable now against the singing in my own head.

Halfway through the round Moore slipped—almost to one knee—not because of anything I had done, but his footing had betrayed him somehow. Laughter rose out of the seats, and almost as if in retribution he jabbed and followed with a long lazy left hook that fetched up against my nose and collapsed it slightly. It began to bleed. There was a considerable amount of sympathetic response and though my physical reaction, the *jab* ("peck, peck, peck"), was thrown in a frenzy and with considerable spirit, the efforts popped up against Moore's guard as ineffectually as if I were poking at the side of a barn. The tears came down my cheeks. We revolved around the ring. I could

hear the crowd—a vague buzzing—and occasionally I could hear
my name being called out: "Hey, George, hit him back; hit him
in the knees, George." I was conscious of how inappropriate the
name George was to the ring, rather like hearing "Timothy" or
"Warren" or "Christopher." Occasionally I was aware of the
faces hanging above the seats like rows of balloons, unrecognizable, many of them with faint anticipatory grins on their faces, as
if they were waiting for a joke to be told which was going to be
pretty good. They were slightly inhuman, I remember thinking,
the banks of them staring up, and suddenly into my mind
popped a scene from Conan Doyle's *The Croxley Master:* his
fine description of a fight being watched by Welsh miners, each
with his dog sitting behind him; they went everywhere as
companions, so that the boxers looked down and everywhere
among the human faces were the heads of dogs, yapping from
the benches, the muzzles pointing up, the tongues lolling.

We went into a clinch; I was surprised when I was pushed
away and saw the sheen of blood on Moore's T-shirt. Moore
looked slightly alarmed. The flow of tears was doubtless disarming. He moved forward and enfolded me in another clinch. He
whispered in my ear, "Hey, breathe, man, breathe." The bell
sounded and I turned from him and headed for my corner,
feeling very much like sitting down.

Lou Stillman had not provided a stool. "There's no stool," I
said snuffily to George Brown. My nose was stopped up. He
ministered to me across the ropes—a quick rub of the face with
the towel, an inspection of the nose, a pop of head-clearing salts,
a predictable word of the old advice ("just jab him, keep him
away, keep the glove in his snoot, peck, peck, you're doing
fine"). He looked out past my shoulder at Moore, who must
have been joking with the crowd, because I could hear the
laughter behind me.

For the next two rounds Moore let up considerably, being
assured—if indeed it had ever worried him—of the quality of his
opposition. In the last round he let me whale away at him from
time to time, and then he would pull me into a clinch and whack
at me with great harmless popping shots to the backs of my

shoulder blades which sounded like the crack of artillery. Once I heard him ask Ezra Bowen if he was behind on points.

But George Brown and Blair Fuller did not like what was going on at all ... I think mostly because of the unpredictable nature of my opponent: his moods seemed to change as the fight went on; he was evidently not quite sure how to comport himself—clowning for a few seconds, and then the humming would rise, and they would grimace as a few punches were thrown with more authority; they could see my mouth drop ajar. In the third round Brown began to feel that Moore had run through as much of a repertoire as he could devise, and that the fighter, wondering how he could finish things off aesthetically, was getting testy about it. I was told Tom Guinzburg, one of my seconds, came up to the corner and threw a towel into the ring ... but whether he was doing it because he was worried or because he knew it would raise a laugh—which indeed it did—I never discovered. But, long after the event, I found out that Brown had reached down and advanced the hand of the time clock. The bell clanged sharply with a good minute to go. Ezra called us together to raise both our arms, and, funning it up, he called the affair a draw. I can remember the relief of its being done, vaguely worried that it had not been more conclusive, or artistic; I was quite grateful for the bloody nose.

"That last round seemed awfully short," I mentioned to Brown.

He dabbed at my face with a towel. "I suppose you were getting set to finish him," George said.

Much of the crowd moved with us back into the cubicle area. In my stall, I was pushed back into a corner. Moore stood in the doorway, the well-wishers shouting at him, "Hey Arch, hey Arch!" There was a lot of congratulating and jabber about the great Yvon Durelle fight. I heard somebody ask, "Whose blood is that on your shirt, hey, Arch?" and somebody else said, "Well, it sure ain't his!" and I could hear the guffawing as the exchange was passed along the gloomy corridors beyond the cubicle wall.

The character of the crowd had begun to change. The word had gone around the area that Archie Moore was up in

Stillman's, and the fight bars down the avenue had emptied. A whole mess of people came up Stillman's stairs, some of them in time to see the final round, others pushing against the striped-tie crowd leaving. "It's over? What the hell was Arch doin' fightin' in Stillman's?"

"I dunno," one of the others pushing up the stairs said. "I hear he kilt some guy."

"A grudge fight, hey?"

They pushed back into the cubicle area. The cigar smoke rose. I caught sight of Lou Stillman. He was frantic. He had found two women, a mother and daughter, back in the cubicle area, which had flustered him; but the main aggravation was that his place was packed with people who had not paid to come through his turnstile. Someone told me that he had become so astonished at the number turning up for the exhibition, at the quantity of coats and ties, signifying that they *could* pay, that finally venality had overcome him; he rushed to the turnstile and the last twenty or thirty people who crowded in had to pay him two dollars a head. Later, I heard that he had tried to recoup what he had missed by charging people, at least those wearing ties, as they *left*.

I sat on my stool, feeling removed from the bustle and the shouting. While I pecked at the laces of my gloves, suddenly in front of me a man turned—I had been staring at the back of his overcoat—and he said, "Well, kid, what did you get out of it?"

He was an older black man, with a rather melancholy face distinguished by an almost Roman nose; his ears were cauliflowered, though very small.

"So far, a bloody nose," I said.

He smiled slightly. "That's the good way to begin; that's the start."

"I guess that's right," I said.

"There's a lot more to it," he went on.

I must have looked puzzled.

"Stick to it," he said. "You've got a lot to find out about. Don't let it go, hey?"

"No," I said vaguely, "I won't."

I never discovered who he was. I thought of him a couple of times later that evening.

Stillman's cleared out, finally. The fighters, who had been standing along the back wall to watch the strange proceedings, took over the premises again; they climbed up into the rings; the trainers sat down in the front seats, gossiping; things returned to normal.

I was told that at seven o'clock or so the duchess d'Uzès had arrived. She was not a duchess then (she had a marriage or so to go before she became one) but she had the airs: she was delivered to the door of Stillman's in a Rolls-Royce. She stepped out and hurried up the stairs. She was famous for being late—even at her own extravagant parties, where her guests stood yawning with hunger, waiting for her to come down the long, curved stair and make an entrance—and she paused at the turnstile, a lovely, graceful girl who always wore long light-blue chiffon to set off her golden hair.

She peered into the gloom. "Where's everybody?" she called. She had a clear musical voice, perfect for cutting through the uproar of a cocktail party.

Lou Stillman approached. I don't know if he produced one of his infinitesimal spittles. Let us say he cleared his throat.

"Everybody is not here," he said.

had assumed that climbing into the ring with a great professional fighter was something that very few ordinary citizens had done, or wished to do, since one would be hard-pressed to think of a more uncomfortable way of spending time. But that turned out not to be the case at all. The list was long—a curious group of eccentrics, braggards, publicity seekers, adventurers, aficionados, slightly addled-sounding aristocrats, a large number of writers, and certain individuals on whom it was difficult to pin a description. Archie Moore himself provided an example of the latter.

"Once," he told me, "I was in Argentina, boxing exhibitions in the little towns in the back country. This small man with very slick dark hair, and a beautiful blond girl at his elbow, turned up at the café where I had dropped in to get the lay of the land, and he said he wanted to box a couple of rounds with me that night. He was a Brazilian, a little sleek Brazilian. He said, 'You are the *most* of the champions. Everybody in Brazil think you are the *most* of the champions.' He was very respectful. But, still, he wanted to box. Perhaps he had said something to the girl and he couldn't back off. He kept saying, 'Everybody in Brazil think you are the *most* of the champions.'

"Well, that night, suddenly, there he was, climbing through

the ropes with these baggy trunks on, spindly sort of legs, and he was carrying his own bucket with a sponge in it. I didn't know how he had done it—bribed one of the officials, I suppose. He had a very weak smile. I didn't see the girl. She must have been sitting out there watching him. So there he was in the ring. The first man on the card. I didn't know how good he was. He looked scared and pretty bad, but you can be tricked. So I tried to find out what he knew. Every time I faked he dropped his hands; I opened up so he could punch and I saw he couldn't do that. So finally I started a big overhand punch, like an Englishman throwing a cricket ball, making it long and easy, like a man stretching and yawning, so this fellow had *plenty* of time to see what I was doing; but when I started to bring the punch down over my head I saw the man couldn't move; he stared up at the punch coming for him and he *accepted* it, just standing there with his gloves down by his sides, his face up, like he was looking into a shower head, and of course the punch connected and down he went. He got up after a while and he was all right. He thanked me very much and he climbed down out of the ring. 'Thank you. Thank you.' He forgot his pail with the sponge in it. I guess he didn't have much use for it after that. 'You are the *most* of the champions.' That's what he kept saying."

Apparently in days gone by it was quite easy to pile into the ring with a professional fighter if one had a mind to. Fifty-nine people tried it against John L. Sullivan in the hopes of winning a purse of five hundred dollars offered to anyone who could remain in the ring with him for four rounds. The majority of the aspirants did not last a round, and indeed one of them, a neophyte of the sweet science named Fleming, from Memphis, Tennessee, was dropped in two seconds. Sullivan kept at it—a "knocking-out tour" he called it—for eight months under the sponsorship of a theater chain. Finally, the word went ahead that the odds of survival for four rounds were not good at all. Sullivan was forced to raise the purse to a thousand dollars to entice victims onstage.

Since Sullivan's purse in this kind of event was for anyone who could last four rounds with him, he was *guaranteeing* in effect that he could knock out this man, whoever he was. People thought they could get away with it by fleeing across the ring. It didn't work. Sullivan caught them. Only on one occasion did he lose his purse: to a man, who said his name was Tug Wilson (he actually had a small reputation as a fighter), who utilized the ploy of collapsing to the canvas every time Sullivan touched him—down nine times in the first round, eight in the second, and in the last two rounds witnesses simply lost count as he hauled himself up and flopped down again like a drunk whose legs had gone on him. Sullivan hovered over him, trying to peg him when he could legitimately do so, but Wilson thrashed around, weaving as he came up, and then collapsed as a glove would go by. Sullivan failed to get him, and had to pay up.

Years later, Stanley Ketchel, the middleweight champion, took off on the same sort of theater circuit. But he was a smaller man; contestants gave him such trouble, the legend had it, that if he felt himself in difficulty, he would bull his opponent across the stage into a curtain that served as the fourth side of the ring. From behind it an accomplice would tap with a lead pipe at the bulge of the challenger's head against the curtain, which was sufficient to slow him down.

Ketchel himself was turned at the last minute on one occasion; he went into the curtain instead of his opponent and got bopped. His knees buckled, and his seconds, staring aghast from the wings, were just able to save him for the next round. By that time his head had cleared, and he had enough strength to bull his opponent into the curtain, where the lead pipe finally found its proper target.

One always hoped that the amateurs in such situations did better, that in the great tradition of the weakling who prevails, the shy man in the back of the crowd would timidly put up his hand—I always imagined him as looking like the actor James Stewart—the giggles rising as he came forward; he would arrive on the stage and take off his coat, but not his tie, and proceed to beat the other fellow to a frazzle ("Okay, I'll pay up, I'll pay up! The thousand is yours!"). Leonard Jerome, Winston Churchill's maternal grandfather (quite a horseman—the Father of the

American Turf, he was called), tried to do such a thing at the age of seventy-four. Wandering down the midway of a country fair, he bridled at a circus strongman's challenge that no one could stay in the ring with him for five minutes; and although using a cane at the time, Jerome clambered up onto the canvas, hung his cane on the middle rope, and is reported to have knocked the strongman senseless. Hard to believe. I rather suspect that the strongman, faced with this wizened, peppery gent, simply took a graceful dive. One can hardly imagine him picking up the ancient Father of the American Turf and tossing him over the ropes back out into the midway. In fact, he might just as well have done so, since Jerome's death not long after was attributed to the strain of his adventure.

I had once talked to Billy Conn about professionals versus amateurs—specifically street fighters. One had always heard rumors of champions being taken out by back-alley fighters. Conn was scornful. "Aw, it's like hitting a girl," he said. "They're nothing."

Conn had a history of testing out his theory. He once broke his left hand on the head of his father-in-law at an Irish postchristening party in Pittsburgh—just before a scheduled fight with Joe Louis—in a tremendous free-for-all in which one of the guests got so excited he fell down the stairs and broke an arm, and even Mrs. Conn got pushed around.

I checked out the story. Conn said, sure, he had hit his father-in-law, and he would again, too.

"What was the argument about?" I asked.

"To begin with, you're talking about a couple of Irishmen," Conn explained. "At the party my father-in-law made some remark about not thinking too much about my marrying his daughter, and I told him that if he felt that way, to get his ass off the sofa and we'd have a go at it. He jumped right up."

"He must have been pretty sure of himself."

"Aw, he'd fight anyone," Conn said. "Only one guy he wouldn't tangle with and that was Jim Thorpe. My father-in-law played ball for the New York Giants under John McGraw—his name was Timmy Smith—and this one time Thorpe dropped a fly ball and McGraw told Smith to go on out to the outfield and tell him he was through for the day. My father-in-law said, 'No sir, Mr. McGraw, you go on out there and tell the Indian yourself.' "

"He didn't want to fool with that Indian," I said, "but he'd take on a guy who was about to fight the champion of the world."

"Aw, sure. Broke my hand on his head. Afterwards, Joe Louis, whenever he'd see me, he'd say, 'So how's your father-in-law? Still knocking the hell out of you?' " Conn roared with laughter.

"You made it up with him?"

"Aw, sure. The Irish are always fighting. Sometimes you have to straighten people out, even a father-in-law. This one time in Ocean City I took my wife into a restaurant where I tried to sit down at this table which I thought was empty. These three guys got upset. So I apologized. It was their table. But they got real aggravated, and what happened was that I had to stretch the three of them."

"You stretched them?"

"I sure did, and not only them but also my wife's cousin, who came hurrying in to help me, and I caught him by mistake with a good punch."

"Your wife's relatives came in for quite a lot of punishment with you," I commented.

"Yeah, I hit him a great shot," Conn said. "Poor guy. He was the only one who got his name in the paper the next day.... Naw, the amateurs have it real bad against a pro. Like hitting a girl," he repeated.

I did find one possible refutation of Conn's insistence. John P. Heinz, a professor of law at Chicago University whose great love is the history of boxing, once put me onto an account in a book called *The Yellow Earl* which actually describes the victory of an amateur over the heavyweight champion of the world, John L. Sullivan, of all people, though predictably there is no mention of the matter in Sullivan's own memoirs. The amateur was Hugh Lowther, the fifth earl of Lonsdale (he was born in 1857 and died in 1944), who was so upset that a championship bout had never been arranged between John L. Sullivan and Jem Smith, the champion of England, that he took the rather extreme step of challenging Sullivan himself.

Sullivan, according to *The Yellow Earl*, received the challenge and, very much in the spirit of taking on people on his "knocking-out tours" or who took umbrage at his behavior in saloons—he was at his happiest and most terrifying in a barroom brawl—agreed to meet the aristocrat. "If he wants a fight he can have one," he is recorded as having bellowed. "And that goes for any other Dooks or Oils he cares to bring with him." (I have always liked "Oils"—an accurate American twang to that—but I don't know how "Dooks" can be pronounced other than "Dukes.")

The match, arranged in great secrecy, took place at the Central Park Academy—which was a riding school in which Sullivan had a financial interest. Lowther wrote an account of what happened in a magazine called *The People* (it is reprinted in *The Yellow Earl*) which is as valuable for its peppery style as it is for its account of what happened:

"For the first round we just sparred and padded around taking each other's measures. I could see that Sullivan was a bit puzzled—just a little bit. I don't think he expected to find daring Mr. Lowther quite such a game proposition.

"I saw him run his eyes over me when I entered the ring, and he seemed—perhaps I imagined it—to be rather surprised.

"In the second round I felt once or twice that I had taken on something that was beyond me altogether. Sullivan got in one or two mighty blows that shook me, and I wasn't able to land any of mine. But I held on grimly and managed to sidestep the worst punches, and in the last few seconds I got in a beauty on the champion's nose.

"Sullivan's face changed when that blow made contact. He began to wear that bear-cat expression which terrified his opponents. But I wasn't easily terrified in those days, and I kept on telling myself that even if I did take the count in the end, I had at least drawn the claret. . . .

"It was in the third round that Sullivan crashed home that

sledgehammer right of his straight into my ribs, and I thought I was done for.

"The blow was a capital one. It took all the wind out of me, and sent me staggering up against the ropes.

"But it really served to put me on my mettle. I felt a fierce shooting pain in my ribs, but I didn't know that Sullivan's fist had done much damage.

"I fought back after that for all I was worth, and got home several stingers on the big fellow's head and face. There was feinting and clinching, and then I put over a rattler of a smack to John L.'s chin.

"All this time, too, I was taking punishment. One of my eyes was closed up, and I had an ugly cut on my shoulder. But though I was certainly hard pressed, I knew quite well that Sullivan was in a much worse plight. I had shaken him up time after time, and he was breathing hard, and finding it difficult to time his punches.

"As he came at me in the opening of the sixth, I decided it was now or never.

"I let fly with my right and caught him solid in the solar plexus, and he went down without a sound, apart from a faint grunt.

"He lay there for several minutes after the final count, and when I went over and put out my hand to shake his, his face wore a dazed sort of smile as he accepted my grip.

"As it half-clasped mine, I could feel its old, instinctive strength, while a shrinking pain ran up the back of my hand between fingers and wrist. This sudden stab made me realize that a bone had been broken!

"But I HAD BEATEN JOHN L. SULLIVAN!

"So, you see, though Jim Corbett got the credit for defeating the Boston Strong Boy as heavyweight champion years later in New Orleans, actually he was vanquished by—me.

"And considering that Sullivan when I met him was quicker, lighter, younger, and in every way a finer boxer than when time, fame and drink had combined to lull him on to a state of complacency, then perhaps you will admit that I may be forgiven for thinking that my victory was no mean one.

"Yes, now after all these years, I can look at my strong right hand and say with truth 'This hand put to sleep John L. Sullivan!'"

As the author of *The Yellow Earl* comments, "Certainly false modesty was never one of Hugh Lowther's weaknesses." He goes on to editorialize that because of the secrecy with which the affair was conducted, no one was quite sure if the fight took place at all, or if it had come out the way Lowther said it did. One of Lowther's friends in New York, Richard K. Fox, owner of *The Police Gazette,* claimed to have been a witness and supported Lowther's version. So did one of the better fighters of the time, Charlie Mitchell (who later fought Sullivan to a draw in a bout in France), who was Lowther's sparring partner and instructor. One thing for sure: Lowther was an enormous physical specimen. Professor Heinz told me he had seen a photograph of him—well over six feet, brawny-looking, and certainly not one to be mistaken for a Walter Mitty-like figure rambling out his fantasies on a street corner.

A far more illustrious name from the English peerage to enjoy "milling"—to employ the word from his time—was, of course, Lord Byron. He had sparred on a number of occasions with John Jackson, who was the champion of the world in the 1790s. Jackson was an immensely powerful man, capable of writing his name, it was said, with an 84-pound weight hanging from his little finger. He had won the title from Mendoza the Jew, largely by the tactic of grabbing his opponent's long hair—these were the bare-knuckle days, of course—and holding him out with one hand while he bopped him with the other, much like holding up a gong and hitting it with the free hand. Despite this somewhat unchivalrous behavior Jackson insisted on being referred to as "Mister" or "Gentleman" Jack Jackson to signify his social aspirations (he was probably one of the few boxers of the time able to write his name, with or without a weight attached to his little finger), and indeed his name in the boxing chronicles has come down to us as "Gentleman Jack" Jackson. Following his ring career he became a boxing instructor with rooms in Bond Street, London, and it was here that Byron boxed him, as did the prince regent who later became George IV, who was a great fancier of the fights and at whose coronation in Westminster Cathedral a choice number of the leading fighters of the day—among them Belcher, Richmond, Cribb, and, of course, Gentleman Jack Jackson—were on hand to act as ushers.

I have seen a print of Lord Byron sparring with Mister Jackson in his Bond Street rooms. Both men are wearing "muffles"—ski-mittenlike gloves which in those bare-knuckled days were used in practice—and Lord Byron is outfitted in what looks like a long embroidered dressing gown buttoned in at the waist. Mister Jackson is wearing knickers and a shirt, and also—being retired from active pugilism—a full length of hair. Byron appears to have been tagged; he is slightly off balance on his back heel. Four dandies are in the gym looking on, ruffled at the throat, and one of them is holding a delicate cane. Byron once said to a friend of his, Isaac Nathan, who recorded it, that he took lessons from Jackson "without anticipation of its being of practical utility. But however," he said to his friend with great formality, "should I at any time be compelled to diverge from the strict punctillio of gentlemanly conduct and be obliged to set-to, the art of self-defense is essential; that is to say, if necessity obliges a man to be a blackguard, he may as well be scientific."

Whether or not Byron considered it departing from the "strict punctillio of gentlemanly conduct," he is said to have been a very tough customer in the ring with his acquaintances, and not beyond laying them low. His temper was considerable, perhaps an hereditary matter since his mother was supposed to have died of a fit of rage brought on by reading an upholsterer's bill.

One of the other peers to spar with Gentleman Jackson in his rooms was the fourth (and last) duke of Queensberry (subsequently the title was moved down a peg to marquis; it was the eighth marquis who wrote the famous Queensberry rules). On one occasion the duke arranged an especially elaborate stag party in London to honor the czar of Russia. After the dinner the duke stood up and announced that a unique entertainment would be offered—an exhibition of the noble art—whereupon Gentleman John Jackson, in his fighting togs, appeared from the pantry and the duke squared off against him. The duke was known as Old "Q," the qualifier not at all surprising since the duke was in his late seventies at the time. A peppery gent he must have been, and quite sneaky, as an account of the exhibition would suggest:

"Tables and chairs having been removed by a corps of servants, the guests formed a ring—Old 'Q' squaring off in approved fashion as the champion's adversary!

"Of course, it would be absurd to suggest that Jackson did *not* pull his punches in the ensuing set-to—but by all accounts he had his hands full to avoid nasty punishment from Old 'Q' suddenly gone berserk! Giving ground before the furious onslaught of his amateur adversary, Jackson presently had his back to a huge sideboard on which reposed a boar's head on a silver salvar. At a signal from Old 'Q' the butler tilted the salvar, allowing the greasy gravy to overflow onto the polished floor—directly behind Jackson.

"The next moment the Champion's feet flew out from beneath him, and he plopped heavily onto the floor in a sitting position. The round was over—and it was Old 'Q''s. Nor did Gentleman Jackson suggest that there be another. How richly he merited that sobriquet of his!"

The account ends there; so, unfortunately, we have no way of knowing, for example, what the czar of Russia thought of all this.

My favorite of the pugilistic English peers of that period was Henry de la Pier Beresford, the marquis of Waterford, more popularly known in his time as the Mad Marquis. It seemed an accurate enough epithet. He had an odd mania for collecting door knockers and bellpulls; in fact, he had the largest (perhaps because it was the only one) collection in Europe. He was a big man, an excellent amateur fighter by accounts, having taken on a number of professional fighters, usually after a drinking bout, and beaten them. He was Irish, and, being something of a dandy, he fought his brawls without divesting himself of his coat. That, incidentally, was the practice when gentlemen fought or sparred with professionals at that time: the latter would fight stripped to the waist, but the gentlemen always fought somewhat hampered by ruffled shirts, sashes, collar buttons, and so forth, or in dressing-gowns, as we have seen in Byron's case; the only concession was the removing of one's top hat and coat, and in Waterford's case he only bothered with his hat.

When the Mad Marquis was not fighting boxers, he had them around as companions. He was the patron of an excellent fighter named Deaf Burke, known as The Deaf 'Un, who was indeed deaf—a very rough-cut specimen whom Waterford took along to social occasions, such as Mayfair high teas.

Perhaps it was not surprising, considering Waterford's entrancement with door knockers and knocking heads, that one year the officials of the London and Greenwich Railway Company received a letter as follows:

SIRS:

   I am anxious to witness a train smash. If you will allow two of your engines to collide, head on, at full speed, I will contribute a sum of 10,000 £s to your funds.

                                        WATERFORD

The startled company officials wrote back and refused. Indeed, they implied in their letter that the request was flagrant enough to suggest that Waterford belonged in an institution.

I had always assumed that closed the matter, but an English friend of mine, a social historian of sorts, told me that Waterford had become so obsessed with his fancy of locomotives colliding that he had pressed on, finally managing to buy a pair of decrepit engines; on a friend's estate, which had a spur of track, he constructed a small pavilion looking out on the spot where the two locomotives were supposed to meet in a fine *bonging* concussion of iron and wheels. Friends were invited. Champagne was served. On the appointed day the two engines, a mile or so apart, were steamed up, and at the signal of a gunshot, their throttles were shoved forward, the engineers hopping off before the locomotives got going too fast, and the two machines began moving toward each other.

My friend laughed. "The damn silly trouble was that one engine came on at a different speed ... so that here came engine number one, whisking around the bend, down the straightaway, going like sixty as it went by the pavilion in front of Waterford's friends, heads turning to see it whiz by, and then it went around a corner behind a hill and banged into the other chap head on— no one to see it happen at *all.*" He could barely contain himself. "All Waterford and his friends got to see was a puff of steam rising from behind the hill."

As eccentric as Waterford was another Englishman, a century later, Arthur Cravan, who arranged himself a bout against Jack Johnson. Related to the family of Oscar Wilde's wife, Cravan was on the avant-garde scene in pre–World War I Paris. He is judged one of the precursors of the iconoclastic Dada movement, publishing a magazine, called *Maintenant,* which was a typical exercise in total denunciation. He performed all the gestures the Dadaists would perform later—delivering a lecture in a jockstrap, threatening to commit suicide in public (by drinking an entire carafe of absinthe)—but when the curious collected, he left them (in typical Dada fashion) disappointed and outraged. He liked to refer to himself in his magazine as among other things "the nephew of Oscar Wilde," "the poet with the shortest hair in the world," "taxi driver and burglar in Berlin," and "poet and boxer." As for the latter, he apparently had immense physical strength but had overtrained it in the gyms of Paris into softness. He fled France upon the declaration of war in 1914 and meandered about Portugal and Spain trying to scare up enough money to get to the United States. In Barcelona, Cravan ran into the heavyweight champion, Jack Johnson, an old crony from the Paris boxing scene, who was on the run himself, being wanted in the U.S. for his conviction on charges of white slavery. Both being short on funds, the two decided to meet in a boxing match which would be billed as the return to the fistic world of the great Jack Johnson, risking his title against "the nephew of Oscar Wilde," "the poet with the shortest haircut in the world," "poet and boxer," etc., etc. Promoters were found. Posters went up all over Barcelona. Articles were published in the local papers, with the result that a great deal of interest was aroused: the arena was packed with the curious on the afternoon of the fight.

The French writer Blaise Cendrars has a lively account of that fight, having learned what went on from an eyewitness:

"As customary, each of the adversaries had an assured purse. The amount doesn't matter too much. The night before the fight Cravan was able to get an advance from the managers, call it five thousand pesetas, and he reserved a place on a steamship which was to leave the next evening for New York. He said nothing of this to his pal Jack: but since he wasn't in shape to go more than three rounds, he did ask the Negro not to knock him down too soon and not to hit him too hard.

"The match in Barcelona took place on a Sunday afternoon in I know not what unused arena. The introductions were made, and at the 'Go!' of the referee, handsome Arthur put up his guard, carrying his two gloved fists in front of his face, lowering his head, pulling in his belly, doubled over in order to cover himself with his two elbows squeezed one against the other while he awaited the fatal blow, his neck between his shoulders, back bowed, without the slightest gesture, not even the hint of a feint resembling a boxer, and contented himself with turning round and round, *trembling visibly.* The Negro prowled around him like a big black rat around a Holland cheese, tried three times in a row to call him in order by three kicks to the rump, and then in an effort to loosen up the nephew of Oscar Wilde, the Negro thumped him in the ribs, cuffed him a bit while laughing, encouraged him, swore at him, and at last, all of a sudden furious, Jack Johnson stretched him out cold with a formidable punch to the left ear, a blow worthy of a slaughterhouse, so fed up had he become. Cravan moved no more. The referee counted him out. The bell sounded the end of the bout. And Jack Johnson was proclaimed victor by a knockout. The affair hadn't lasted a minute. The Negro then had to defend himself against the Catalan public which protested with vehemence and invaded the ring and demanded its money back, sacked the arena, and set fire to the benches. As the rioting spread it was necessary to escort the champion of the world to the police station, and the managers were forced to comply with the crowd's demands: the box office take was refunded.

"Big Jack was furious; he spent the night in the calaboose shouting for Arthur, swearing to have his skin, and the sergeant of the guard had to threaten him several times with a strait-jacket.

"While the Spanish promoters were looking for Cravan, while they were searching all over the city, handsome Arthur was locked up in his cabin on board the steamship which was plunging through the ocean on its way to America, where he was sponging his left ear that was red, not from shame, but from the violent blow it had received. And from what I knew of him, he must have been thinking that he had come off pretty well and was doubtless saying to himself, 'To save face is fine for the Chinese! Me, keeping my portrait intact is what counts, and it's still there, my precious mug!' And he must have smiled at himself in the mirror, placing his compresses with care."

As for the United States, it too had its amateurs, many from the highest levels of society, who had been in the ring with the great boxers of their time. In Philadelphia, the senior Anthony Joseph Drexel Biddle was an internationally known amateur boxer who sparred (always with his shirt on, I have been told) against Jack Johnson, Jim Corbett, Bob Fitzsimmons, Philadelphia Jack O'Brien, and Jim Jeffries. He introduced his son and namesake to boxing (and its displeasures) when the boy was only ten years old by inviting Bob Fitzsimmons, who was then the heavyweight champion, to their Philadelphia mansion to spar with the youngster. A parity was established by having Fitzsimmons sit on a bench so that he was at eye level with the boy. The champion got things started by tapping the boy with a slap—I've always imagined it as the sort of blow that Baloo gave Mowgli to introduce him to the Ways of the Jungle—and in a youthful rage the young Biddle reared back and threw a short blind punch that to everyone's surprise happened to connect on the end of Fitzsimmons' nose. The champion moved his left hand a few inches in reflex, and the youngster was sent reeling back against a wall, knocked out cold.

When he came to, Fitzsimmons was still seated on the bench. The boy heard his father saying, "He is a very light boy, Bob, but even at that I have never seen a better short punch."

The two of them chatted and nodded while the youngster hauled himself off the floor; when Fitzsimmons noticed him he said, "So there you are. You will never forget this, young man. The reason I could hit you was because you lost your temper. Never lose your temper."

I would have thought this sort of lecture, especially with one's ears ringing, might well have meant the end of any interest in boxing or its practitioners. But the young Biddle grew up to be a great supporter of boxing, even when years later, after a bois- terous party he gave for the boxing fraternity in the St. Regis Hotel in New York, some of the guests stole the silverware and a number of fighters were caught trying to work a piano down the service stairs.

Of other social figures, I had always heard that Raymond Guest, the former ambassador to Ireland, who is a Virginia squire and a horse owner, had once been in the ring with Max Baer when Baer was the heavyweight champion. I had heard the story for years, and it held that Baer had been given a terrible time by Guest, who was famous for his strength. In Palm Beach circles he was remembered for having wrestled an alligator out of a swamp behind his house in West Palm Beach and making a golf bag out of him.

I reached Mr. Guest by phone at his Virginia plantation. I introduced myself and asked if it were true that he had been in the ring with Max Baer.

"What's that?"

I repeated the question.

"No."

"It's not true?"

"No."

"Oh."

"No, I'm afraid I can't help you there," he said. His voice was elegant and rather distracted, and I had the sense that he was sitting in a deep print-covered armchair by a bay window, peering out on a paddock at some horses grazing there.

"You never were in the ring at all?"

"Well, I was my school's boxing champion, but I never thought much about it."

"Do you think you would have stood a chance against Baer?" I asked foolishly.

"Hell no."

"Well, I guess that's that. I'm sorry to have bothered you."

"Not at all. I wish I could have helped."

"Could I ask one more question—if it's true that you wrestled an alligator out of a swamp?"

He brightened considerably. "Well, yes," he said, "though it isn't accurate to say that I 'wrestled' him out of the swamp. I caught him on a trap line, actually, and sort of 'horsed' him out of the swamp. Interesting thing about alligators is that they won't take a bait that's underwater. So I laid the bait on a plank floating on the water, and when I'd shoved it out there, the alligator took it almost immediately. All of this took place right in the middle of what is now West Palm Beach; we lived in the only house north of the Breakers Hotel."

"And did you make him into a golf bag?"

"Of course I did. He was a very large specimen—eight feet six inches."

"Good heavens!"

"Yes, that's all quite so. I'm sorry I can't help you with the other matter. It would be a nice story, wouldn't it, getting into the ring with that chap. But I'm afraid I must be truthful."

Another large class of persons who ventured into the ring against champion boxers was composed of authors. Ostensibly these writers had a reason for doing so: they wanted to go through the experience of confrontation in order to write about it. Perhaps the best known of the literary pugilistic amateurs was the author Paul Gallico—the famous chapter "The Feel" from his book *Farewell to Sport* was what inspired me to try my hand at participatory journalism—who as a cub reporter assigned to the training camp at Saratoga, N.Y., where Jack Dempsey was preparing for the Luis Firpo fight, persuaded the champion to go one round with him. He wanted to find out what it felt like to be in the ring with Dempsey. Gallico had never boxed before, but he felt that four years' rowing in a Columbia racing shell would stand him in good physical stead. It did not at all. Dempsey, who quite simply did not like to have other people in the ring with him, stalked him and pole-axed him. ". . . a ripping in my head and the sudden blackness, and the next thing I knew, I was sitting on the canvas . . . with my legs collapsed under me, grinning idiotically. How often since have I seen that same silly, goofy look on the face of a dropped fighter . . . and understood it. I held on to the floor with both hands, because the ring and the audience outside were making a complete clockwise revolution, came to a stop, and went back again counterclockwise."

Even earlier than Gallico in the New York newspaper field was a journalist named Albert Payson Terhune, who subsequently became famous for his fiction about dogs, especially collies. For twenty-one years he was a reporter on the Pulitzer-owned New York *Evening World* (he started in 1894 at fifteen dollars a week). He scored a great journalistic coup when he happened to be on hand in June, 1906, to see Harry Thaw shoot Stanford White in the Madison Square Roof Garden. He rushed to a phone booth, and, bodily removing a man who was inside talking to his girlfriend, he phoned in to the paper what was then called a "flash," which made the next editions.

His managing editor at the *World* was a big, gruff, intensely disliked man named Nelson Hersh. Terhune was called into his office one day and asked to take on a somewhat unusual assignment for the feature page—to box three rounds against the six best heavyweights of the day and write about his experiences. The six were Jim Corbett, Kid McCoy, Gus Ruhlin, Jim Jeffries, Bob Fitzsimmons, and Tom Sharkey.

Terhune jumped at the chance. He was an excellent amateur fighter (he had been trained as a youngster by an ex-fighter named Professor McDermott, the Daddy of Footwork); he was built like a heavyweight—six foot four and so strong that he was always called on to act as a pallbearer when a member of the *Evening World* staff died. Not only did he know most of the fighters he had been asked to box, but he had already sparred with some of them. He saw his assignment as an easy way of coming up with six good features for his paper.

To his surprise, each of his opponents—even those he thought of as friends—really whacked him around. By the time he had finished with the six sparring matches, his left hand was broken, two teeth were gone, and his face was puffed and stitched. He said of the experience, "I used to limp back to the office in a deplorable condition to write my daily tale of the carnage."

What Terhune did not know was that Hersh, who hurried over to get a firsthand account of the day's bloodletting every time his reporter staggered into the building, had been around to see each of the professional fighters in advance, offering a half-page feature story to the boxer who knocked Terhune out. Apparently, he wanted a story which truly described what it was like to be in the ring with a champion, no holds barred.

Terhune eventually found out about the bribe (a staff member fessed up a year later) but there is no record that he went in and socked his managing editor around as a result. Certainly it was to his credit as a fighter that he never went down for good against any of the six, and perhaps it was enough compensation to remember what Corbett had told him after their set-to—that he was the best amateur in the country.

Ernest Hemingway was, of course, an active boxer from his early newspaper days with the Kansas City *Star*. He sparred whenever he had the chance. Indeed, his friendship with F. Scott Fitzgerald supposedly evaporated as a result of an incident during a sparring session between Hemingway and the Canadian writer Morley Callaghan in the America Club following a lobster thermidor lunch at Prunier's. Fitzgerald got so excited watching the proceedings that he let a round, which was supposed to last one minute, go four, at the end of which Hemingway got caught by a counterpunch and was dumped, bloodied, on his back on the canvas.

One of the best men Hemingway sparred against was Tom Heeney, who fought Gene Tunney for the championship in 1928, just before Tunney's retirement. Hemingway was fond of saying that his Heeney scuffles—which took place on the beach at Bimini—were so ferocious that finally Heeney said, "Hey, Ernie, the two of us ought to quit this ... or get paid for what we're doing." The story got better with each telling. George Brown was predictably skeptical. Imagining the two of them on the beach, he laughed and said the only way Hemingway could have hit Heeney was if the professional got bogged down in the sand and couldn't move. This could well have been the case. Heeney was very large indeed. Mary Hemingway told me once that years later she and her husband, driving up from Key West, had stopped in a bar Heeney was running in Miami at the time. Miss Mary had not met Heeney before. "He was an absolutely *vast* man," she remembered. "I didn't think he could have walked on a beach without dropping in. I had a trick at the time of being able to heft quite big men off the ground—sneaking up behind them, locking my arms around their middles, and hoisting them up an inch or so off the floor. I tried it on Heeney—he was deep in conversation with Ernest—but I couldn't budge him ... not even a millimeter. He was like a tree rooted to the floor. I'm not sure that he even noticed."

I had often heard a rumor that Hemingway had sparred with Tunney himself and had had such an ugly time that he never talked about it. I checked it out with Tunney's son and I could see why. It happened at the Finca Vigía, Hemingway's home outside Havana, where Hemingway was always trying to get Tunney, whenever he came to visit, to spar bare-fisted, especially if the two had polished off some of the frozen daiquiries that were brought out in a thermos from the Floridita Bar in town; Tunney would grumble and get up on occasion to do it, though mostly he looked up at Hemingway from his armchair and said no. He had once hurt Eddie Egan, the president of the New

York State Boxing Commission, quite badly in a sparring
session—Egan had hurt *him* with a sneaky punch, and he had
retaliated and popped the commissioner with some exceedingly
stiff shots and had damaged him—and he knew that the same
sort of thing could happen with Hemingway. The problem was
that neither Hemingway nor Egan knew how to spar; neither
could resist taking advantage of an opening. There *were* amateurs Tunney enjoyed sparring with—Bernard F. Gimbel, my
friend Peter's father, and James Forrestal, among others—excellent exercise, shuffling around, half shadowboxing, half sparring—but the thought of fooling with Hemingway always made
Tunney wince. Sure enough, on this occasion at the *finca,* the
two began shuffling around the big living room, and Hemingway
did what Tunney half expected: he threw a low punch, perhaps
out of clumsiness, but it hurt. It outraged Tunney. He feinted his
opponent's guard down, and then threw a whistling punch,
bringing it up just a millimeter short of Hemingway's face, so
that the fist and the ridge of bare knuckles completely filled the
other's field of vision, the punch arriving there almost instan-
taneously, so that immutable evidence was provided that if
Tunney had let it continue its course, Hemingway's facial
structure—nose, cheekbones, front teeth, and the rest—would
have snapped and collapsed inwardly, and Tunney looked down
the length of his arm into Hemingway's eyes and said, *"Don't
you ever do that again!"* This simple child-warning admonition
was delivered with such venom and authority that on subsequent
occasions at the *finca,* Hemingway would get up and look at his
friend, and pad around, and Tunney could see that he had it on
his mind to ask him to spar, but he never did.

Among Hemingway's contemporaries, A. J. Liebling, the great
New Yorker writer (especially on the subjects of food and
boxing), enjoyed sparring with professional fighters; indeed, he
was a habitué at George Brown's gym on Fifty-seventh Street,
where he moved ponderously around on goutish legs but was
possessed (according to Brown) of an excellent left hook when
he could move himself into position, rather like a battleship
jockeying around in a fjord, to throw it. He boxed Philadelphia

Jack O'Brien on one occasion, and he wrote a lovely paragraph in his book on boxing, *The Sweet Science,* commemorating his membership in the brotherhood:

"It is through Jack O'Brien, the *Arbiter Elegantiarum Philadelphiae,* that I trace my rapport with the historic past through the laying-on of hands. He hit me, for pedagogical example, and he had been hit by the great Bob Fitzsimmons, from whom he won the light-heavyweight title in 1906. Jack had a scar to show for it. Fitzsimmons had been hit by Corbett, Corbett by John L. Sullivan, he by Paddy Ryan, with the bare knuckles, and Ryan by Joe Goss, his predecessor, who as a young man had felt the fist of the great Jem Mace. It is a great thrill to feel that all that separates you from the early Victorians is a series of punches on the nose. I wonder if Professor Toynbee is as intimately attuned to his sources. The Sweet Science is joined onto the past like a man's arm to his shoulder."

To my regret I had never met Mr. Liebling. He called me on the phone within an hour of my experience with Archie Moore (he had heard about it somehow)—finding me in the offices of *Sports Illustrated,* where I had gone to wind down. He wanted to know what had happened; he was glad I was interested in boxing, and he told me that he himself, after a long layoff, was going to start writing about boxing again for *The New Yorker*—the subject was one which he could not stay away from.

If we had met in person I think I would have stared at his nose, which had been poked by Philadelphia Jack O'Brien, and I like to think that he would have looked briefly at mine—perhaps still bulbous from what Archie Moore had done to it—since it was by these respective appendages that we were both pegged onto that splendid genealogical tree that led back to Jem Mace.

Of the writers of more contemporary times, Norman Mailer, of course, is an enthusiast. Mailer has sparred with a number of fighters, starting with an early father-in-law whose record in the professional ranks was 2 won and 2 lost, at which point his wife made him stop because in donnybrook fashion he either murdered his opponent (Norman reported) or *was* murdered, with neither condition endearing him to her.

Mailer's most exalted competition was Jose Torres, the world's light-heavyweight champion in the mid-sixties. One summer in Vermont, when Torres had a house down the road, they sparred almost every day out on the front lawn—two-minute rounds, with a minute of rest. "Sometimes they were one-minute rounds with two minutes of rest," Mailer remembered. "Torres occasionally gave me a hole to hit through so I couldn't get demoralized, but he didn't like it. He said it made him feel wrong. So he made me work very hard ... it was like boxing a puma."

Once, by accident, Mailer landed a right hand, which so excited Torres, the proud instructor, that he ran around the lawn shouting, "He hit me with a right, a *right!*"

The two of them actually performed in public—on the Dick Cavett television show (Torres was promoting a book he had finished), on which Norman appeared wearing a somewhat frayed bathrobe over a sweatshirt and short pants. Torres, very fancily got up in what he would wear for a championship fight, got influenced by the public's being on hand and hit Mailer in the stomach much harder than he intended, grimacing as soon as he had done so, much as one would dropping a vase, as if he expected Norman to disintegrate on the floor. Torres was so relieved that Mailer had withstood the punch that later he called up Cus D'Amato, the distinguished fight manager, and cried out, "Cus, I hit him hard in the stomach and he didn't go down. Not *hard,* but hard."

There were others. Roger Donoghue, an excellent middleweight who cut his ring career short when an opponent with the sweet name Angel Flores died after a Madison Square Garden bout in 1951, had also sparred with Mailer. Donoghue liked his balance. He told me, "His hook off a jab isn't too good, but he can hook off a participle."

"What's that mean?" I asked.

"Which means that he's not bad, but he's a much better writer."

Donoghue had also gone four rounds with Budd Schulberg, the author of *On the Waterfront* and *The Harder They Fall.* Donoghue described Schulberg's style as follows: "He gets very low to the ground, in a huddled sort of crouch, and he peers up at you over the rim of his gloves like a woodchuck looking out of a hole. It's very hard to foul him. He looks at you sorrowfully, like he knew what you had in mind to do, and he feints you with his eyebrows."

Of all the accounts I had heard and read about, perhaps the most appealing matchup between an amateur and a professional was one which took place at the turn of the century, initiated by the startling defeat of the British heavyweight champion, Bombardier Wells, by Georges Carpentier, the Orchid Man, just then beginning to advance his career. Carpentier knocked out Wells in the seventy-third second of the first round in Covent Garden. The punch that finished Wells was very much like the solar-plexus blow that Bob Fitzsimmons used to finish off James Corbett: Wells was fully conscious as he lay on the canvas, unable to move hand or foot, staring into the face of one Danny Maher (as he later recounted), a famous jockey of the time, a midget figure staring sadly up at him from his ringside seat.

For the English, Wells' defeat was particularly galling, since the heavyweight crown, indeed the institution of the sport of boxing itself, was a homegrown property, and here it had been removed—by a "Frog," what's more—less than two minutes into the evening. A considerable amount of sulking and heavy drinking went on, especially among members of the National Sporting Club, which had sponsored the match.

Then, a peculiarly English reaction developed. The members of the club decided that if a member of their organization could stay in the ring against Carpentier longer than Bombardier Wells had—those seventy-three seconds—it would somehow reestablish the boxing prestige of England. A clubmate named George Mitchell, a family man from Yorkshire, was persuaded to try—he was the best amateur boxer in the club—and in a long formal letter Carpentier was challenged. He was bet £100 he could not knock out Mitchell inside of seventy-three seconds (this was to insure a bona fide, out-and-out competition), and he was offered £200 simply to agree to the match.

Carpentier wrote back by return mail. He said he would be delighted to accept the challenge. The bravado of the whole thing pleased him.

Nothing is recorded of Mitchell's reaction. I have imagined him just finishing his breakfast, his clubmates rushing in with the news from the morning post, slapping him on the back, brandishing the letter from Paris, cries of "Bully for you, George," while in truth he sat there with his eyes staring, a piece of breakfast muffin crumbling in his fingers.

The fight took place in Paris, in the gymnasium of a "physical-culture professor" named Lerda, where a ring had been set up. A number of Mitchell's friends arrived to support him, many of them fellow Yorkshiremen who kept up a steady cry of "Up Yorkshire, George, up Yorkshire" as soon as the two contestants were waved together.

Their yelling was brief. Almost immediately, Carpentier knocked Mitchell to the canvas twice, then worked him into a corner, feinted his guard down, and knocked him out with a right cross. But according to various stopwatches, Mitchell had lasted a few seconds longer than Bombardier Wells. Since this was the hope of Mitchell's Yorkshire friends, they jumped into the ring shouting, picked Mitchell up, and carried his semi-conscious form around the professor's gym in triumph.

Mitchell and Carpentier subsequently became good friends (I read about this in Carpentier's autobiography), and when the Yorkshireman was killed in the 1914–1918 war, Carpentier, when he was brought the news in his home, went and stood in a corner, "where I bit my lips so that blood came from them, and cried."

Fortunately, I had read this account of the Carpentier-Mitchell fight *after* my fray with Archie Moore. Otherwise, in order to insure the legitimate nature of the bout, I might have been fool enough to arrange the sort of conditions that were set up in the professor's gym. I might have persuaded *Sports*

Illustrated to put up a purse that would have diminished the longer I survived in there with him. What nonsense! I once asked Moore how long it would have taken him to dispose of me had he been required to do so in jig-time. He looked at me speculatively. "'Bout the time it would take a tree to fall on you," he said. "Or for you to feel the nip of the guillotine."

"Very descriptive," I said.

"And very accurate," he said. "You must remember that I am the *most* of champions."

6

Ernest Hemingway was interested in what had gone on in Stillman's Gym with Archie Moore. George Brown had told him about what had happened, and I was surprised to hear from Hemingway, because he and I had had a falling-out over a *Paris Review* interview I had done with him on the craft of writing. He had sent me a savage letter saying that I had wasted his time and diverted his attention from more important things. I had felt rotten about it, as much for the disappointment of realizing how much venom he could let loose as for having monopolized his time.

Hemingway was famous at the art of making enemies, especially of people who were close to him. Archibald MacLeish once told me about the time Hemingway had been badly injured in an automobile accident in Montana. MacLeish had set out across the country to comfort his friend (an arduous enough trip to take in the late twenties when this happened), and had arrived only to be lambasted by the patient. "He somehow got the idea in his head that I had come to gloat over his impending death. He looked like anything but a dying man to me. He was growing a black beard, and Pauline, his wife, had to fight to keep the nurses off him." Increasingly, this bitterness seemed to become a part of his character. During his latter days in Cuba, when he would get cranky, he would go up to the tower of the *finca* to shoot at the vultures coming over the trees in the air currents, pretending that they were people he did not like ... the critic Bernard de Voto, William Faulkner ... the latter an ironic choice in that Faulkner had said (indeed, in a *Paris Review* interview) that he wanted to come back in his next life as a buzzard. It occurred to me, of course, to wonder if *I* had ever been responsible for the end of a vulture, one just tilting across the big ficus by the front of the house, idly musing how nicely he was digesting a long-gone mouse he'd found, when *puff!* he was hit and dropped like a black feather duster onto the little baseball diamond below the hill.

What made it especially taxing to be acquainted with Hemingway was not only the unpredictable nature of the sort MacLeish (and a great many others) experienced but also Hemingway's constant testing of his friends to see if they measured up to expectations. And it did not take much to fall swiftly from grace. Peter Viertel, a dashing novelist-sportsman very much in the Hemingway mold, was disgraced one afternoon simply because he got seasick aboard the *Pilar,* Hemingway's boat, out in the Gulf Stream. Although Viertel's distress was thought to have been brought on by a turtle soup Hemingway insisted on his sampling, Hemingway's feelings about him changed abruptly. Viertel was required to leave the *finca,* where he had been staying as a houseguest, and to move to a hotel in town. Although he was working on the screenplay of *The Old Man and the Sea,* Hemingway would not talk to him. No one could patch it up. "He gets sick," Hemingway would say.

"But you really must speak to him."

"What for? He gets *sick.*"

In my own experience with him I had been tested a few times. Once he asked me to come with him and shoot live pigeons in competition at a gun club outside Havana—"You're good with a gun, huh?"—and before I could tell him that I knew almost nothing of the art he said that he was going to get some good bets down on me. In the predawn hours of the day of the shoot the phone rang in the room of the Ambos Mundos Hotel, where

I was tossing nervously, and I can remember the relief with which I heard his voice, scratchy and weak over the connection, telling me that the gun club had been closed for a period of mourning: the president of the place had committed suicide just the evening before.

"Oh God!" I cried, as if the president were a blood relative and it was the first I had heard of the news. "Oh God!"

Then the falling-out had come along, nonetheless, over the *Paris Review* interview, and I doubted I would ever hear from him again. But one day in New York he rang up, and I heard his tentative voice at the other end—I always had the sense that he disliked phones, or that he was uneasy with them—and he said he had heard about the Archie Moore fight; he wanted me to come around to the Sherry-Netherland Hotel.

I went around and told him about my experience in the ring. He was glad to see me and he was good company. He was very pleased about the notion of the fight, and told me he wished I had come out and trained with him in Ketcham, Idaho. "You'd have done better," he said. Sometimes I think he got the priorities mixed up, thinking that it wasn't to provide material for notebooks that I was fighting as much as to undergo a physical test—truly as if what I was after was Archie Moore's championship. When I said things had been difficult, he said, "If you'd have come out to Ketcham, we'd have made a *strong* fighter out of you." He urged me to get into the ring again as soon as possible. "The elephant hunter," he said, "can't begin to call himself one until his fiftieth elephant."

"Good God," I said.

"Truly, and even then he's only just beginning to understand the character of his game."

He himself had started boxing when he was fourteen. Big for his age, he had been invited to spar in a Chicago gym with Young A'Hearn, who was a fair middleweight. He got laid out with a smashed-in nose, but it didn't seem to discourage him. He went back to the gym for more lessons.

"I knew he was going to give me the works the minute I saw his eyes. . . ."

"Were you scared?"

"Sure. He could hit like hell."

"Why'd you go in there with him?"

"I wasn't that scared."

That was the start of it, and since then Hemingway had turned the tables and pummeled a lot of people.

George Brown told me Papa was a dirty fighter who took every advantage that he could, and on a number of occasions when the two of them had sparred he had tried to knee George. Once, he brought his fist down on the top of George's head during a clinch, and George had to "cool" him. He wouldn't explain quite how he had done it; he smiled and looked away.

"Don't even fool with him," he told me.

"Well, I don't mean to."

"It may happen."

"Well, you won't tell me what to do."

"Well, I lean on him," he finally told me. "I joke with him, and tell him how *strong* he is, and all the time I'm hanging over those big shoulders of his, digging him a few shots in the kidney region, always talking to him, though, to keep him calm, like talking to a duck whose throat has been cut, and soon enough the strength drains out of him and he feels more like sitting down than fighting. That's how to handle him."

"Oh, yes," I said.

"You have to be careful. He's not predictable."

George was right. That spring, I flew over from Florida to see the Hemingways in Cuba. He seemed so gracious and friendly. I remember standing with him on a fisherman's wharf where he had docked the *Pilar*—we'd had a first-rate day fishing out on the Gulf Stream—and he was in such a good mood as we stepped off the boat and proceeded up the dock that I thought I would press him with a question about a literary device that had always puzzled me.

"Papa," I asked, "what is the significance of those white birds that sometimes turn up in your, um . . . sex scenes? I've always . . ."

I mentioned this in a high, cheery voice, as if it were a natural enough matter to come up in conversation; actually it always *had* puzzled me, especially the white bird that flies out of the gondola in the love scene between the young princess and Colonel Cantwell in *Across the River and Into the Trees.*

He stopped and whipped around toward me and I could see that I had made a mistake. His whiskers seemed to bristle like an alarmed cat's. "I suppose you think you can do better," he shouted at me.

"No, no, Papa," I said. "Certainly not."

I noticed how small his eyes had become, suddenly, and bloodshot, as if affected by the flush of rage that showed on his cheekbones, and if I had not been carrying a very excellent picnic hamper of his with some wine left over in it and some cheese, he might well have bulled me off the dock into the bay.

I hoped he would calm down. The next day at lunch at the *finca* there were three of us, the Hemingways and myself, not counting Christobal, who was Hemingway's favorite cat, and who lolled next to his plate—a sort of Roman emperor of a cat who from his supine position occasionally dropped his head back, his jaws agape, and accepted a morsel of food from his master's fingers as if a grape were being dropped down a pipe. He was absolutely inert; his tail never moved—a calico-marked receptacle.

I was remarking on this to myself when suddenly the Hemingways began to have an argument—a sort of Mr.-and-Mrs. dispute, except that they were arguing not about who was going to set out the garbage the next morning but about how many lions they had seen on a particular day during their latest safari in Africa. As soon as the argument started, the cat snapped its jaws shut and began to look edgy. I've forgotten exactly what the discrepancy of the numbers was; Hemingway said that they had seen eight lions, and Miss Mary said eleven, something like that, and she could prove it by looking it all up in her diary. Hemingway said her diary wasn't reliable; it took someone who was truly experienced to count lions milling around a waterhole, and she was probably counting the same lion twice. Miss Mary had something sharp to say in reply to that, and while this niggling was going on, Hemingway suddenly looked across the table and saw me sitting there.

He looked at me almost as if he had noticed me for the first time. Since lions were the nub of their dispute, that was the first quick impression—the big-cat character of the large grizzled head turning, the intense curiosity of that first formidable look, all of this compounded by the evident testiness, so that one had the forboding sense of what a gazelle must feel when he looks up to find a lion staring at him over a bush.

Hemingway pushed back his chair. Its legs shrilled on the tile floor and Christobal jumped off the table.

"Let's see how good you are," Hemingway said.

I had no idea what he was talking about. But then, as he came around the end of the refectory table, I could see that he was assuming a semicrouch, his hands bunched at his waist, and I realized he wanted to spar—he wanted to take a look at George Brown's pupil.

But of course it was something else, too; he was belligerent now, and he wanted to lash out at someone. Perhaps he remembered my impertinent question about the white bird the day before. I pushed back my chair and stood up to face him—my hands up in front of my chin—and I put on a tremendous smile to indicate that I hoped he'd calm down and all of this was going to be in good fun. I put out my left hand, flicking it an inch or so off his whiskers, to keep him away, and he stepped past quickly. His hands were rolled at belt level, and one of them came up in a left hook and I was banged hard alongside the head, past my guard, and I staggered backward and my chair went over. I felt the sympathetic response at work, the tears beginning to spring out; my smile wobbled; I moved around behind the fallen chair, keeping it between us, and I leaned over it and kept my left out. I noticed once again how small the eyes were in his face, and furious like a pig's, and yet how surprising and utterly unnatural it would have been actually to hit out at those whiskers.

In the corner Christobal was playing with a Ping-Pong ball, quite oblivious of the shuffling of feet, of the chair's going over, as if he had his own workout to conduct, and I remember the sharp *toc* sound of the ball as he slapped it round the tile floor: A side glance: I could see Miss Mary sitting, head down, picking at her salad. No relief there.

I thought of George Brown's instructions—to drape myself over his shoulders and talk to him like a farmer's wife to a dying duck. But under the circumstances that seemed quite illogical; it meant getting close to him, and to the fists beginning to roll once again in tight quick circles at his waist.

But then suddenly I was inspired—perhaps not even consciously; could it have been simple resignation?—to stop and drop my hands by my side.

"How do you do that?" I asked, trying to keep my voice contained, as if a question which I could not understand had come up in a math class.

"Huh?"

"I mean, I don't understand how you did that," I went on. "That punch."

He looked pleased. "Pretty good, huh?"

"I mean, to be able to do that with your hands hung so low."

"Yes." Across the chair his hands stopped their rolling movement; he flexed his fingers as if tired of bunching them. "Counterpunch," he announced. "Look here," he said. He was as pleased as an inventor showing off a machine. "The principle..." He came around the chair to show me. He said, "No, no, no, not that way," and he pushed my hands around until I was doing it properly. I was cuffed around a little bit more, but it was to illustrate a point in the art of the counterpunch and not as a target of his frustration. I kept asking him questions. How come his knuckles were so flat? Was that from fighting? He stopped and rubbed them. No, they had flattened out over the years, he said, a couple of them when he was trying to punch out a dent in a German helmet. He looked pleased to have been asked.

"Oh, yes," I said.

Miss Mary looked up from her salad and smiled at us. I remember hoping she wasn't going to butt into the nice time we were having and insist on the number of lions she'd seen on that day long past. . . .

7

One thing that Ernest Hemingway had always told me was that it was a bad idea to get to know an active fighter and become interested in his career. Sooner or later he was going to get hurt in the ring, and beaten, and it would be an almost unbearable thing to see if he were a friend.

But the upshot of my experience with Archie Moore was that I ignored Hemingway's advice and followed the fighter around the way a fan might pursue a rock group or a professional football team. I went to his speeches ... to his fights ... to watch him receive awards. I rushed up to him on the streets. I'm not sure he knew who I was, looming up, with a big hero-worshipping smile, because he often looked rather tentative and he got my name wrong. "Well, er, hello, Bill." I was not deterred. In gratitude for his cooperation in the sparring match (and possibly in relief for his not having extended himself) I ordered him a thin and quite expensive penknife from Tiffany's with a silver chain attached—I can't imagine why—and sent it to him in San Diego, where he lived. He wrote back to thank me: "Dear Roger ..."

When I was on the West Coast I invited myself down to his

house—he called it, somewhat ingloriously, the Chicken Shack, commemorating the original use of the premises as a fried-chicken stand. It had been built on to, and now it was quite grand—a ranch house surrounded by a picket fence. His name appeared on a painted sign above a pair of boxing gloves; another sign on the gatepost itself read THE MOORES, and inside the gate the name appeared once again, this time inscribed in the cement of the paving-stone walk leading to the front door. Off at the corner of the front yard a small swimming pool was formed in the shape of a boxing glove, the steps leading down where the glove's thumb would be. Inside the house, Moore took me to a large living room where an enormous picture window looked out on the traffic going by on the freeway. "What I like about this view," Archie Moore said at my elbow as we looked out at the big trucks passing, "is that it is always changing." He showed me the bathrooms, with their gold leaping-dolphin faucets, and in each one he flushed the toilets, which were of purple enamel, and we stood over them and stared down into the bowl as the water swirled. "Very nice," I found myself saying.

The house had a complete intercom system, which hummed faintly and never seemed to be turned off. The Moores used it to keep track of each other.

"Joan, where are you?"

"I'm over here, by the stair."

A pause.

"Where are you?"

"In the den."

They used the system like children. "Where are you now?"

"I'm still here, Joan."

It was on all day. In the guest room where I spent the night I could hear them murmuring as they got ready for bed.

Archie was a fine host. He loved showing things off. He even showed me some of his ring secrets: one, a can of what he called his "magic oil," a sort of milky fluid which he rubbed into his skin—"The stuff penetrates your muscles and keeps them loose"—and which he said with a straight face was emu-bird oil from Australia. "Very hard to get your hands on emu-bird oil," he told me. "Very hard to get your hands on the bird and *very* hard to get the oil off him." He never made it clear to me how this was done—my mind troubled with the thought of fleet-footed men corraling these ostrich-sized birds and moving toward them with suction cups and pliant sponges—and Moore would never elaborate on the process itself, except to say that he had "powerful connections" who provided the stuff for him.

As for his famous "secret diet," Moore said he had obtained it from an Australian aborigine—"You never see a fat aborigine"—and this turned out by my own observation in the Chicken Shack to be not so much a diet as a system of eating during which he never swallowed anything. At the dinner table, he chewed everything he put in his mouth very thoroughly, chomping down and squeezing out the juices and whatever, and then, as decorously as possible under the circumstances, he would reach in and deposit what was left on a plate off to one side.

His more strenuous physical training was done out at a place in the country he sometimes called the Salt Mines, sometimes the Bucket of Blood. He drove me out to see it. It was sweltering when we got there. He told me he had bought 120 acres' worth of the forlorn dun-colored rocks. The place was once a nudist camp, and among the rocks were flat cement shelves where the inhabitants of the camp could lie out among the rocks like marmots. There was a canopied outdoor ring. Many of the larger rocks had been painted in bright red with the names of prizefighters—STANLEY KETCHEL, RAY ROBINSON (a form of decoration Muhammad Ali was later to copy at his camp in Deer Lake, Pennsylvania)—and especially with Archie Moore's own name, which appeared, as it did around the Chicken Shack, a number of times. I noticed one crag on which a rude likeness of him had been chisled out with the legend underneath: ALL-TIME K.O. CHAMP. He took me over to a flat terrace—one of the sunbathing spots—where his name had been painted flat in huge letters, which he told me was to let people flying overhead in the airliners know they were above his camp.

"Do you think someone can read that from thirty thousand feet?" he asked.

"I would think so," I said truthfully.

Moore told me that Cassius Clay, who was then beginning to make a considerable stir in fight circles, had been out to the Salt Mines to train, but the young fighter would not adhere to the rules of the place: he refused to take a shift in the laundry, or to clean dishes, or to clear the cabins. "I didn't come out here to learn to be no pearl diver," Archie told me he had said.

"What's that mean?"

"A guy that washes dishes. No, sir, he wasn't going to do that." Archie grinned and said that one of Ali's early advisors had complained to him that it sounded, judging from the reports from the Salt Mines, as if Clay needed a spanking.

"I remember telling him that he sure did," Moore told me, "but that I didn't know who was going to give him one, including me."

Of course, Clay eventually arranged a fight against his former mentor. It took place in Los Angeles. I wanted to go out for it, but I couldn't. I thought Archie Moore would show him up. I was very much hoping that he would.

There was the usual palaver before the fight. Clay (of course, this was before he changed his name to Muhammad Ali) described himself as one of the two "greats" left in the world (the other one was Britain) and said that against such might it was inevitable that Archie Moore would fall. In fact, he was going to fall in the fourth round, and the poem describing that event went as follows:

> When you come to the fight
> Don't block the aisles
> And don't block the door
> For you may all go home after round four

There was more: In acknowledging Archie's advanced years, Clay hired a few elderly citizens down in Miami to join his camp, sparring gently with them to see how these venerables moved around. One of them was a Mr. Pop Mobely, a somewhat bewildered tailor in his mid-sixties. When he moved his training quarters to Los Angeles just before the fight, Clay hired an ancient named One Round Andrews, a fighter long retired from the ring whose sobriquet was not particularly honorable since it was gained, in fact, by Andrews' career-long inability to last into a second round.

Moore bridled splendidly at all this. "The only way I'll fall in four," he said, "is by toppling over Clay's prostrate form. He belittles people too much. Even his contemporaries hope I beat the socks off him. As I've said, Clay can go with speed in all directions, including straight *down*, if hit properly. I have a good, solid right hand that will fit nicely on his chops."

I went to see the Moore-Clay fight on closed-circuit television in the Academy of Music Theatre on East Fourteenth Street. The place was full. A great cheer went up when Moore clambered heavily into the ring. Almost everyone there wanted to see Moore successful with his right hand to Clay's chops—a punch he had entitled for the occasion the Lip-Buttoner. A few catcalls went up when Clay ducked through the ropes and began to jog up and down, very slender-looking, every motion fluid and easy. Moore looked jowled and tired.

Of course, Clay won the fight quite easily, knocking Moore out in the fourth, just as he said he would. I sat in a fever of despair in that ancient theater, watching my friend—he was dressed in a pair of overlong boxing trunks hiked up so that his waist seemed at breastbone level—get pummeled around. At one point his mouthpiece was knocked out of his mouth, and when he finally subsided to the canvas, the young Clay, not even bothering to head for a neutral corner, did a strutting prance over him, stomping up and down in his white ring boots like a Masai warrior. I felt awful. I remembered what Hemingway had told me.

I drove uptown and stopped in an Eastside cocktail lounge where a girl bored by fights and not wanting to watch was waiting at a table. She was bent studiously over a match-box cover on which she was drawing or writing something. A tall drink with a straw in it stood by her left ear. I sat down.

"Well, my gosh, look at you!" she said. She swept her hair back from her eyes. "I guess your man didn't exactly *win* or anything, did he."

"Been waiting long?" I asked.

"No," she said.

"It was pretty awful," I said. "Clay did this miserable victory stomp—Archie on his knees trying to get up."

"I'm sorry to hear all that," she said. "Did he fall in four?" I had told her about Clay's prognosticative verses.

"I'm afraid he did."

"How sad for him."

"Listen," I said. "I was thinking coming up here how much I'd like to challenge Ali for what he did. Get him in the ring."

"You big fat rabbit," she said evenly.

"What do you mean?" I said. "What's wrong with that?" I could feel my ears getting red.

"Don't you grin at me," she said. "I know you. You mean every word of it. You truly do."

"Well, perhaps," I said. "It was so sad."

8

It looked as though my surrogate avenger of Archie Moore's sad showing against Muhammad Ali was going to be Sonny Liston, then the heavyweight champion of the world, who had an awesome reputation, built mostly on his destruction of Floyd Patterson in the first rounds of their two bouts, and whom Cassius Clay had challenged for his title. The fight was to be in Miami, but very little interest had been generated since it was considered a gross mismatch. The odds on Liston went as high as nine to one, higher than the odds when Joe Louis fought his bums of the month.

But I went nonetheless, increasingly curious about the fight game, and certainly about the young fighter who had humiliated my hero, Archie Moore.

I kept notes, and when I returned to New York, I wrote up the account which follows.

Clay did most of the preparation for his fight in the Fifth Street gym, south on the beach, removed from the mainstream glitter, in an area of gas stations, one-story rooming houses, hardware stores featuring fish tackle, and shoe-shine parlors. The gym itself was up a wide wooden stairs on the second floor, hot and low-ceilinged, its walls a montage of unframed posters and fight photographs curling and peeling in the heat, some signed in faded ink, one by Barbara Buttrick, in leotard fight togs and fists at the ready, who hails from Lancaster, England, and is the female boxing champion in what must be a somewhat limited field. It cost fifty cents to come and watch the fighters work out or hit the heavy boxing bags creaking on their chains. The facilities were somewhat wanting—water to refresh the fighters kept in liquor bottles in a cardboard box at ringside: a fighter assigned himself a particular brand name: a Melrose Rare Blend bottle, he may use, or Old Stagg Bourbon. Two open showers were in back, in a dark dressing room full of crumbling lockers, and there was a ladies' room out front with a triple legend gracing the door: LADIES, it read, then on the next line FOR WOMEN ONLY, and finally, in massive letters, FIGHTERS KEEP OUT. There were more girls than usual in the gym to watch Clay—and one was always sure to find artists in there trying to get the fine tawdry inelegance of the place down on their sketch pads.

From behind the ropes, Bundini, Clay's trainer, in a pink-striped sport shirt and *his* golfing cap (these caps were standard equipment in both fighter's camps, and for the press) watched his charge train. He kept snapping his fingers, and his foot tapped slowly in some empathetic rhythm that he felt with Clay. His face mirrored wonder, a faint smile always on it, and his eyes would pop with pleasure when Clay got a good punch in. His enthusiasm was not shared.

"Look at that!" said Jimmy Cannon, the Scripps-Howard columnist. "I mean, that's terrible. He can't get away with that. Not possibly." He was sitting next to me.

Cannon was referring to Clay's major bad habits. He has two, according to the purists. He carries his hands too low to pick off punches. And, second, he leans back from a punch, which puts him off balance, and unable to counter. Learning to slip a punch, letting it slide past the ear, and then countering from a well-set position to the area left defenseless by the opponent's extended arm is a fundamental move in boxing.

"No, no," said Cannon. He made another hopeless gesture with his hands.

"Perhaps his speed will make up for it," I said.

"He's the fifth Beatle," said Cannon. "Except that's not right. The Beatles have no hokum to them."

"It's a good name," I said. "The fifth Beatle."

"Not accurate," said Cannon. "He's all pretense and gas, that fellow . . ." He went on nodding up at Clay. "No honesty."

I looked in his columns later to see if the "fifth Beatle" designation turned up. It seemed too good not to use—even if it was inaccurate. I never could find it. Cannon was a man of his word.

There was very little enthusiasm for Clay. I remember Joe Louis, in Liston's camp, replying to someone who wanted to know how *he* would advise Clay, said that (1) Clay ought to stay away from the champion, and (2) well, to stay away *faster*. He was thoughtful. His hand drifted up to touch a monkish bald spot at the peak of his head, and it was obvious he was not trying to be clever or smart-alecky—simply concerned, in his manner, to answer honestly.

Even Angelo Dundee, Clay's manager, slipped up. A reporter asked him what would happen if Liston hit his fighter a good shot, and Angelo said, "Well, if he gets hit, he's gonna *get up*," at which guffaws rose around the room at the admission, conscious or not, that anything Liston hit was going to fall down.

The challenger's press conferences were tumultuous affairs. The old sportswriting hands disapproved of them; certainly they sat through them with disapproving frowns, sniffing slightly, as if tradition and decorum were being flouted. In the past they had put the required questions to the fighters ("How's your weight? What did you have for breakfast?") and they would write WT GD, 6 EGGS, 1 STEAK on their pads with a sense of accomplishment. Now the same sort of questions served only to unleash an hysterical monologue of self-assertion—snatches of poetry, home-grown aphorisms, punctuated with a brandishing of canes, cries of "Rumble, man, rumble!"—which might have been interesting the first time, but certainly wasn't the third time around. Still, I was always surprised the writers couldn't get any fun out of it at all. They stared down at their pads, and sometimes they said under their breaths, "Aw, come off it, Clay." They rarely looked up at the fighter.

Norman Mailer once told me that he felt men didn't like to look at Clay—he emphasized just about everything they were not, and it cranked up all sorts of antagonisms they were ashamed to admit to—much as one avoided looking at a beautiful girl at a cocktail party for fear of a disruption of equanimity. I never could quite understand Mailer's notion. In Clay's presence, such as at those press conferences, I always found myself staring at him, my jaw slightly agape, and always a smile in the works somewhere, because so much of him came out in little digs and flourishes that we had to be on our toes to catch.

Clay made a short, final address to all of us. "This is your last chance," he said. "It's your last chance to get on the bandwagon. I'm keeping a list of all you people. After the fight is done, we're going to have a roll call up there in the ring. And when I see so-and-so said this fight was a mismatch, why, I'm going to have a little ceremony and some *eating* is going on—eating of words." His manner was that of the admonishing schoolteacher. The press sat in their rows at the Miami Auditorium staring balefully at him. It seemed incredible that a smile or two wouldn't show up on a writer's face. It was so wonderfully preposterous. But I didn't see any.

The Liston people made a production of the champion's training—a well-made theatrical event that cost fifty cents to see and was worth it. It took place in the Surfside Civic Auditorium in North Miami Beach every afternoon until just a day or so before the fight. The auditorium was a cheerful place, with two or three hundred blue-leathered chairs facing a stage, which had a grand piano at its foot, off to one side, flanked by American and Florida State flags. It was on the second floor. Downstairs there was a recreation hall with teenagers playing Ping-Pong, a "library," which always seemed locked, and a swimming pool, a large one, with just a step or so down to the beach and the sea.

The production opened with a film shown on a screen set up in front of the stage—a twenty-minute "official" film of Liston's destruction of Floyd Patterson in the first round of their second fight, in Las Vegas. Much of the film footage promoted Las Vegas and certain of its hotels, but the minute or so of the fight was shown twice, once in slow motion, so that the concussive force of Liston's attack became shockingly apparent, the anatomy of destruction, every blow, alternate hooks, one after another, absolutely predictable because in slow motion each was telegraphed: Patterson's body quivered like a struck custard as he sailed to the canvas, bounced once gently and then could not rise.

During the slow-motion footage the sound track of the crowd was very loud—a long, sustained yell—and when the film was suddenly over, the last shot showing Patterson, on his feet, being comforted by Cus D'Amato, his trainer, and the lights went up, applause began, and a young man wearing a University of Miami sweatshirt came out and removed the screen. Behind it, on the stage, a ring had been set up and standing in the middle of it, expressionless, huge, we saw the perpetrator of the execution we'd just seen, the champion, dressed in close-fitting black trunks and a shirt promoting the Thunderbird Hotel in Las Vegas. Applause began again. An announcer stepped forward with a microphone and introduced the champion's entourage. They stepped forward and bowed stiffly. They rarely took their eyes off the champion. They all had towels and when the champion finished an exercise they rushed forward to mop him off, two of them kneeling on the stage floor to get at his legs. Willie Reddish, the trainer, being the top dog, had the privilege of working the towel across Liston's features—the faintly pouted lips and the hard eyes searching the audience—dabbing at them, then covering them carefully with the towel, and then, with the towel's removal, the features emerging as they went in, exactly, as if what was being mopped off were stone.

The announcer presented each exercise; first, Liston in a shadowboxing session with a sparring partner, the two wearing very light gloves and never actually establishing contact. The announcer warned that no one in the audience would be allowed to take photos with a flashbulb, which might temporarily blind the champion and cause him to miscalculate and hit his sparring partner by mistake. A low whistle went up at the thought of what would happen. No bulbs. The shadowboxing went three rounds. Liston looked fast and tireless. His opponent skipped and wheeled, his ring shoes squeaking on the canvas, moving very fast, as presumably Clay would do; but Liston always seemed to loom above him, an attendant thunderhead. We were seeing the part of the show that emphasized Liston's speed. Heavy applause when it was done, and up front a row of small girls whacked their hands together like applauding seals.

The ring was removed by stagehands. Liston stood off to one side, among his attendants and their towels. The announcer came forward again. "The champion at the light bag," he said. The attendants backed away and Liston cruised slowly over and went to work, a powerful *rat-tat-tat* on the light bag, minute following minute, until after a while people began to suck in their breath at his physical stamina, and when the act finally ended, with one last concussive whack at the bag, more applause broke out as the attendants moved quickly for him, fresh towels in their hands. You could see the people in the audience looking at one another, shaking their heads. Then came the phase which emphasized the indestructibility of the champion. Reddish would pick up a fifteen-pound medicine ball, and, grunting and wheezing (perhaps a bit more than he had to), he would wind up and heave the thing at the champion's stomach. The champion would brace himself. It would hit with no effect other than a loud *thwack,* bounce to the floor, where Reddish would retrieve it, and he'd back off and try again. Finally, after ten heaves or so, Reddish tottered off, hamming it up, the champion un-budged, staring after him. It was a good show, though it didn't prove much. "What they are trying to tell us," said one wag, "is that a medicine ball ain't going to make it to be champion of the world."

Following a series of limbering exercises, we came to the finale: a record of *Night Train;* Liston skipped rope on a flat plank that acted as a sounding board. The tread of his gym shoes and the percussion section of the band on the record hammered at the stomach. The record went on and on, the phonograph arm resetting on the opening measures as soon as the record finished.

"Note," said the announcer, "that the champion's heels never touch the board. He does all this off his toes."

We looked and it was so. We watched, hypnotized, the swing of the skipping rope, the churning motion of his legs, until the human quality seemed to leave him. When it was over, a good stage manager would have drawn the curtain, and let us go to remember that suspended rage. But at this point an attempt was made to humanize Liston. He was toweled off, fetched up in a gold-trimmed robe, and those in the audience who wanted to have their picture taken with him were invited to a table at the foot of the stage to pay ten dollars for the privilege. Many in the audience pressed forward to do so, paying, then stepping up on the stage and walking across to where Liston waited in front of a white screen. They walked toward him somewhat stiffly, some with tentative smiles. A photographer's assistant held their handbags and coats for them, and they stepped up beside the champion and turned to face the camera. Liston's face was always the same—he was at rest now, and had something of the look of a contented cat. If a girl stood beside him, he would drape a hand across her shoulder. Once he bent slightly and picked up a black woman, wearing a flowered hat, who weighed two hundred pounds. The camera shutter clicked. A piece of costume jewelry fell off her and crashed to the floor. Her body shook as she giggled. Liston continued to hold her aloft. One of his cuadrilla produced a high, keening wheeze of appreciative chuckling, leaning forward to pound his knee. Liston set her down and looked for the next. The woman, her hat now gone askew, retrieved her jewelry. She seemed relieved to get off the stage.

When the photographing was over, members of the press were asked to stay for a press conference. Almost everyone hung around. We couldn't get enough of him. I was hoping he would say something. I had heard that he had once said about one of his managers, a man named Katz, that if he ever got the electric chair, he hoped he could arrange for ten percent of the "juice" to go to Katz. I thought that was quite sharp. A red curtain was drawn across the stage, and after the fifteen minutes or so it took

Liston to shower and change, he came out in front to answer questions. His cuadrilla was with him. A chair was brought out for him, which he sat down on, and his people arranged themselves around him as if for a formal group photograph. He had a golfing cap on, a two-toned sweater, and he wore a big ring on his little finger which had the effect of magnifying the bulk of his hand. Willie Reddish stood next to him. Questions were asked for. Someone in the press wanted to know if Liston had ever hit anyone as hard as he could. Liston looked interested, but Reddish answered the question for him. "No," he said. "No fighter ever hits as hard as he can. He's never set for it. His target is always on the move, even if the fellow he's hittin' is out on his feet and ready to go down." Liston seemed pleased with the answer.

A reporter raised his hand. "Sonny, I'd like to know what you're going to look for when Clay comes out in the first round."

The champion spoke for the first time, after some consideration—a voice surprisingly soft and silky: "I look for him to pull a gun."

The cuadrilla rocked with laughter—Beau Jack, the ex-fighter, ex–shoeshine boy, now as fat as a turnip, almost going to his knees with his guffawing. They all kept their eyes on the champion as they laughed. He remained expressionless. It took a moment or so for the room to quiet down, a little longer for the people up on the stage.

At the fights in Miami one was sure, sooner or later, to run into King Levinsky, a second-rate heavyweight when in his prime (he was one of Joe Louis' bums of the month) who had probably fought too long, so that it had affected him. He was now an ambulatory tie salesman, working out of a cardboard suitcase. He would appear in the Municipal Auditorium around the press headquarters displaying his wares; they were decorated with a pair of boxing gloves and he'd get rid of them in jig-time by reason of a formidable sales technique: he would single out a prospect and move down the corridor for him fast, like a fighter cutting the ring; and sweeping an arm around the fellow's neck, he would pull him in close, to within range of a hoarse and somewhat wetly delivered whisper to the ear: "From the King? You buy a tie from the King?" The victim, his head in the crook of the fighter's massive arm, would mumble and nod weakly and fish for his bankroll. Almost everyone had a Levinsky tie (I had three), though I didn't see too many people wearing them. When the King appeared around a corner, the press would scatter, some into a row of phone booths set along the corridor. "Levinsky!" they'd call out to one another, and move quickly. Levinsky would peer around like a puzzled bear and then he'd spot the crowded phone booths. He'd set his cardboard box down; he'd pick out some poor writer, staring wide-eyed out from his booth, like a goldfish in a drinking glass, and the King would begin to shake the booth gently. You'd see him watching the fellow inside; then the door would open and the writer would come and buy a tie. It only cost a dollar.

Levinsky was a discomforting presence. I remember Clay came down the corridors of the Municipal Auditorium after the crazy Sonny Liston weigh-in proceedings and Levinsky bounded after him, the ties spilling from his cardboard box. "He's gonna take you, kid!" he hollered. "Liston's gonna take you, make you a guy selling ties.... Partners with me, kid, you can be *partners* with me." The challenger's entourage was moving at a lively clip, canes on high, shouting that they were ready to rumble, so it was doubtful the chilling offer got through.

At the late-afternoon press parties in the bar of the Roney Plaza the promoters had a more presentable fighter at hand named Marty Marshall, a personable black heavyweight who was the only man to have beaten Liston. The promoters brought him down from Detroit, his hometown, to impress the writers that Liston wasn't invincible, hoping that this notion would appear in their columns and help promote a gate lagging badly since the fight was universally considered a mismatch. Marshall had met Liston three times in the ring, winning the first time, then losing twice, though decking Liston in the second, always baffling him with an unpredictable attack. Liston blamed his one loss on his making the mistake of dropping his jaw to laugh at

Marshall's maneuvers, and *bam!* getting it broken with a sudden punch.

Marshall doesn't strike one as a comic figure. He is a tall, graceful man, conservatively dressed, with a pleasant face, small, round, delicate ears and a quick smile. Greeting him was a complex matter, since he was attended for a while by someone who introduced him by saying, "Shake the hand that broke Sonny Liston's jaw!" Since Marshall is an honest man and it was a left hook that did the business, his *left* would come out and one had to consider whether to take it with one's own left, or with the right, before getting down to the questions. There was almost always a circle around him in the bar. The press couldn't get enough of what it was to be in the ring with Liston. Marshall didn't belittle the experience.

"When I knocked him down with that left hook in the second fight, he got up angry," said Marshall. "He hit me three shots you shouldn't've thrown at a bull. The first didn't knock me down, but it hurt so much I went down anyway."

"Jeezus," said one of the reporters.

"Does he say anything—I mean when he's angry? Can you see it?"

"No," said Marshall. "He's silent. He just come for you."

"Jeezus," said the reporter again.

We all stood around, looking admiringly at Marshall, jiggling the ice in our glasses.

One of the writers cleared his throat. "I heard a story about the champion this morning," he said. "He does his roadwork, you know, out at the Normandy Golf Course, wearing that hooded sweatshirt, and there was this greenskeeper working out there, very early, pruning the grass at the edge of a water hazard, the mist coming off the grass, very quiet, spooky, you know, and he hears this noise behind him and he looks over his shoulder and there's Liston there, about ten feet away, looking out of his hood at him, and this greenskeeper is so scared he gives a big scream and pitches forward into the water."

"Yeah," said Marshall. He was smiling. "I can see that."

Each fighter had his spiritual adviser, his *guru,* at hand. In

Liston's camp was Father Murphy, less a religious adviser than a confidant and friend of the champion. In Clay's camp was Malcolm X, who was then one of the high officials of the Black Muslim sect, indeed its most prominent spokesman, though he subsequently defected to form his own black nationalist political movement (and eventually was assassinated for doing so). For months he had been silent. Elijah Muhammad, the supreme leader, the Messenger of Allah, had muzzled him for making intemperate remarks after the assassination of President Kennedy. But he had been rumored to be in Miami, and speculation was strong that he was there to bring Cassius Clay into the Muslim fold.

I was riding in a car with Archie Robinson, who is Clay's business manager and closest friend—a slightly built young man, not much older than Clay, one would guess, very polite and soft-spoken—and he asked me if I'd like to meet Malcolm X. I said yes, and we drove across Biscayne Bay to the Negro-clientele Hampton House Motel in Miami proper—a small-town hotel compared to the Babylon towers across the Bay, with a small swimming pool, a luncheonette, a pitch-dark bar where you had to grope to find a chair, with a dance floor and a band which came on later, and most of the rooms in balconied barracklike structures out back. It was crowded and very lively with people in town not only for the fight but also for an invitational golf tournament.

I waited at a side table in the luncheonette. Malcolm X came in after a while, moving by the tables very slowly. Elijah Muhammad's ministers—Malcolm X was one of them—are said to emulate him even to the speed of his walk, which is considerable. Seeing the ministers moving in a small group was not unlike watching parade marshals coming around a corner in an old speeded-up newsreel: they scurried. But the luncheonette was not set up for a swift entrance. The tables were close together, and Malcolm X came by them carefully—a tall, erect man in his thirties, a lean, intelligent face with a long pronounced jaw, a wide mouth set in it which seems caught in a perpetual smile. He was carrying one of the Cassius Clay camp's souvenir canes, and with his horn-rimmed glasses, his slow stately walk, and with Robinson half a step behind him, guiding him, I thought for a second that he'd gone blind. He sat down, unwrapped a package of white peppermints which he picked at steadily, and began talking. Robinson sat with us for a while, but he had things to attend to and he left the pair of us alone.

I took notes from time to time, scratching them down on the paper tablecloth, then in a notebook. Malcolm X did not seem to mind. He said he was going to be unmuzzled in March, which was only five days away. He himself wrote on the tablecloth once in a while—putting down a word he wanted to emphasize. He had an automatic pen-and-pencil set in his shirt pocket—the clasps initialed FOI on one (Fruit of Islam, which is the military organization within the Muslim temple) and ISLAM on the other. He wore a red ring with a small crescent.

Malcolm X's voice is gentle, and he often smiles broadly, but not with humor. His manner is distant and he asks, mocking slightly, "Sir?" when a question is not heard or understood, leaning forward and cocking his head. His answers are always skilled, with a lively and effective use of image, and yet as the phrases came I kept thinking of Cassius Clay and *his* litany—the fighter's is more limited, and a different sort of thing, but neither of them ever *stumbles* over words, or ideas, or appears balked by a question, so that one rarely has the sense of the brain actually working but rather that it is engaged in rote, simply a recording apparatus playing back to an impulse. He is intractable—Malcolm X—absolutely dedicated, self-assured, self-principled, with that great energy ... the true revolutionary.

"The extremist," he said, "will always ruin the liberals in debate—because the liberals have something too nebulous to sell, or too impossible to sell—like the Brooklyn Bridge. That's why a white segregationalist—what's his name, Kilpatrick—will destroy Farmer, and why William Buckley makes a fool of Norman Mailer, and why Martin Luther King would lose a debate with me." "Why Mr. King?" I asked. "Because integration is ridiculous, a dream," Malcolm X replied. "I am not interested in dreams, but in the nightmare. Martin Luther King, the rest of them, they are thinking about dreams. But then really King and I have nothing to debate about. We are both indicting. I would say to him: 'You indict and give them hope. I'll indict and give them no hope.' "

I asked him about the remarks that had caused him his muzzling by Elijah Muhammad. His remarks about the assassination had been taken out of context, he said, though it would be the sheerest hypocrisy to suggest that Kennedy was a friend to the Negro. Kennedy was a politician (he wrote down the word on the paper tablecloth with his FOI pencil and circled it)—a "cold-blooded politician" who transformed last year's civil-rights march on Washington into a "crawl" by endorsing the march, joining it, though it was supposed to be a protest against the country's leaders . . . a politician's trick which tamped out the fuse though the powder keg was there. Friend of the Negro? There never had been a politician who was the Negro's friend. Power corrupts. Lincoln? A crooked, deceitful hypocrite, claiming championship to the cause of the Negro who, one hundred years later, finds himself singing "We Shall Overcome." The Supreme Court? Its decision is nothing but an act of hypocrisy . . . nine Supreme Court justices expert in legal phraseology tangling the words of their decision in such a way that lawyers can dilly-dally over it for years—which of course they will continue to do . . .

I scribbled these phrases, and others, on the paper tablecloth, mildly surprised to see the Muslim maxims in my own handwriting. We talked about practicality, which is the weakest area of the Muslim plans. Malcolm X was not particularly concerned. What may be illogical or impractical in the long run is dismissed as not being pertinent to the *moment*—which is what the Negro must concern himself with. He had a peppermint and smiled.

I changed the subject and asked him what he did for exercise.

"I take walks," he said. "Long walks. We believe in exercise, physical fitness, but as for commercial sport, that's a racket. Commercial sport is the pleasure of the idle rich. The vice of gambling stems from it." He wrote down the word "Promoter" on the tablecloth with his FOI pencil and circled it. "The Negro never comes out ahead—never *one* in the history of sport."

"Clay perhaps."

"Perhaps." He liked talking about Clay. "I'm interested in him as a human being," he said. He tapped his head. "Not many people know the quality of the mind he's got in there. He fools them. One forgets that though a clown never imitates a wise man, the wise man can imitate the clown. He is sensitive, very humble, yet shrewd—with as much untapped mental energy as he has physical power. He should be a diplomat. He has that instinct of seeing a tricky situation shaping up—my own presence in Miami, for example—and resolving how to sidestep it. He knows how to handle people, to get them functioning. He gains strength from being around people. He can't stand being alone. The more people around, the better—just as it takes water to prime a country well. If the crowds are big in there tonight in the Miami Auditorium, he's likely to beat Liston. But they won't be. The Jews have heard he's a Muslim and they won't show up."

"Perhaps they'll show up to see him taken," I said.

"Sir?" he said, with that slight cock of the head.

"Perhaps . . ."

"When Cassius said, 'I am a man of race,' " Malcolm X went on, "it pleased the Negroes. He wouldn't eliminate the color factor. But the press and the white people saw it another way. They saw him, suddenly, as a threat. Which is why he has become the villain—why he is booed, the outcast." He seemed pleased with this.

Wasn't it possible, I asked, that the braggart, the loudmouth, was being booed, not necessarily the Black Muslim? After all, Clay had been heartily booed during the Doug Jones fight in Madison Square Garden, and that was before his affiliation with the Muslims was known.

"You, *you* can't tell," replied Malcolm X. "But a Negro can feel things in sounds. The booing at the Doug Jones fight was good-natured—I was there—but the booing is now different . . . defiant . . . inflamed by the columnists, all of them, critical of Cassius for being a Muslim."

"And as a fighter?"

"He has tremendous self-confidence," said Malcolm X. "I've

never heard him mention fear. Anything you're afraid of can whip you. Fear magnifies what you're afraid of. One thing about our religion is that it removes fear. Christianity is based on fear."

I remarked that one could say that the Muslim religion, since it has its taboos and promises and threats, is also based on fear— one remembers that British soldiers extracted secrets from terrified Muslim captives by threatening to sew them up for a while in a pig's skin.

Malcolm X acknowledged that the Muslims had to adapt and shift Islam to their purposes. "We are in a cage," he said. "What must be taught to the lion in a cage is quite different from what one teaches the lion in the jungle. The Mohammedan abroad believes in a heaven and a hell, a hereafter. Here we believe that heaven and hell are on this earth, and that we are in the hell and must strive to escape it. If we can adapt Islam to this purpose, we should. For people fighting for their freedom there is no such thing as a bad device."

He snorted about peaceful methods. "The methods of Gandhi?" Another snort. "The Indians are hypocrites. Look at Goa. Besides, they are the most helpless people on earth. They succeeded in removing the British only because they outnumbered them, out*weighed* them—a big dark elephant sitting on a white elephant. In this country the situation is different. The white elephant is huge. But we will catch him. We will catch him when he is asleep. The mice will run up his trunk when he is asleep.

"Where? They will come out of the alley. The revolution always comes from the alley—from the man with nothing to lose. Never the bourgeois. The poor Negro bourgeois, with his golf clubs, his golfing hat"—he waved at the people in the lunchroom—"he's so much more frustrated than the Negro in the alley; he gets the doors slapped shut in his face every day. But the explosion won't come from him. Not from the pickets either, or the nonviolent groups—these masochists ... they *want* to be beaten—but it will come from the people *watching*—spectators for the moment. They're different. You don't know. It is dangerous to suggest that the Negro is nonviolent.

"There *must* be retribution. It is proclaimed. If retribution came to the Pharoah for his enslavement of six hundred thousand, it will come to the white American who enslaved twenty million and robbed their minds."

"And retribution, that is in the Koran?"

"Sir?"

"The Koran . . . ?"

He said, "Chapter twenty-two, verse one-oh-two."

I put the numbers down, thinking to catch him out; I looked later. The verse reads: *"The day when the trumpet is blown. On that day we assemble the guilty white-eyed (with terror)."*

"These are the things you are teaching Cassius?"

"He will make up his own mind."

He popped a peppermint into his mouth. We talked a little longer, somewhat aimlessly. He had an appointment with someone, he finally said, and he stood up. The noise of conversation dropped noticeably in the luncheonette as he stood up and walked out, erect and moving slowly, holding his gaudy souvenir cane out in front of him as he threaded his way between the tables; the people in the golfing hats watched him go.

I went out into the hotel lobby, just stood around feeling low. The cars were whipping by on the turnpike. A phrase from Kafka, or rather the idea of some phrases from *The Trial*, came to mind. I looked them up when I had the chance. "But I am not guilty," said K. "It's a mistake. Besides, how can a man be guilty? We're all men." "True," said the priest, "but that's how the guilty talk."

Mid-morning on the day of the fight the weighing-in took place. The weigh-in ceremony is traditionally a low-key affair, where reporters, ex-fighters, hangers-on, stand around, renew acquaintanceships—big hellos with always the hope that a photographer will be on hand to record them. It is hard to work up much excitement over the climax of a weigh-in, which is the presentation of the fighters' weights, though the statistics are intoned with solemnity and listened to with respect. True, the fighters themselves, at the scales, usually impassive, are scru-

tinized with care, not as one looks at a horse in the paddock—
that is, not speculatively—but as one probes the human condition, as if something could be divulged of the state of mind of a
fighter facing the enormity of a championship bout only hours
away. And sometimes in the first confrontation of the day
between the two fighters, a few psychic blows can be thrown.
Archie Moore used a weigh-in to intimidate his opponent with a
hard stare, and before his fight with Floyd Patterson he was
noticed standing on his toes trying to intimidate with size—
puffing himself up like a toad. At a weigh-in in 1962, Benny
Paret's death in the ring that night was ordained when he twitted
his opponent, Emile Griffith, about his manhood, and they
almost had their first round on the scales. So, occasionally, things
of moment do occur. But for sheer malarkey the Liston-Clay
weigh-in eclipsed them all.

The proceedings took place in one of the auditorium's big
high-ceilinged rooms. The scales were set on a large wooden
stage with steps going up at one end which were guarded by
police. The sociology of a championship is controlled by a strict
caste system, and even at the height of lunacy a knot of angry
people continued arguing with the police that they were privileged to be up on the stage.

Clay had put in an early appearance—about a half hour before
the ceremony was to begin. He swept in and swept out, traveling
at a good clip, shouting, "It's my time to *howl*. . . . I'm going to
rumble, man, rumble. . . ." His entourage tried to keep up with
him, the canes which they all affected raised, and then he was
gone. It was evident he was working himself up, and when,
almost an hour later, he returned and tore up the stairs and onto
the stage—now thick with officials and the privileged—he had a
frenzied rhythm to him, the speed of his walk stuck fast, as if
only a cataleptic seizure would relieve him of his dervish
whirlings. When Sonny Liston entered and slowly stepped up the
stairs, Clay stormed and carried on, leaping up within the circle
of his people. In the uproar it was difficult to hear what he was
shouting. Once I heard him yelling, "You can't scare me with
that look"—and indeed Liston was staring at him with a look

that may have been baleful but that also seemed puzzled to me, perhaps awed, and he shook his head a few times to indicate utter bewilderment. It was the kindliest set I had seen to his features.

I kept my eye on the commission doctor. He was a small, bespectacled, completely studious man with a job to do—measure the fighters' heartbeats and take their blood pressures—and he kept at it doggedly, doing Liston first, who sat looking out over the crowd, occasionally raising two fingers to show he would take care of Clay in the second round. The doctor then moved for Clay, who was on the rear of the platform shouting "Chump! chump! chump!" and being restrained by Sugar Ray Robinson, who had his arms around him. Teddy Brenner, the boxing promoter, was reported in Red Smith's column in the *Tribune* the next day to have remarked that Clay was the first fighter Sugar Ray, who was getting on, though still fighting, has been able to tie up in a decade. Clay's efforts were mostly vocal, but he was straining within the circumference of Sugar Ray's arms and the two of them stumbled about the rear of the platform, ringed by people shouting at Clay to behave himself. The doctor got through this perimeter, his eye on Clay, and kept after him, his stethoscope outstretched and at the ready, and when he had his target in range, he darted forward with two little jerky steps and planted the stethoscope on Clay's chest, getting perhaps a thud of that racing heartbeat in his eardrums before Clay's klipspringer leap threw him off. He tried it a few times, a doughty figure doing his best. He was only able to get his job done when it was announced over the public-address system that the commissioner had fined Clay $2,500 for his behavior. Clay sat down at that, and was more tractable, though his shouting continued. Later, the doctor reported that Clay's pulse was up to 180, and that it was his impression that Clay was "scared to death."

I managed to wedge into Clay's dressing room after the weigh-in. One of Clay's people nodded at a policeman and I was allowed past. It was quiet in there, a very small room with just enough space for a training table and a few chairs. Outside you could hear the hubbub. We all watched Clay. I was surprised. I half expected his own people would be tending him, trying to quiet him down. He was absolutely calm. He sat on the edge of the training table. "What do you think?" he asked. No one answered. "He was really shook up," said Clay. "He was little, and he was short, and they're telling me he was so big." He paused. "I think he was shook up."

He stripped off his clothes, Bundini blotted at him with a towel, and he put on a fresh pair of trousers and an orange shirt.

"Let's have the cane," he said.

Moving for him, one of his seconds knocked over a waste-paper basket. It clanged—everybody jumped—and rolled on the floor.

"That's the big ugly bear goin' down," the second said.

"Yeah," said Clay. "I'm not scared," he said again. He sat down again on the edge of the training table. No one said anything. He could have been an introspective ten-year-old testing his reactions to find out about them more exactly. Everyone in the room stared at him, watching him do so.

I had a seat in the auxiliary press section, a long way back, behind the $250 "sportsman" seats and the $100 seats. Many of them were empty—whole rows of them—but no one seemed to move forward into them. A $25 top and there'd have been quite a press forward at the last moment, but slipping into someone else's $250 seat did not seem something to do with impunity.

The man sitting next to me gave me the once-over and announced that he'd been going to prizefights for thirty, forty years, and if you asked his opinion, Liston and Clay were both bums. "Just bums," he said.

Clay came into the ring first. He came down the aisle very fast, leaving his entourage and the police escort trailing behind him as he moved at that storming pace of his, hopped between the ropes, and went immediately to his corner. He was wearing a white terry-cloth bathrobe, a shift-length thing you might find on a Brazilian beach or in a fashion magazine. It had THE LIP in red script across his shoulders, and also a hood, down, which flopped on his back as he scraped his gym shoes in the rosin box and began to jog in his corner, looking calmly out over the crowd. Gloria Guinness, one of the world's great fashion figures, who was covering the fight for *Harper's Bazaar*—the first fight she'd ever seen—took one look at him and reported later to me that she had nearly fainted. "He was simply to die over," she said in her manner. She couldn't take her eyes off him.

As for what he looked like as a prizefighter, that was promising, too—no nonsense about him. There had been rumors that if he arrived in the ring at all, he was going to mess around in Liston's corner—jaw at him, stand in his rosin box. But there was none of this. He kept up his jogging, his back—with the bouncing hood and that inscription, THE LIP—to Liston's corner. "He looks like maybe he's come to fight," I said to my companion.

"A gah-damned cream puff," he replied.

Liston came in, hooded in white, as usual, moving slowly down the aisle, people on chairs craning to see, and quite a roar greeting his arrival. The crowd noise had awe in it, as if a large piece of important machinery had turned up to get a job done, the sort of applause that a tank receives in a military parade. Clay's was more partisan, and frantic—shriller, probably the female contingent—and as for the booing he got, I wasn't able to gauge whether it was antibraggard, or anti-anti-Jew, as Malcolm X had prophesied, or simply good-natured.

During prefight ceremonies Clay did something which caught the fancy of many people. Sugar Ray Robinson, very gaudy in a black-lapeled pepper-gray suit, was introduced to the crowd, and when he got into the ring, Clay stopped his jogging and bowed to Robinson, a low, obeisant bow, heels together, very formal indeed. He was clowning: he has great respect for Sugar Ray but the bow was so exaggerated as to put him nearly on his face. The crowd liked that. The assumption was that if Clay wasn't an hysteric in the ring, he'd come in zombie stiff, gape-jawed, and await his extinction. What they saw was a fighter supremely confident, his senses very much alive—not past playfulness—and you could feel the crowd warm to him.

*   *   *

Sure enough. He survived the first two rounds easily enough. Then, in the third round Clay, increasingly contemptuous, threw a quick right hand and it opened up Liston's cheekbone: a sheen of blood appeared. It is not a dangerous place to be hit, beneath the eye, but Liston reacted like a bull under the sharp pain of the banderillas—bucking, nearly, with rage—and he leaped after Clay, who had a somewhat pop-eyed, startled look, his white mouthpiece shining in his face, as he backpedaled, as if he couldn't quite believe what he'd done. Blood did not seem appropriate to Liston, it was said later—lox, perhaps, or liquid hydrogen—and Clay seemed as surprised as anyone. He must have been very pleased with things. He jeered at Liston in that round and when he got back to his stool he began mugging it up for the press packed around the ring, peering down at them between the ropes as his handlers worked on him, and dropping his jaw to give them the Big Mouth. I could see his trainer, Angelo Dundee, shouting at him in the uproar, presumably telling him to keep his mind on the business at hand.

The fourth was the only slow round of the fight; Liston slowed down, and Clay was not quite ready to go over to the attack. During the round some of the caustic solution on Liston's cut was transferred, probably by Liston's glove, to Clay's forehead, where it got down into his eyes, causing the wild bunkum of the fifth round.

The fifth round, like the weigh-in, did not properly belong to the boxing spectacle. Everyone watched in amazement. It was a vital moment in heavyweight history since, reflecting back, it was evident that boxing, which was not in the healthiest condition, could have been corked up and finished in that round. Consider: Clay didn't want to come out for the round at all. He told me later he was at the door of the Near Room—the place with the trombone-playing alligators and the screaming snakes. He almost went in. He said that his eyes hurt so much from whatever it was in them that he told Dundee to "cut the gloves off." The warning buzzer which gives the handlers ten seconds to get out of the ring had sounded and the referee was within a second or so of awarding the fight to Liston when Dundee finally got his fighter moving, pushing him toward the center of the ring, shouting at him that it was "the big one, Daddy" and to *"get going."* If Clay had not made it, the crowd in the auditorium and in the closed-circuit theaters across the country would have whooped it up and started smashing things—I don't think they would have stood for it—and since the odds had gone from 8-1 to 9-1 at fight time, reflecting late heavy money on Liston (probably due to Clay's psychotic behavior at the weigh-in), a fixed fight would have been indicated.

As it was, it looked as if the fix had been set for Clay to go down in the fifth and that he was being sulky about it. None of us, of course, was aware of what had happened to his eyes. We saw a flurry of corner men around Clay until the bell sounded, and then Clay himself, listless, his hands down, shaking his head, moving out flat-footed, all the celerity, the cockiness, gone from him. Liston began to move for him. Everyone stood up and began to yell. A row of chairs went over in front of me with a crash I couldn't hear for the noise around me. My companion began to yell, "The fix is in, the fix!" jabbing his finger at the ring. I could barely hear his voice.

I suspect Clay could see much better than he allowed later, when he said that Liston was just a vague blur. Surely his eyes hurt, but like a small child, he wanted everyone to know it and to feel sympathy for him. A show of this sort is all right at the age of eight—bitten by a yellowjacket at a Sunday picnic, to stand off with the corners of your mouth down—but in a prize ring which has Sonny Liston in it such petulance is not much short of lunatic. But Clay got away with it. He got tagged a few times, and you could see his head snap back from the blows, but he survived, and he was able to make Liston miss enough so that by the end of the round he had the champion arm weary again, worn, almost motionless. He was actually able to hold Liston off with an extended arm. It had been an extraordinary feat.

There was almost as much noise between rounds as there had been during the fifth, the sharp babble of onlookers leaning in on their neighbors to find out what they'd seen. My companion was shouting in my ear, "The champ's gone; his gloves are full of *mush,* I tell ya; he's gotta be finished." He was chewing gum extremely fast. "The kid sticks an arm out like that, he's gotta get *kilt,* he's gotta get *ruint.* But the champ can't do it. He's wore out."

At the bell opening the sixth Clay came off his stool fast and lively, back to his usual style. He threw the first two punches of the round—sharp picture-book jabs—and he began circling, always to the left, away from the champion's power. Liston, no longer on the offensive, revolved in the center of the ring, occasionally plodding two or three small steps and setting himself. It seemed the sort of round fighters use to pace themselves in a long fight. When the bell sounded, there wasn't the slightest suspicion that it wouldn't sound again.

Clay himself must have known first. He was up off his stool at the warning buzzer for the seventh, jogging, looking across at Liston, counting down the seconds to the bell—"ten ... nine ... eight ..."—when suddenly his jogging became frenetic and his arms went up. He'd seen Jack Nilon remain in the corner, making no move for the ropes, and then he'd seen Liston spit out his mouthpiece.

For the rest of us, astonishment swept across the arena once again: "Wha'? Wha'? Wha'?" We didn't know that Liston's left arm had gone numb from a strain of a muscle.

I went around with the new champion the next day to the house he had rented for himself and his seconds. The living accommodations for Liston and Clay had been as different as their fighting styles. Liston had a big place on the beach, a sixteen-room house next to Yankee owner Dan Topping's, reportedly very plush, wall-to-wall carpeting, with each room set up like a golf-club lounge, a television set going interminably, perhaps someone in front of it, perhaps not, and always, invariably, a card game.

Clay's place was on the mainland, in North Miami, in a low-rent district—a plain, white one-story home with louvered windows, a front door with steps leading up to a little porch with room for one chair, a front yard with more chairs set around and shaded by a big ficus tree with leaves dusty from the traffic on

Fifth Street. His entire entourage stayed there, living dormitory style, two or three to a room. Outside the yard was worn almost bare. There wasn't a neighborhood child on his way home from school during the time Clay was training in Miami who didn't pass by to see if anything was up. Films were shown there in the evening, outside in the yard, the children sitting quietly until the film started. Then the questions and the exclamations would come, Clay explaining things, and you could hardly hear the sound track. Only one film kept them quiet. That was the favorite film, shown two or three times, *The Invasion of the Body-Snatchers*. The children watched wide-eyed within the comforting sounds of the projector's whir and the traffic going by occasionally on Fifth Street. When the big moths would show up suddenly in the light beam—almost as big as white towels, they seemed—a yelp or two would go up, particularly if a body was being snatched at the time, and the children would sway for one another.

The children were waiting for Clay when we drove up. They came for the car, shouting, and packing in around so that the doors had to be opened gingerly. Clay got out, towering above them as he walked slowly for a chair in the front yard. The litany started almost as soon as he sat down, the children around him twelve deep.

"Who's the king of kings?"

"Cassius Clay!"

"Who shook up the world?"

"Cassius Clay!"

"Who's the greatest?"

"Cassius Clay!"

"Who's the ugly bear?"

"Sonny Liston!"

"What round d'he get beat in?"

Confusion here—almost as much as there'd been in the auditorium—some yelling six, some seven, and others, the smaller ones, simply puzzled. Clay would get them back on safe ground soon enough.

"Who's the prettiest?"

"Cassius Clay!"

I went inside while this was going on. The main room, with an alcove, had sofas along the wall. The artifacts of the psychological campaign against Liston were set around—signs that read SETTIN' TRAPS FOR THE BIG BEAR, which had been brandished outside his training quarters, and, standing next to an easel in a corner, a valentine as tall as a man, complete with cherubs, which had been offered Liston and which he had refused. Newspapers were flung around—there had been some celebrating the night before—and someone's shoe was in the middle of the room. Souvenir canes were propped up by the side of the stove in the cooking alcove. It was fraternity-house clutter. I was standing next to Howard Bingham, Clay's "official" photographer. "It was fun, wasn't it?" I said. "I mean, it would have been fun even if the title hadn't come with it."

"Oh my," he said. "We have the *best* time here."

Bingham had joined up with Clay after the George Logan fight, in California. He was about Clay's age, younger perhaps, and shy. The others got on him. They nicknamed him Oh Please, which was what he'd say when they'd josh him. He stuttered a bit, and he told me that he didn't take their kidding lying down. He said, "I walk around the house and ... sc-sc-scare people, jump out at them. Or they'd ... doze off on the ... c-c-couch, and I sneak around and tickle them on the nose, y'know, with a piece of string. Why, I was agitating ... C-C-Cassius for half an hour once when he was dozing off. And I give the hot ... f-f-feet around here and a lot of that. We had a high time."

I asked what Cassius' winning the championship meant for him.

"Well, of course that must make me the greatest ph-ph-photographer in the world." He couldn't keep a straight face. "Oh please," he said. His shoulders shook. "Well, I'll tell you. I'm going to get me a mo-mo-mohair wardrobe, that's one thing."

Clay was going strong outside, his voice rising above the babble of children's voices: *"Who shook up the world?"*

"Cassius Clay!"

I wandered back to his room. It was just large enough for a

bed, the mattress bare when I looked in there, an armchair with clothes, including his *bear-huntin'* jacket, thrown across it, and a plain teak-colored bureau which had a large-size bottle of Dickinson's witch hazel standing on it. A tiny oil painting of a New England harbor scene was on one wall, with a few newspaper articles taped next to it, illustrated, describing Clay at his most flamboyant. A training schedule was taped to the mirror over the bureau. It called for all to rise at five A.M. The bedclothes were in a corner. One corner of the mattress was covered with Cassius Clay's signature in light-blue ink, flowery, with the *C*'s tall and graceful, along with such *graffiti* as CASSIUS CLAY IS NEXT CHAMP; CHAMPION OF THE WORLD; LISTON IS FINISHED; THE NEXT CHAMP: CASSIUS CLAY.

Outside, it had all come true. His voice and the answers were unceasing. "You," he was calling, ". . . you all are looking . . . at . . . the . . . champion . . . of . . . the . . . whole . . . wide . . . world!"

9

had heard somewhere that Muhammad Ali (by this time he had changed his name) would be driving his bus and his whole entourage of sparring partners and cooks and hangers-on from Miami to Chicopee Falls, Massachusetts, where he planned to set up his prefight training for the second Sonny Liston fight, and that there were seats available if any sports journalists wanted to come along for the ride. I arranged a spot for myself, flew down from New York and took a taxi out to where the bus was waiting at Ali's place in North Miami.

Just before we set off, the new champion stood on the bus steps and made a short speech in which he described the blessings those on the trip (there were four journalists, counting myself) would enjoy: food, coffee, the new heavyweight champion at the wheel; he would tell us jokes, do dance routines and other entertainments; and he had only one request—that we all eat heavily before crossing the state line into Georgia, because we weren't going to be "flying" over the state. I didn't know what he meant at the time.

We set off. Ali called his bus Big Red, which was one of

Malcolm X's nicknames, but the bus was more likely named for its gaudy circus-wagon color. Inside, Ali had picked the decor—an eye-tiring silver roof with uneven patterns of burnished gold. Some of the seats had their supports removed so that they collapsed back on the seat behind; in them the sparring partners slept a lot, lying on their backs with their big hands folded comfortably on their coverall fronts. One of them was Cody Jones, whom everyone called the Porcupine for his swept-up hairstyle. Indeed, he *was* a hairstylist, and a barber as well, which was practical at the training camps where he sparred. He cut George Chuvalo's hair for the Floyd Patterson fight, and later on, when Cody's mother saw a rerun of the fight on television, he said to her, "See that fellow getting hit with that right cross, Ma? That's my haircut he's wearing."

As we headed north, the stops were frequent—just places where Ali felt like pulling over to the side, usually lonely places with the pines stretching away from the ditches on either side of the macadam highway, and just the faintest whir of insects in that breathless heat, so that everyone walking away from the bus seemed to talk in low voices so as not to jar the stillness too much. The sparring partners squatted in a row and chucked pebbles into the cattails in the ditches. The cooks stayed in the bus. Ali dug down with his hands to where the earth was cool, sniffing at it as it trickled through his fingers, and then he made compresses of it, and spread them on the bare arms of those around him to show them how cool it was. Back down the highway from the bus Jimmy Ellis, who was one of his sparring mates then, found a dead snake in the weeds—a chicken snake nearly three feet long. He got ahold of it with a piece of stick and came high-stepping along, giggling, meaning to lob it at the champion, it was obvious, who watched him come for a while, and then jumped up and went down the creek bed at a great clip. Ellis kept after him, but lost ground steadily because of his burden, which was difficult to handle, and he was slowed by paroxysms of laughter, practically to a standstill, and finally he looked as if he were going to fall down for laughing so hard at the champion's haste. I could see the cooks looking out the bus window, grinning and pointing. The sun rose and the heat began to shimmer off the macadam. Ali wandered back. He took a pistol out of the bus and fired it at the sky, four shots shattering the quiet, as if he were signaling for someone; the pinewoods absorbed the echoes. We heard the click of the trigger pin. "Hey, is there some more bullets?" he called out to one of the cooks in the bus. "They is some lying aroun' in the box with the croquet set."

The cook's face disappeared for a while. Then he reappeared at the window and shook his head.

Bundini was smoking a cigar. The blue smoke drifted out across the ditches. "We have no bullets for that pistol? Oh, my goodness. We is defenseless. When the Klan turns up tonight, nothin' to do but help them with the nooses."

Bundini was the most expressive character in the Ali camp; he looked not unlike the champ, and was occasionally mistaken for him, except that he had a hugely mobile face that brought his emotions close to the surface. He often launched into a sort of helter-skelter holy-roller rhetoric which must have put the Black Muslims on edge. I am not sure they accepted his close friendship with Ali easily. At the time, Bundini was married to a large Jewish woman named Rhoda Palestine; he wore the Star of David on a chain around his neck and though his religion was a hodge-podge he had put together himself (he liked to refer to God as a personal friend of his named "Shorty"), he certainly was of no mind to become a Muslim. The Muslims certainly tried. He told me that Elijah Muhammad had described him as someone who would be worth ten battalions of ministers to the movement.

Ali and Bundini had met for the first time just before the Doug Jones fight in Madison Square Garden (which I would always remember because Ali ate some of the peanuts disgruntled fans threw at him from ringside). Bundini had been taken up to his room in a "raggedy" hotel called the American, where he found the young fighter lazing around in a clutter of clothing tossed every which way, shoes underfoot, and fight equipment hardly suitable for such a bright newcomer to the boxing scene. Bundini had asked, "Who takes care of you?" Ali said, "He do," and he pointed to a white man seated in a corner, smoking a cigar. Bundini looked over and suggested that the fighter's shoes needed polishing, and he mentioned what sort of wax should be used, and that his socks needed washing, and that the man had best *move* to care for a fighter packing people into the Garden up to the rafters and the seats where before there was nothin' there but *pigeons!* Ali listened to this in astonishment, being a Southern country boy who had never heard a white talked to in such a fashion.

"How did he react to this—this fellow in the corner?" I had asked.

"Why, he stepped right up and started in," Bundini said. "But the champ had his eye on me. The night of the fight I rode with him in the limousine to the Garden. We couldn't find a place to park, so I tol' the chauffeur to drive the car up on the sidewalk. The police came runnin' up, but I tol' them they had Cassius Clay there in the car, and if it warn't for him, they wouldn't be out there on duty. Sugar Ray, they let *him* park on the sidewalk. So they let us stay there, and that opened his eyes even mo'. He took me to the dressing room, but Angelo, he didn't know who I was, or why I was in there . . . so they made me wait outside . . . 'cept when they came out on the way to the ring I got close in behind Clay and started rubbing his neck muscles, just hanging on until we got to the ring posts. They couldn't budge me from the corner. I never seen this man box befo', but then I see Doug Jones—they call him 'Cueball'—hit him with a right hand in the fourth or fifth that just bounce him off the ropes, and when I saw him git over that, and how he bear down in the seventh round and start beatin' the man to death, he made me fall in love. I was with him from that fight on. That night, I tol' him to go to the hotel and get some Epsom salts and soak in a bath . . . but he went up to a birthday party at Small's Paradise in Harlem and got sick right on the birthday cake from exhaustion and they carried him out of there stiff as a board. I said, you listen to *me* from now on."

Bundini's friends liked to say he had supplied and nurtured

much of his young charge's wit, and the routines, and the rhymes; certainly he was responsible for the famous slogan "Float like a butterfly, sting like a bee." I thought he would perform on the bus, but he seemed curiously subdued on the first part of the trip. Perhaps he was thinking of his hometown in the North of Florida where we were planning to stop so he could meet family folks he had not seen in years. When we were once again on the road, and Ali had turned the wheel over to the Muslim driver to put on his show as promised, Bundini stayed in the back of the bus—and it seemed to me he was sleeping back there.

Ali started his show with a tap dance in the door-well in front of the bus, scarcely keeping his balance in the bus's motion but doing some very fancy and noisy stepping with his big tan work boots to a musical accompaniment provided by Howard Bingham, singing "The Darktown Strutters' Ball" into his cupped hands. Jokes then followed by the dozens, the champion telling each with immense enthusiasm, usually with the punch line repeated, guffawed over, and then offered again, perhaps three or four times. "This cat had him a car, a special-built car, that do hundred and eighty and which he use to agitate the cops—they come after him on this three-hundred-mile-long stretch of highway and he just *toy* with them. But this one time, this cop keep up to him. When he do hundred, the cop do the same. So he shove her up to hundred thirty, but the cop holds on. He let her out to a hundred *fifty,* and the cop is still stuck to him, the siren goin', and so this cat he shoves her down to the floor, a hundred *eighty,* and man, he don't budge an *inch* from that cop. So, he give up and pull over t' the side of the road. He say, 'You take me to jail, you do *any*thing to me, but first allow me one look under the *hood* of yo' car.' So you know what he find under the hood of that car? He look under there an' he find six niggers wearing *sneakers.*"

He told us he could use the word "nigger" and it was all right. "You understand?" he said. He told the joke again, as if to show us. Our laughter began to sound forced. When the show was over, he came down the aisle and visited with us. He kept us entertained.

Once, he sat down beside me and began talking about the Muslim religion—the homegrown part about the space platform manned by "men who never smile" which circles the world loaded with bombs that at the Armageddon will be dropped a mile deep into the earth and level everything. The platform was designed and set up by Allah in the person of Master Wallace Fard in 1930, and it whips through the sky at 18,000 miles per hour and can stop on a dime, revolving until the earth's collective guilt calls for the destruction to begin. Ali took out his wallet and showed me a frayed photograph of Wallace Fard, quite a pale-looking black, staring down at a book in his lap. Fard was Elijah Muhammad's instructor (Ali said that Elijah had never seen the Master asleep; he'd look through a keyhole at night and there Fard would be, working on his papers) and his "vision" was that the holocaust would come soon, in 1970, and that 154,000 Negroes would survive (almost all the figures in the Muslim mythology are exact) to get things going again. Ali had seen the platform many times, and if it wasn't cloudy out, we could see it in the night sky. Cody Jones, sitting in the next seat, nodded. He'd seen it at five A.M. one morning while out on roadwork with the champ—a bright light darting in the sky (I didn't dare say I thought it was probably Venus or Jupiter)—and the champ had told him what it was, and about the bombs and the men who never smile.

I asked Ali to tell me about the Muslims' concept of the universe, and how everything had come to be. He allowed that he was not a minister, but from a long singsong explanation, almost like a litany, it was possible to piece together the following:

The black man originally inherited the moon—"people of the moon" is how they refer to themselves. There was no earth then—trillions of years ago—just the moon. Then one of the great scientists became disenchanted because he couldn't get everyone to speak the same language, and he caused, in a great rage, an enormous explosion which tore the "moon" into two parts—the larger one, the earth as it now is. There were some survivors of the explosion. The first people to inhabit the earth were all black—members of the tribe of Shabazz. But among them was an evil genius, Yakub (here Ali's voice dropped to a conspiratorial level), the devil of the Black Muslim religion. Yakub invented the white man in his laboratory, a job that took him six hundred years. He is the father of the Caucasian race and was finally cast out of Paradise along with 59,999 of his inventions ... who nonetheless came to overwhelm the blacks and subjugate them. The guilt is piling up on the white, and the date of retribution is quite exact. The men who never smile will push the bombs over. The blacks will get eight to ten days' advance notice; they will be informed by pamphlets in Arabic dropped from the platform and the righteous will be told where to go to survive. I asked Ali if he expected to be one of the lucky 154,000 survivors, and he said, well, that was in the hands of someone else. He had no way of knowing. The dreadful platform came over the earth twice a week, in the night. Cody Jones nodded.

It was almost evening when we reached Sanford, Florida, which is where Bundini was reared. "Goose Hollow," he told me, "just back of Sanford, where the poor people walks on sand, and the white man, he has concrete to walk on." Bundini came and sat on an arm rest as we pulled in. He said that when Joe Louis fought, amplifiers were strung up in the pines out by one of the cabins and the folks sat around in the darkness to listen and cheer, and he remembered that a storm was whipping the pine forest during one of the broadcasts, so the words from Madison Square Garden, or wherever, were shredded away, people running around in the wild darkness trying to find out what was going on as if the words whirling off were corporeal, retrievable, like panicky chickens.

While Bundini was inside talking to his folks, the new champion sat on the porch steps, and from down the dusty street the people began cruising up to gawk. An elderly gentleman with a black stick for a cane picked his way up the path as tentatively as a heron: "Champ, you look good. You feel pretty confident?"

"He must fall," the champion said, scarcely looking up.

As usual, the children were the easiest with him, careening around corners, slowing up and casing him speculatively, and showing off as noisy as jays, and he always had a hold of the shiest of the crowd—a small girl, usually—and he'd ask her if she knew that the person talking was the champion of the whole wide world.

He motioned me over. He had an autograph book in his hand. The small boy who had given it to him leaned back against the crook of his arm. Its title page read THIS BOOK BELONGS TO COOL DADDY RODNEY THAT IS MY NAME NOT MY NUMBER. On the page opposite was written PRESIDENT KENNEDY DIED, the date, and under it, also in the block letters stark as initials in tree trunks, the name Sam Cooke, an ex-con country singer, and the date *he* had been shot. The champion riffled the pages and found all of them blank, so he went back to the beginning and signed the first ten pages. "That'll get you started," he said to the youngster. He swung his arm open and let him loose.

We set off again in the bus.

Bundini Brown said, "Let's stop and eat. I empty." No one said anything. It was dark outside, the pine forests stretching back from the road, their thin trunks showing up sticks of gray in the headlights. Four or five miles up the road the driver—he was one of the Muslims—slowed down and turned the bus into a truck stop near the Florida-Georgia border. Yulee was the name of the place. The big gas pumps with the PURE FIREBIRD gasoline emblems stood in pools of light from overhead standards, and there were a few truck trailers parked across the macadam-topped lot. The restaurant had a small neon light in the window. The champion's brother, Rachaman, said, "You're goin' watch a man face reality—that's what you're goin' to see."

Bundini climbed down from the bus and headed for the restaurant. With the bus motor switched off it was quiet outside, and warm, with the day's heat still rising from the macadam. I got out with the other journalists to go with Brown.

Ali and his group and the sparring partners left the bus, but they stayed back near the pumps.

The restaurant had a screen door that squeaked, and the people inside, six or seven couples sitting in the booths, looked up when Bundini came in. He sat down at the counter, and we flanked him on stools to either side. The waitress looked at us and put her hands together. The manager came out from behind the counter. "I'm sorry," he said. "We have a place out back. Separate facilities," he said. "The food's just the same." Through the serving window we could see two black cooks looking out. "Probably better," the manager said with a wan smile. He talked at us as if Bundini were not there. Bundini's face began working. The journalists began intimidating the manager, whipping whispered furious words at him. He stayed calm, tapping a grease-stained menu against his fingertips. "In this county—Nassau County—they'd be a riot," he said simply. In the booths the people continued eating, watching over their forks as they lifted the food and put it into their mouths.

Bundini said, "The heavyweight champion of the world, and he can't get nothing to eat here." He spoke reflectively, and he spun around on his stool and stood up.

The screen door squeaked again and slapped shut. Ali stood in the room, leaning forward slightly and staring at Bundini. "You fool. What's the matter with you—you damn *fool!*" His nostrils were flared, his voice almost out of control. "I tol' you to be a Muslim. Then you don' go places where you're not wanted. You clear out of this place, nigger; you ain't wanted here, can't you *see.* They don' want you, nigger . . ." He reached for Bundini's denim jacket, hauled him toward him and propelled him out the door in an easy furious motion. Bundini offered no resistance. He stumbled out on the macadam as if he had been launched from a sling.

The champion rushed after him, pushing him for the bus, still vilifying him, and then Ali broke away and began leaping among the gas pumps and out across the macadam under the flat, eerie light, circling among the trailers, one with a multithousand-dollar yacht balanced in its cradle—a lunatic backdrop for a frenzy that suddenly became as gleeful as a child's. "I'm *glad,* Bundini!" he shouted. "I'm glad! You got *showed,* Bundini, you got *showed.*"

Bundini's shoulders were hunched over and he was looking down. "Leave me alone," he kept repeating. "I'm good enough to eat here!" he shouted suddenly. "I'm a free man. If a man is a puppet, go tell Henry Ford to give him a nose and an eyeball and a new heart. God made me. Not Henry Ford."

The champion whooped with delight. He leaped high in the air and circled Bundini. "Don't you know when you not *wanted?* Face reality and dance!" he shouted.

Bundini cried back at him, "I'll be what I was, what I always been. In my heart I'm a free man. No slave chains round my heart." He escaped into the bus.

The rest of the group stood by and watched the champion, who was still capering and shouting, begin to wind down. His brother stalked about, his face lit with excitement, repeating like a litany, "A man has seen reality, seen *re-al-i-ty.*"

I went to look in through a window at the room in back. It was off the kitchen, a table with six chairs. An old magazine lay tossed in a corner. I turned back. Everyone was sitting in the bus. The tree-frog buzz began drifting across the macadam lot from the dark pinewood and swampland.

But when the Muslim driver got the bus moving again, the turmoil started afresh. Ali leaned over the top of his seat and kept railing Bundini: "Uncle Tom! Tom! Tom! Tom!" He muzzled him with a red pillow. He shouted, "This teach you a lesson, Bundini!" He leaned over and pushed down on Bundini's head. "You bow your head, Bundini."

"Leave me alone!" Bundini shouted. "My head don' belong between my knees. It's up in the stars. I'm free. I keep trying. If I find a waterhole is dry, I go on and find another."

The exchange was carried on in full volume, the rhetoric high-blown, as if delivery were from a memorized morality play.

"You *shamed* yourself back there!" the champion shouted.

"They were ashamed," Bundini said.

"What good did that do, except to shame you?"

"That man," said Bundini, "that manager, he'll sleep on it. He may be no better, but he'll think on it, and he'll be ashamed. I dropped a little medicine in that place."

Ali whooped. "Tom! Tom! Tom!" He whacked a series of quick blows at Bundini with the red pillow. "You belong to your white master."

It got to Bundini finally, and he began to cry. His grief is unbearable to watch, his face a perfect reflection of the mask of tragedy. The champion looked at him.

"Hey, Bundini," he said softly. He mopped at Bundini's face with the red pillow—clumsy but affectionate swipes.

"Leave me alone," Bundini said, barely audibly.

Ali tried to make him laugh. "Hey, Bundini," he said. "What sort of crackers was they back in that restaurant?"

Bundini did not want to answer.

"I'll tell you what kind of crackers. They was not Georgia crackers; they was soda crackers. And if they're soda crackers, that makes you a graham cracker. That's what you are—a *graham cracker.*"

Bundini did not say anything.

The champion gave a great whooping laugh and belted Bundini on the top of the head with the red pillow.

Bundini's shoulders finally began shaking from laughter.

"Champ," he said, "les' just train and fight—none of the other stuff. Why you make us come this way?" he said resignedly. "We could have flown over all these miserable miles."

"Don't fly over it, Bundini," Ali said, in an odd shift of mind which I remembered thinking was part of the paradox of him and made him so difficult to judge. "You fight it out, Bundini," he said, ". . . like your aunts and uncles have to do."

Not far down the road, Bundini, seeming to take his counsel, said again, "I'm empty. I want to eat. Lookee yonder! A Howard Johnson's coming up."

"We'll stop," the champion said grimly. He was again a Muslim. "This is Georgia, Bundini. You haven't been *showed?*" he asked incredulously.

When the bus was parked in the lot, Bundini stepped out, and this time the sparring partners, none of whom were Muslims, decided to join us, a grim group moving up the path for the restaurant, with its bright windows and the illuminated orange-peaked cupola roof; behind, the Muslim contingent stood by the bus, with the champion's brother once again calling out, his voice tense with excitement, "You facing reality, Bundini—reality!"

The restaurant, which was nearly full, fell silent at our entrance; a cocktail ensemble playing "Tea For Two" over the

Muzak was nearly deafening. In the booths forks and spoons were poised perhaps not surprisingly: we must have seemed a forbidding bunch; we were apprehensive, considering what had happened in Yulee, very grim and walking stiffly, eyes flicking everywhere to see where the first rebuff would come from; a formidable group, too, with the boxers part of it, tattoos showing on their broad black arms. A sheriff, if he had been sitting there, might well have stepped up and arrested us on general suspicion.

We gathered around a long table and sat down. A waitress appeared with a stack of menus. "You all look *hungry*," she said brightly. She began passing out the menus.

Bundini began giggling. "My," he said, "no one mind if I sit at the head of the table?" The seats were rearranged, and Bundini pointed out the window at the Muslims standing by the bus. "I'm going to eat three steaks standing up so's they can see," he said.

He waved at the Muslims like a child. They looked like waifs standing out there in the dark.

Ali came in after a while, striding through the restaurant, the people watching him, and those with children getting ready to push them up for autographs.

"What you doin' here?" Bundini said smugly. "This place only for integrators. Soda *and* graham crackers."

The champion smiled at him and sat down. He had his meal, and when his coffee came, he said, "Bundini, I'm goin' to integrate the coffee." He poured some cream into it. "When it's black, it's strong."

Bundini shook his head. The two were smiling at each other. "Champ," said Bundini once again, "les' just train and fight—none of the other stuff."

10

After the bus trip, I got to know Muhammad Ali better; at least he knew that I wrote about him, and if he saw me in a crowd, he would say, "Hey, look who's here," and then he would try to remember my name, though he rarely could. "Author," he would say, or "the Writer," as in "let's put the Writer in the backseat of the car so's I can talk to him," and sometimes he called me Kennedy because he thought I bore a resemblance to that clan.

He was always accommodating. Once, I arranged a tea for Marianne Moore, the distinguished poet, to meet him. He was quite agreeable. She and I were working on a project together— going to various events, mostly sports contests, and seeing how our artistic view of each compared: mine, predictable and pedestrian; hers, quirky and unexpected and illuminating. One saw something of the poetic process while sitting with her. We had been to a World Series game together, and a football game, a zoo ("I am foolish about gorillas"), and a prizefight—the Floyd Patterson–George Chuvalo fight at Madison Square Garden.

She loved athletes; she did not know how to account for people who could be indifferent to miracles of dexterity, though

I often wondered how much she actually *knew* about sports—I mean in the sense of the experts in the Third Avenue saloons who sounded like assistant coaches if you eavesdropped on them; they all seemed to know Tucker Frederickson, the ex-Giant, personally; they could labor a whole afternoon over trivia questions, such as what major-league ballplayer had been an active player through four decades of baseball. Marianne Moore did not care about this sort of thing. I am not even sure at the end of the games we attended that she knew who had won. She was interested in the way pigeons dropped down out of the rafters, or how a player wore his socks. She would have been entranced not by Minnie Minoso's longevity record (he was the one who played in four different decades) but by his first name, and she would have written it down in a tiny notebook she carried, just the name Minnie in a delicate spidery scrawl so that she could ponder it later. She loved ballplayers' names, and they would suddenly arrive in her conversation, quite unexpectedly, like a sneeze. Vinegar Bend Mizelle was a particular favorite when he played with the Mets, and she would say his name when she had a fancy to.

Another was Bill Monbouquette, then a Yankee pitcher. One fine summer afternoon, when a small group of us were up at the stadium as guests of Mike Burke and the Yankee management, Marianne Moore peered out over the railing of the second-tier box and noticed that Monbouquette had a most disturbing habit at the end of his delivery, which was to cup his groin at the jockstrap and give it a little heft, as if to rearrange what was within. "That is interesting, what he does at the completion of his toss," she had said, and our little group stared transfixed as, sure enough, he did it every time. It was an integral part of his pitching motion, surely quite unconscious since it was hardly a gesture one would think of oneself doing in front of twenty thousand or so people, time after time. We discussed whether he should be told, whether an umpire should come out and say, "Hey, don't do that, please . . . our sensibilities!" or whether the television cameras ever lingered below his waist when he was pitching, and if he *was* told, what it would do to his pitching abilities ... to realize suddenly that for the fifteen years or so of his career he had been displaying across the country this faintly obscene peculiarity of his—like being told one's fly had been open for *years*. It might have kept Monbouquette from ever picking up a baseball again without blushing and having to drop it. Miss Moore was quite serene about what she had discovered. "There is an insouciance in that gesture which is appealing," she said. "He should not be told. We should keep mum." She wrote his name down in her little book. "Monbouquette," she said, barely audibly. " 'My little bouquet.' Absolutely correct."

The rules, statistics, tactics, and structure of the games we watched were of little interest. Indeed, she seemed lost in those vast sports arenas and people rushed to help her, the tiny, delicate lady under the great hat she was famous for. I remember she caused a considerable flurry at the Belmont Race Track by trying to bet fifty cents on a horse at the ten-dollar window, a long line behind her, the great hat, and those immediately aft of it trying to get around it to tell her she couldn't do such a thing.

We had a fine time going to the events and corresponding about what had happened (her letters were wonderful, tremendously personal expressions not unlike her conversation). I was relieved, because one would always worry about exploiting that gracious lady. She wrote me once that *McCall's* magazine had prevailed on her to divulge what she would do if she were the president of the United States. "I worked all afternoon," she wrote. "I found it most inconvenient. They are so good at concocting these traps. Darkness fell. I found it cruelty. I shouldn't be exhibited. One is wiser as one grows older. The Chinese think so anyway. But I'm a house cat. They came with very complicated recording apparatus. It didn't record a word. We have deadlines they shouted at me. They were very polite but rather frantic."

Until she met Ali, her favorite boxer had been Floyd Patterson. She had met him at an autographing party to which she had been taken by a neighbor. The hostess was "Miss Negro Bookclub"—a titular choice Miss Moore found arresting—and Sugar Ray Robinson was the chairman of the event. "His competence and unsensational modesty were very pleasing," she wrote me about the occasion. "I met Floyd Patterson and Buster Watson also, his assistant trainer. Floyd was very courteous and I was very rude, interrupting Buster when he was talking to two other men. I resolved never to be so rude again. I bought books for some boys ... and another for myself in which Floyd wrote my name and 'all the best.' "

She read the book with care—*Victory Over Myself.* She remembered phrases from it: "I never thought of boxing as a profession; it was a grind ... but a way out for me and my family"; "boxing is supposed to be a dirty business but it has made me clean and enabled me to do some good for others." I think she was also moved by the description of Patterson's childhood: he was so intimidated and shy that he hid from the outside in a cubbyhole he found in the foundation of an elevated subway trestle in the Bronx.

I arranged for a row of seats for his fight against Chuvalo. It was not at all clear that Marianne Moore was going to enjoy the evening. She had not been to a prizefight before, and people hitting each other was an activity she could not condone. A few days before the fight she wrote me, "Marred physiognomy and an occasional death doesn't seem an ideal life objective. I do not like demolishing anything—even a paper bag. Salvaging and saving all but dominate my life."

I asked her in the cab on the way to the fight if violence had ever intruded; it seemed an odd suggestion to apply to such a fragile person.

"In Brooklyn I intercepted a small boy who laid down his schoolbooks to slug a classmate," she replied. "When I said, 'If you don't stop, I'll beat you up,' he said, 'he cursed my mother.' I said, 'Then it's justified, but lay off him.' "

She closed her eyes, as if in thought, and then she said, "One time I was driving in a taxi going through the Bowery; I looked out and saw a man with a knife creeping up on another. The car was going quite fast, about as fast as we're going now, and I can't tell you what the end was." She made a small snorting sound. "Violence! I didn't know what it meant. If I was wild

enough to come home late at night, I didn't know enough to be
timid. Once, I was amazed when my friend asked, 'Do you want
me to go in with you to see if anyone's in the house?' I was
astonished. 'Someone in the house?!' But now I have been
trained to call out, 'Who is it?' and look out the little peephole,
and when I see my good friend, or a neighbor, I feel craven."

Miss Moore was wearing her famous tricorne hat, with its
pointed-prow effect; when she turned to speak, it gave a sort of
thrust to what she was saying, much like talking to a miner in
the beam of the light from his helmet. Her tricorne fit nicely in
the cab. She had other hats which would have required some
jimmying around to fit—a great cartwheel of a stiffened felt hat
that if one were walking along beside her one had to get under,
crouching along Groucho Marx–like, to hear what she was
saying in her soft, erratic voice. She told me that she had picked
the tricorne for the fight "because my other hats keep anyone
behind me from seeing."

We picked up some friends to join us at the fight. Just as we
were nearing the Garden, Miss Moore heard something from
one of them about Chuvalo that shook her support of Patterson—namely that Chuvalo was so incredibly poor at the start of
his ring career that on one occasion he drove across Canada with
his wife in a car so decrepit that the accelerator pedal had come
off, and a part of the accelerator arm; Mrs. Chuvalo had had to
crouch under the dashboard and at a signal from her husband
depress or raise what was left of the accelerator by hand. "Bring
her up a touch; we're coming into a town." Miss Moore was
moved by this nearly to the point of shifting her allegiance. She
asked to be told the story again.

It was obviously on her mind during the fight. We had good
seats in the mezzanine, far enough away so that the physical side
of the fight was not too pronounced. Still, small gasps erupted
from Miss Moore at a solid blow. Once, I heard her call out,
"George!" Another time, "Floyd!" She had a very small pad and
pencil with her, though I never saw her write anything down.
She seemed relieved when the fight was over. "Well, that's that,"

she said brightly, as if something especially wrenching had been completed, like a frightening circus act.

She wrote me subsequently when she had had time to consider things: "I did not enjoy the Patterson-Chuvalo fight at all until Floyd began to win and in the end suffered no major damage." But she could not rid herself of the Chuvalo accelerator story. "A moralist at heart, my notions of psychic adaptiveness and creativeness of muscular as well as mental endurance were enlarged by Mrs. Chuvalo's scars of battle with life when she held a finger in a fixed position to replace what should have been an automatic device in the car."

She wrote that she had also been taken by the referee's performance: "The assiduous precision of the referee in seizing the angle most advantageous from which to see every trifle, impressed me most—and his impeccable appearance—nothing sticking out or dangling. Swift and compact, the embodiment of vigilance."

She had also noticed Muhammad Ali at the fight; he was sitting on the far side of the ring and jumped up into it to talk with Patterson at its conclusion. When I next saw her, I asked if she would like to meet him. She nodded. "I do not see any reason why I should not meet someone who assures everyone 'I am the greatest' and who is a poet nonetheless."

Some weeks later I was able to arrange our tea with Ali through Hal Conrad, the fight publicist. For reasons I have forgotten, we had it at Toots Shor's establishment, in mid-Manhattan. The place was almost empty when Miss Moore and I arrived—a slack time in the place, about four in the afternoon. Toots Shor himself was there, but knowing that Ali was expected, he did not sit with us. He did not approve of Ali then, or perhaps ever, and he sat at the opposite end of the room, studiously ignoring us. From our banquette Miss Moore looked over and was impressed by Shor. She had heard that he had started in the restaurant business as a bouncer. I think she expected, or hoped perhaps, that he would "bounce" someone. "His haunt is quite peaceful," she said to me. "It makes the offices of bouncer seem hearsay; no killer instinct had made itself evident."

"No, no," I said. "I think he has other people to do that for him these days. Besides, there's no one in here for him to bounce except the waiters and you and me."

"Fancy," she said.

Presently Muhammad Ali arrived with Hal Conrad. He slid in behind the table and arranged himself next to Miss Moore. He gazed at her hat, which was the same tricorne she had worn to the fight. Almost immediately, as if she had yet to arrive, he turned to Hal and me and asked who she was and what he was expected to do. Had a photographer arrived?

Miss Moore listened attentively to what Conrad and I had to say about her—a great sports fan, one of the most distinguished poets in the country. . . .

"Mrs. Moore," said Ali, turning and looking at her, "a grand-mother going to the fights? How old is she?" he suddenly asked, turning toward me and whispering loudly. I was taken aback.

"Oh, forty," I said idiotically, producing the first number that came to mind.

"Is that so?" commented the champion. "The way you settled her down in here so careful I reckon she's got to be a grandmother, seventy-nine going on eighty, or maybe ninety-six." He inspected her. "They have these women up in Pakistan," he confided in me loudly, "who live to be one hundred and *sixty*. They haul pianos up and down these hills. They eat a lot of yogurt."

Miss Moore sat patiently through this, smiling faintly. The fighter turned to her suddenly and asked, "Mrs. Moore, what have you been doing lately?"

"I have been subduing my apartment," she said in her high, thin voice. "I have just moved in from Brooklyn to a new apartment which is strange to me and needs taming."

"Is that so?" The champion ordered a glass of water. "Yes," he said to the waiter. "We is tiptop at Toots." He turned back to Miss Moore. "Well, I am considering farming, myself," he said. "I'd like to sit and look across the fence at the biggest bull in the

world—jes' sit and rock back and forth and look at him out there
in the middle of the field, feeding."

"Oh yes," Miss Moore said. She was quite shy with him, ducking her head and peeking at him. "Can we come and look with
you?"

"You can sit on the porch with me, Mrs. Moore," Ali said.

She made a confused, pleased gesture and then had a sip of
her tea. He ordered a bowl of beef soup and a phone. He announced that if she was the greatest poetess in the country, the
two of them should produce something together—"I am a poet,
too," he said—a joint-effort sonnet, it was to be, with each of
them doing alternate lines. Miss Moore nodded vaguely. Ali was
very much the more decisive of the pair, picking not only the
form but also the topic: "Mrs. Moore and I are going to write a
sonnet about my upcoming fight in Houston with Ernie Terrell,"
he proclaimed to the table. "Mrs. Moore and I will show the
world with this great poem who is who and what is what and
who is going to win."

"We will call it 'A Poem on the Annihilation of Ernie
Terrell,' " Miss Moore announced. "Let us be serious but not
grim."

"She's cute," Ali commented.

A pen was produced. Ali was given a menu on which to write.
He started off with half the first line—"After we defeat"—and
asked Miss Moore to write in Ernie Terrell (which she misspelled
"Ernie Tyrell" in her spidery script) just to get her "warmed up."
He wrote most of the second line—"He will catch nothing"—
handing the pen over and expecting Miss Moore to fill in the
obvious rhyme, and he was quite surprised when she did not.
She made some scratchy squiggles on the paper to get the ink
flowing properly. The fighter peered over her shoulder.

"What's that say?" he asked.

"It doesn't say anything. You could call them 'preliminaries.'
Terrell should rhyme nicely with 'bell,' " Miss Moore said tenta-
tively. I could see her lips move as she fussed with possibilities.
Finally, Ali leaned over and whispered to her, " 'but hell,' Mrs.
Moore."

"Oh, yes," she said. She wrote down "but hell," but then she wrestled with it some more, clucking gently, and murmuring about the rhythm of the line, and she crossed it out and substituted, "he will get nothing, nothing but hell."

Ali took over and produced his next line in jig-time: "Terrell was big and ugly and tall." He pushed the menu over to her. His soup arrived. He leaned low over it, spooning it in, and glancing over to see how she was coming along. While he waited, he told Conrad and me that he was going to try to get the poem out over the Associated Press wire that afternoon. Miss Moore's eyes widened, perhaps at the irony of all those years struggling with *Broom* and the other literary magazines, and now to be with a fighter who promised instant publication over a ticker machine. It did not help the flow of inspiration. She was doubtless intimidated by the presence next to her, especially at his obvious concern that she, a distinguished poet, was having such a hard time holding up her side: speed of delivery was very much a qualification of a professional poet in his mind. He finished his soup and ordered another. The phone arrived and was plugged in behind the banquette. He began dialing a series of numbers—hotels, most of them—but the room numbers he requested never seemed to respond.

Finally, seeing that she had not got anywhere at all, he took the poem from her and completed it. It was not done in a patronizing way at all but more out of consideration, presumably that every poet, however distinguished, is bound to have a bad day and should be helped through it. He tried some lines aloud which he eventually discarded: "When I hit him with my right/ He'll become a colored satellite. . . .

"Now, let's see," he said as he began to write. He had moved close to her, so that she appeared to be looking down the long length of his arm to watch the poem emerge. "Yes," she said. "Why not?" as he produced a last couplet. The whole composition, once he had taken over, took about a minute. With the spelling corrected, it read as follows:

After we defeat Ernie Terrell
He will get nothing, nothing but hell,
Terrell was big and ugly and tall
But when he fights me he is sure to fall.
If he criticize this poem by me and Miss Moore
To prove he is not the champ she will stop him in four,
He is claiming to be the real heavyweight champ
But when the fight starts he will look like a tramp
He has been talking too much about me and making me sore
After I am through with him he will not be able to challenge Mrs.
    Moore.

The stratagem of involving her in the poem, particularly as a pugilist herself, was clever: Miss Moore nodded in delight, despite its being a truncated sonnet. She made a tiny fist. "Yes, he has been making me sore," she said.

A photographer arrived—something of a surprise. He was from one of the wire services. I suspect that Muhammad Ali, knowing that he was meeting someone of distinction, if not quite sure *whom,* had arranged for the photographer so that the event could be recorded. Miss Moore did not seem to mind. She allowed Ali, who continued to dominate the afternoon, to dictate the poses. His idea was to have the photograph show the two of them working on the poem. "We've got to show you *thinking,* Mrs. Moore," he said. "How you show you're thinking hard is to point your finger into the middle of your head." He illustrated, jabbing his forefinger at his forehead, closing his eyes to indicate concentration. She complied, pursing her lips in feigned concern as she pondered the poem. The photographer clicked away happily.

Miss Moore then expressed a wish to see the Ali shuffle—a foot maneuver Ali occasionally did in mid-fight which looked like a man's trying to stay upright on a carpet being pulled out from underneath him. Ali said he would be delighted to show her the shuffle. He thought it would be best to do it out in the street where he had room to do her a really *good* shuffle. But when we walked outdoors, a crowd immediately collected—I think the word was around the neighborhood that the fighter was in Toots Shor's—so we came back through the revolving door and he did the shuffle right there in the foyer. Miss Moore was delighted. She asked him to do it again, and when he went out and did the shuffle for the people in the street, she watched him through the revolving door.

"Well," she said when he had left, "he had every excuse for avoiding a performance. But he festooned out in as enticing a bit of shuffling as you would ever wish to see."

"He 'festooned'?" I asked.

"He certainly did. He was exactly what I had hoped to meet."

Subsequently, I wrote Miss Moore to ask her what she had thought of her afternoon at Toots Shor's. What was her opinion of Ali as a poet?

She wrote, "Well, we were slightly under constraint. And the rhyme for Terrell ["Hell"] being of one syllable is hardly novel. . . . Cassius has an ear, and a liking for balance . . . comic, poetic drama, it *is* poetry . . . saved by a hair from being the flattest, peanuttiest, unweariest of boastings."

She was especially pleased that the poem (which she now thought might be titled "Much Ado About Cassius" rather than "A Poem on the Annihilation of Ernie Terrell") showed a strong sense of structure, which indeed involved herself: "He begins by mentioning a special guest and concludes with mention of the same."

Yes, that *had* entranced her—the conceit of stepping into the ring against the "ugly and tall" Terrell, wearing one of her less-encumbering hats, and taking Terrell out with a hook."

She then went on to produce a whizbang of words about Ali.

The Greatest, though a mere youth, has snuffed out more dragons than Smokey the Bear hath. Mighty-muscled and fit, he is confident; he is sagacious, ever so, he *trains*. A king's daughter is bestowed on him as a fiancée. He is literary, in the tradition of Sir Philip Sidney, defender of poesie. His verse is enhanced by alliteration. He is summoned by an official: "Come forth, *Cassius.*" He is not even deterred by the small folks' dragons. He has a fondness for antithesis; he will not only give fighting lessons, but falling lessons. Admittedly the classiest and the brassiest. When asked, "How do you feel about being called by the British, "Gaseous Clay," his reply is one of the prettiest in literature. "I do not resent it." Note this: beat grime revolts him. He is neat. His brow is high. If beaten, he is still not "beat." He fights and he writes.

> Is there something I have missed?
> He is a *smiling* pugilist.

II

It was not more than a few hours after he had refused to step forward to be inducted into the U. S. Army, in April, 1967, that a telephone call came through to Muhammad Ali's hotel in Houston informing him that the New York State Athletic Commission had lifted his title, the first of the commissions—eventually all of them followed suit—to do so. "I expected that," Ali said. "I am not surprised." He had been lying gloomily on his hotel bed. When Bundini Brown heard the news, he ran into the bathroom and locked the door, and Ali could hear him crying. Ali stood it for a while, and then he went to the door. "Hey, Bundini," he called out, "how much money will it take you to stop that?" The crying stopped abruptly, almost as if Bundini were truly considering what he *would* charge, until finally he could not contain himself any longer, and he started giggling.

Afterward, while Ali's case was working its way up through the courts, Ali put the best face on the matter he could. "I'm still the champion," he told me once. "That mean that every day when you wake up you feel good. It stays with you always. You can be overweight, with an old pair of shoes, and an old coat, but you can always wake up and think back."

Committees were formed to try to do something about getting him reinstated. I was on an informal one composed largely of writers—Pete Hamill, Norman Mailer, and others. We sat around in one another's apartments and complained loudly that the commissions had no right to deprive Ali of his means of making a living—any more than a plumber should be prohibited from keeping at his job if *he* refused induction. We went to see influential people. Once, I found myself in a touch-football game at Hickory Hill, the Robert Kennedy place in McLean, Virginia, playing opposite Supreme Court Justice Byron "Whizzer" White. By our own preference we were situated far out on the flanks of the game, removed from the center of things where Ethel played, and her husband, and the children, and often a very large Newfoundland named Brumus, and guests who wanted to make an impression, and where things were very hectic. I had once been bitten on the ankle in there—not by Brumus. So the Justice and I played out where the wide receivers set up, peacefully jogging up and down in the shadows of the line of pines bordering the lawn. The Justice was out there . . . well, Lord, he had nothing to prove, having been an All-American who had played for the Detroit Lions and the Pittsburgh Steelers, and besides, he was playing in his stocking feet, and my impression was that he was also wearing his round steel spectacles, touching them with a finger to keep them in place as he ran. We gossiped. Suddenly I said, "Mr. Justice, isn't there something very wrong about the Muhammad Ali business—I mean, that the boxing commissions can deprive him of his right to function in his profession? . . ."

The Justice started. He said he was not really allowed to discuss such a matter—he was sorry; conceivably it could be brought before him and the other justices for a ruling—he was sorry.

I was embarrassed to have asked. As we stood there I wondered how often the justices had to do that sort of thing—bust into a conversation and close it off because of a possible conflict. Were their social lives compromised as a result, full of "Ahem, ahem, wait a minute there," or having to get up from the dinner table, or clapping one's hands over one's ears at a luncheon club downtown ... and being only truly happy and at ease in a vast miasma of small talk, just champing to hear about the welfare of someone's pet cat because it meant that the conversation probably would not have to be cut off?

I wanted to ask Justice White, but Senator Kennedy called out from the center of the field and wondered why we weren't putting more vim into our efforts out where we were. Were we spectators, or players? At least we could attend the huddles. So, dutifully the Justice and I trotted in toward them to see what was going to be required of us.

Back in New York, I tried again. I went to see Howard Cosell in his little office in the ABC building. Mostly known then as a boxing broadcaster, he was on the edge of considerable prominence. He was sitting at his desk with his back to the window. Most celebrated people are quite different when away from their public—Muhammad Ali was so often withdrawn and subdued when removed from his admirers—but Cosell always struck me as being exactly the same in private as in public: the voice throbbed; his vocabulary bristled with circumlocutions. Partway through my introductory remarks about Ali, he held up his hand. "Let me articulate my position," he said. "Georgie-boy, I'd be *shot,* sitting right here in this armchair, by some crazed redneck sharpshooter over there in that building"—he motioned over his shoulder—"if I deigned to say over the airwaves that Muhammad Ali should be completely absolved and allowed to return to the ring. I'd be *shot*—right through that window!" he said, his voice rising as if he were broadcasting the event. "My sympathies are obviously with Muhammad." His voice became mellow. "He has no greater friend among the whites, but the time, at this stage in this country's popular feeling"—the voice rising and empathetic—"is not correct for such an act on my part."

"But, Howard, no one's going to shoot you from that building," I said. "That's the Bankers Trust."

"To begin with, it's *not* the Bankers Trust. And secondly, I know whereof I speak. I would be *shot,"* he cried out, "and right through this window. There is a time and a place for everything, and this is not it. I am referring, of course, to the matter of Muhammad Ali's reinstatement, not to being shot from what you so incorrectly refer to as the Bankers Trust."

Later, of course, Howard Cosell became a leading and vocal proponent of Ali's reinstatement to boxing; but at the time, he appeared to reflect a universal disinclination toward the Ali case . . . an attitude which seemed to infect the fighter himself.

I went up to see Ali in Chicago. He was living in a small house with Herbert Muhammad, one of Elijah's eight sons. The matter of his banishment from the ring did not seem to concern him. I brought it up, but he wanted to take me for a ride in his newest car—an enormous limousine with a flamingo-red feather-like rug in the back. As we got into it, he told me that in a car as impressive as this one it wasn't proper to have two people sitting in the front. He asked me to sit in the back; he would drive. I agreed, and climbed in; my shoes were almost submerged in the red rug; we talked through an intercom system, which he seemed to want to test out, because he never bothered to roll down the glass partition windows between us. So I talked to him about his dilemma, lolling in the backseat of the limousine, speaking into a microphone. "What could we do? What could we do?" I saw his shoulders shrug through the glass partition and his jawline move as he replied. He wanted to show me Elijah Muhammad's mansion—"The Leader's House"—and we drove down a side street and by it so fast that I asked him over the intercom if we could go by again. The second time around we went by just as fast. "See it! See it!" he shouted into the intercom as we roared down that street at fifty miles per hour. Something was obviously strained in his relationship with the Muslims, or perhaps he didn't want the Leader to peek out the window and catch him chauffering a white person around on a neighborhood sightseeing tour.

Despite Ali's torpor, we kept at it back in New York. Committees were continually talked about. The writers, especially Pete Hamill, then of the New York *Post,* wrote columns. We continued to buttonhole powerful people we thought might help. I spoke to Senator Javits, of New York. It was not under the best of circumstances—a cocktail party his wife was giving in their New York apartment ... a large number of artistic people shouting at each other cheerfully. Beyond the senator's head a large surrealistic portrait of his wife hung on the wall; she was smiling down at us, composed, and somewhat regal, despite a long Indian arrow which had gone in one temple and halfway out the other, changing her expression not one jot.

"Write me a letter about it," the senator said. "Put everything in there—*facts,* not soft-boiled theories, no sir, I want the legal background, precedents ..."

I was trying to edge around so his wife's eyes ...

"... that's what I'm down in Washington to do—listen to my constituents and their problems—but I can't function for them if their complaints are half-baked and emotional." He sounded angry, but perhaps that was because he was shouting to be heard over the roar of his wife's guests.

So I thought about it. At home I started composing a letter:

DEAR SENATOR,
   I think you'll agree something is wrong here.

That was as far as it went. I kept notes, but they had nothing to do with what the senator wanted. Sometime, I thought, I'd write the senator about what an obviously extraordinary American institution Ali was, and how essential the preservation of that institution was. Had not the senator seen him move in the ring? Why, as an *intellect,* much less a fighter, he had uttered four statements which would probably find their way into Bartlett's *Familiar Quotations*—certainly "I am the greatest!"; then "Float like a butterfly, sting like a bee" (with a footnote explaining that it had actually been composed by Bundini Brown); and then the famous comment, suited with the action of his not taking that step forward in Houston, which had caused the difficulties with the authorities, "I ain't got no argument with them Vietcong." No one would ever find a more succinct way of expressing what a huge group of Americans felt about that war. And then he had produced a poem considerably shorter than the record holder ("the world's shortest poem") in Bartlett's. The incumbent was (and still is) a poem with the title "On the Antiquity of Microbes." The poem reads, "Adam/ Had 'em." Not bad, but Ali's poem, which by rights should displace it, goes, "Me/ Whee!" Not as clever, and it did not have a fancy title, but certainly it was shorter. Marianne Moore would have approved of its candidacy. What was it she had said about him ... "A smiling pugilist." She would have written a good letter to the senator. She had always liked Ali's having landed in London for the Henry Cooper fight and having stepped off the plane wearing a crown. What for? the British press wanted to know. "Well, you have a queen here," Ali had explained, "but I is the *King!*" Arms aloft, that gleeful face. Miss Moore loved that ... and she would have written about it.

But all that would have been discarded. The senator wanted "legal precedents," which we were not equipped to provide. I pegged above my desk the letter I had started, as a reminder to get back to it. I never did. It fell away one day. Or perhaps I made a paper airplane out of it and soared it out a window. It was a pretty good message—"Something is wrong here." It applied to just about everything at that time.

12

I could never remember our wan efforts without thinking of Kenneth Tynan, the English critic and theater personality, and his involvement in an episode in Cuba and what he might have done if he had been committed along with us to the Muhammad Ali cause. I had known him from Europe; we shared a common interest in the bullfights and I would see him at the arenas in Spain, a tall floppy figure dressed invariably in an ill-fitting American seersucker suit. I enjoyed his company. He was very much the *enfant terrible* then, and already a great number of legends had emerged about him. One, I remember, was that he had leaned forward during an editorial meeting of the *Daily Express,* for which he was the theater critic, and blown a smoke ring into Lord Beaverbrook's open mouth.

Tynan was paying his first visit to Cuba—it was just after the revolution there, in 1960—to write a travel article and to meet (he hoped) Fidel Castro. There were a number of other foreigners in town who were curious about the change in regimes, among them Tennessee Williams.

Tynan and I wandered around Havana. The prerevolution sin

which had flourished to such a degree had been shut down: the whorehouses were closed; the casinos were functioning, but just barely, as if in the libertarian glow of revolution, regular customers (if there were any left in Havana at all) did not think it appropriate to hang out there. The night clubs were closed. Superman, the star of the "exhibitions" in the Blue Moon, was gone, along with his successor, Superboy—to Miami, one supposed, where one wondered what sort of trade they were prepared to pursue. Tynan wanted to see a pornographic movie of the sort that had been shown in the taxi halls during the Batista regime. Our guide was very skeptical; things had changed. But finally it was arranged. We were taken to a small apartment in which quite a large family and its pets subsisted, among them a white hen and a large turtle. Our host was very nervous. He set the projector on the floor, about four feet from the wall. The image of the film, no larger than a postcard, flickered on the wall. Tynan leaned forward and squinted at the little rectangle as if he were trying to read it. Beneath it, the turtle appeared, scraping across the bare floor; the light beam briefly flickered on the curve of his shell. "Down in front," said Tynan.

The place where everyone hung out was a restaurant-bar called the Floridita. It was in the old section of Havana and had been Hemingway's favorite spot; he would call and say to meet him there. The bar of the Floridita was so dark that it took one a couple of minutes to become acclimatized; at first entrance, one maneuvered in the faint glowworm light that seemed to emit from the linen jackets of the men seated along the bar stools; one fluttered one's hands in front going down the line—"Sorry, sorry"—like seating oneself in a pitch-dark theater. Eventually, details began to emerge. Down at the end of the bar, with his back to the wall, Hemingway sat in his corner, his *querencia,* always an odd sight in that light because immediately behind him a bronze likeness of him was set in a niche, a life-size bust, so that one was confused by an astigmatic quirk of seeing double … the corporeal Hemingway, his face in its faint half halo of whiskers, his teeth shining in a smile, and then peering over his shoulder another Hemingway, quite a sombre likeness, this one, as if to offer visual evidence of a darker side of the subject's nature; it was emphasized because the bust was ill sculpted, something savage and manic in the dead stare of those bronze eyes so that at first sight it was as startling as looking up and seeing a strange face staring in a country-house window.

When one had got settled, the drinks served in the Floridita were incredibly cold, very likely ready made and chilled for hours in an icebox, because even a small sip produced such a pain, behind *my* eyes at least, that, as with an extra-large gulp of ice cream, I had to pinch the bridge of my nose to keep from yelling.

Sometimes the door outside to the street would open and a great piercing shaft of sunlight would burst in, as if a searchlight had been wheeled up to the entrance and fired in on us, and we would all squint and turn away. Whatever muscles exercise the pupils of the eye got a lot of workout in the Floridita, adjusting from pinpoints in that searchlight glare to the agate-marble size of owls' when the door swung to and we were back in the darkness.

One afternoon Tennessee Williams opened the door and stood there blinking with the sunlight blazing around him like St. Elmo's fire. He was wearing white flannels, a blue blazer, and a yachting cap, a machismo outfit he had apparently decided would be appropriate for his first meeting with Ernest Hemingway. He groped toward us uncertainly. There were three of us waiting—myself, Ken Tynan, and Hemingway. I had asked Hemingway at the *finca* the day before if he would enjoy meeting the playwright. "Sure," he had said. He had seen one of Tennessee's plays—I think it was *Cat on a Hot Tin Roof*—which he admired.

We had waited in the Floridita for Tennessee for almost an hour. I have always imagined that he was back in his hotel room desperately trying on various combinations he thought would be appropriate for meeting Hemingway—cowboy, guerrilla, retired military, rude fisherfolk, or whatever—and having a drink or two to fortify himself. I don't think the meeting went very well for him. Tennessee began by saying that when he lived in Key West he had known Hemingway's former wife Pauline.

"How did she die?" Tennessee suddenly asked.

Hemingway peered at him in the gloom. After a while he offered an explanation that seemed lifted from a freshman Hemingway parody: "She died and then she was dead."

A silence ensued. Quite an awkward one, and it served to remind Tennessee—(and he went on to describe it) of the first time he had met William Faulkner. This had occurred in a small restaurant in Rome where Faulkner had sat, overcome with shyness, staring down at a red-checked tablecloth; finally he raised his eyes and looked at Tennessee, who was so affected by the sadness he discovered there, some sense of the martyred, that he burst into tears.

Hemingway leaned forward again. "Good effort," he said.

I think Hemingway was slightly puzzled by the encounter. Afterward the two of us drove out to the *finca* in a big canary-yellow convertible with the top down, Hemingway sitting beside the driver with a drink held between his knees. He was thinking about Tennessee. "Not a predictable sort of man," he said. "Is he the commodore of something . . . that yachting cap?"

I said I didn't know. I doubted it.

"Goddamn good playwright," Hemingway said.

The Floridita was the scene of the exercise in commitment that I came to admire so in Tynan. It began in the annex to the bar—a pleasant patiolike dining area off the back; it blazed with light out there like a summer meadow compared to the dark corridor of the bar. A group of us were sitting around a table eating club sandwiches: Tynan and his wife, Elaine; Tennessee and a United Fruit Company heiress he was traveling with who was referred to as the Banana Queen. Hemingway had thought about joining us, but he had decided to spend his day out at the *finca*.

An American joined our circle. He announced himself as Captain Marks, a soldier of fortune who had been fighting in the hills with Castro and who had marched in the triumphant entry into the city. He looked like a tourist. He wore a linen shirt, but he had on a wide military belt, and after a while he said that Castro had given him an interesting job over in the Morro Castle, on the other side of the harbor—he was in charge of the execution squads. He was being kept very busy, especially in the evenings, and sometimes his squads didn't get through with their work until one or two in the morning. We all stared at him. In fact, Captain Marks went on, that very evening there was going to be quite a lot of activity over in the fortress and he'd be just delighted if we would consider joining him as his guests at what he referred to as "the festivities." He made the invitation as easily as he might have offered a round of cocktails at his home. He counted us: "Let's see ... five of you ... quite easy ... we'll drive over by car ... tight squeeze ... I'll pick you up at eight. ..."

At this point there was a sudden eruption from Tynan. He had been sitting, rocking back and forth, in his chair; he came out of it almost as if propelled. He began to shout at Captain Marks. Tynan stutters slightly, and on words which are difficult for him his lips pucker, and his eyes squint shut in his effort to make what he wishes to say emerge.

At first, I don't think Captain Marks was aware that these curious honked explosions of indignation from this gaunt arm-flapping man in a seersucker suit were directed at him, but then Tynan got his voice under control, and Captain Marks could see his opened eyes now, pale and furious, staring at him, and the words became discernible—shouts that it was sickening to stay in the same room with such a frightful specimen as an executioner of men ("l-l-l-loathsome!"), and as for the invitation, yes, he was going to turn up all right, but in order to throw himself in front of the guns of the firing squad! He was going to stop the "festivities"—the word sprayed from him in rage—and with this he pulled his wife up out of her chair, and as she flailed in his wake like a miscreant child, he rushed for the exit. We heard from him once again, out beyond the heads turned to watch him go past, some indistinguishable cry of dismay.

"What the hell was that?" Captain Marks asked. He shook his

head and rolled his eyes; he smiled at us; surely we would all agree that the poor man was looney in the head; wasn't it a shame?

He sighed and went on with his plans with us for the evening as if the tumult caused by Tynan had been as idle a distraction as a police siren going by on the street outside. He would meet us at the such-and-such hotel, in the lobby, at eight o'clock ... plenty of time to drive through the tunnel to the fortress on the far side of the harbor. He would take whoever turned up.

I was ashamed that I wanted to go. I mentioned it to Hemingway that afternoon out at the *finca*. He was sitting by his swimming pool with the week's mail and journals bound up in rubber bands beside him on the flagstones. The graves of his pets, cats mostly, were there by the side of the pool—small headstones of cement. Black Dog's grave was there; Hemingway told me that when he went swimming, Black Dog would wait with his head resting on his sandals at poolside. Batista's soldiers had killed him just a few months before in the final flurries of the revolution; they came to the *finca* looking for arms when Hemingway was abroad and Black Dog had barked and wouldn't let them in until finally they dispatched him with a rifle butt. In the pool, leaves as big as plates floated on a surface as opaque as a disused cistern's. Down the hill, out of sight, a baseball game was going on; the thin cries drifted up through the thick hillside foliage. It was hot, but with a cool wind blowing. The evening seemed a long way off. I told him about the executions scheduled, and that I was not at all sure about my own attitudes. The idea appalled me—that anyone (always in the newsreels the victims seemed to be wearing freshly laundered white shirts outside their belts) should be stood up and shot. But I was curious, admittedly so, along with being outraged at myself for not having the same attitude of disgust and the commitment to stopping it as did Tynan. I described Tynan's behavior admiringly. "Damn, you should have seen it, Papa. The face on that man Marks, just stunned, with Ken flapping at him with those long arms, just *steaming* with rage, saying he was going to throw himself in front of the guns. Just grand, with everyone turned around in his chair in the Floridita to see what was going on."

Hemingway allowed that it was too bad; it had been a mistake to ask Tynan. Seeing such a thing might shift his perception of the revolution since his emotional makeup, while okay, just was not suited to accept such things. He'd give the revolution a bad name.

But he felt I should go. He said it was important that a writer get around to see just about anything, especially the excesses of human behavior, as long as he could keep his emotional reactions in check.

So I went that night to the hotel down by the esplanade to wait for Captain Marks. Tennessee was there with the Banana Queen. No sign of Tynan, of course. No one seemed to know what he was doing. Perhaps he was already in the fortress across the harbor entrance, crouched upon some wall, looking down on the floodlit courtyard with the stake in the sand pit and the men standing around in their stiff parade-ground military hats which turned as they occasionally looked toward the door through which the principals of the "festivities" would come.

We had all arrived at the hotel early. The conversation was desultory. We were ashamed of one another, and of ourselves. We talked about our reasons for being there. I was armed with what Hemingway had told me. Tennessee had discovered from Captain Marks that a young German mercenary was scheduled to be shot that evening, and he felt that if he had the chance to do so, he'd get close enough to give him a small encouraging smile. He said that there was a tradition of ministers in his family and so it was quite appropriate for him to offer this little service. I wasn't sure that a "small encouraging smile" from Tennessee was what one hoped for as one's last view on earth, but it seemed as reasonable an excuse as any.

Captain Marks arrived. We all stood up and looked at him, horrified.

"It's been called off," he said. We hardly listened to him. "Circumstances . . . difficulties . . . postponement." He said all this perfunctorily. He did not seem especially anxious to keep in touch with us about the matter—no jotting down of hotels and room numbers. He had doubtless concluded that we were an odd lot: our own doubts so obviously seethed; we didn't seem grateful; we kept staring at him with our mouths ajar.

Frankly, I have no idea whether Tynan was actually responsible for the evening's "festivities" ' being canceled. I like to think that he was; that the officials had got wind of his outraged reaction to Captain Marks in the Floridita, especially his statement that he was going to throw himself in front of the guns. No, it was best to let things cool down; to let this weird fanatic clear off the island. At least they would not have to worry that just as everything was going along smoothly, the blindfolds nicely in place, not too tight, just right, Tynan's roar of rage would peal out of the darkness ("St-st-stop this in-in-infamous be-be-behavior!") and he would flap out at them across the courtyard, puffs of dirt issuing from his footfalls as he came at them like a berserk crane.

Some time after this, Tynan got into a tremendous set-to with Truman Capote which began with a review of *In Cold Blood* in *The Observer* in which Tynan criticized the author at great length for doing less than he might have, despite his being opposed to capital punishment, to save the two murderers in the book, Perry Smith and Dick Hickock, from the Kansas hangman.

I had always thought that Tynan had been fortified in his stance by his show of commitment in Havana. I once mentioned this to Elaine Dundy, his ex-wife, and she was quite scornful. "Oh my goodness, no. His pique at Truman was just jealousy. He wanted to write that book *In Cold Blood* himself. What was *he* doing—*Oh Calcutta!* Oh, no, it was just jealousy."

Whatever, with the appearance of Tynan's review, a predictably violent reaction erupted from Capote, who replied to *The Observer* and spoke of Tynan's allegation as coming from one "with the morals of a baboon and the guts of a butterfly."

The feud went on for years, and every time I thought of it, or ran into either of the principals, I thought of Tynan and the "festivities" in Cuba. I never told Capote about it. I would not have dared; his rage was deep seated. Once, I was sitting in a restaurant having dinner with Capote and suddenly, for no apparent reason, he began describing a fantasy to me he had about Tynan. I had the feeling he had turned it delectably around in his mind for years, like rolling a never-melting candy drop against the back of his teeth.

It started with a kidnapping, an abduction on a quiet city side street, with Tynan bundled into the back of a Rolls-Royce—the appurtenances of Truman's story were all very grand—in which he was taken off to a smart clinic in the country, with a long gravel drive up past the stone gateposts, lawns stretching out on either side, where he was deposited in a very well appointed hospital room with a comfortable bed, a bellpull for the nurse, and a pleasant view over the grounds. The meals were excellent. The members of the hospital staff were polite and sympathetic to his every need, almost unctuously so, and well they might have been, because on occasion Tynan was wheeled off to surgery somewhere in the clinic and a limb or an organ would be removed.

Truman announced this chilling detail quite cheerily, as if describing a hat-check girl helping someone off with his coat. We were sitting in an Eastside Italian restaurant which Truman went to less for the food than for its supposed Mafia connections. At that time the criminal world absorbed Capote, his only reading, according to friends, being detective pulp magazines—they lay throughout his country home in Long Island in thick heaps. He waved for a drink. He told me our waiter was a Mafia hit man. "He's killed just barrels of people," Capote said. He leaned comfortably back in his chair and went on about Tynan, describing how carefully the operations in the clinic were done: with every consideration for the patient; the very best teams of doctors involved; extensive postoperative procedures thought of; flowers set along the windowsill with notes of sympathy pegged to them; careful diets, and therapeutic exercises to get what was left in good shape; then, as soon as the patient was beginning to feel sprightly, why, in they would come to cart him off, the nighthawks wheeling outside in the evening, to remove something else, either a limb or an external organ, until finally, after months of surgery and recuperation, everything possible had been removed except one eye and his genitalia. "Everything else goes!" Truman cried gaily.

"Then what happens *is*"—he leaned far back in his chair for effect—"that the door to his hospital room opens and in is wheeled a motion-picture projector, a screen, along with an attendant in a white smock who sets everything up and shows *pornographic films,* very high grade, enticing ones, absolutely *nonstop.*"

Capote rocked back and forth, relishing his hospital-room scene. "Can you think of anything more frustrating?" he called out. He went on to say that eventually what was left of Tynan was taken off and dumped somewhere—Times Square, I think he said—but it was an untidy and uninspired ending; he wasn't putting his mind to it; he yawned.

Graphic as Truman can be at his best—which is in a Mafia restaurant, late in the evening, with a hit man to point out and a carafe of wine at hand, along with some attentive listeners—I had always found myself less taken with his one-eyed torso (thank the Lord!) than with my own mental dramatization: Tynan in the battlements of that dark fortress in Havana, sputtering with rage as he crept toward the courtyard; then his cry pealing out of the darkness ("St-st-stop this in-in-infamous be-be-be-havior!"), and the image of him dropping down to the ground and setting out for the group of men, the peaks of their military hats turned toward him, to do something about what outraged him. . . .

13

What a coming-out party it was! The Ali-Quarry fight. Atlanta, Georgia, forty-three months after that day in April of 1967 when Ali refused to step forward and accept induction into the Army. The boxing commissions, which had decreed Ali guilty without trial, were allowing him in to practice his craft again. The peacocks from Harlem came down to celebrate, their enormous purple Cadillacs parked along Peachtree Street, the curious staring in at the dashboards, and the chrome doodads, and the carpets, with the phone boxes resting on them; and I never saw crowds as fancy as those in the lobby of the auditorium at fight time, especially the men—felt hatbands, and the feather capes, and the stilted shoes, the heels like polished ebony, and people smoking odd meerschaum pipes. In the lobby invitations were passed out to the grandest of these people to a private celebration in a suburban ranch house later that night, and that was where a spectacular robbery took place: a gang of men and a girl (we heard) holding shotguns on a crowd that was largely underworld—pimps and pushers and mobsters—and they were forced to strip to their underwear and lie on the basement floor, whole rows of them, glaring while belongings were swept into piles with kitchen brooms and then carted away in pillowcases. A great heist, and hardly a writer in Atlanta for the fight who heard about it the next morning didn't crave to begin a hotshot novel or at the very least a screenplay or teleplay to describe this, and then to speculate what happened next—how these underworld people began going about revenging themselves and recovering what they had lost.

I went down to cover the fight, and also because it was a celebration for some of us. Our efforts had very little to do with Ali's being allowed to fight; it was more that the mood of the times was changing, and the public was beginning to relate to what he had said about having "no argument with them Vietcong." But I think Muhammad Ali knew that we had tried to help. He let me stay with him up to the moment he left for the ring. This meant I could try to write something I had long hoped to do—a portrait of a fighter's last thoughts and actions before his commitment:

Ali's contingent had been there for six weeks, in a cottage by a small dun-colored lake in suburban Atlanta, thick woods in back, with the autumn foliage still and heavy from a rain that had come through the night before. The railroad tracks were a half mile or so back through the woods, with the freight trains going by once in a while—long, heavy loads, they must have been, because the whistle would die mournfully in the distance while the wheels of the last cars still clicked slowly and distinctly across the sidings on the far side of the ridge.

The cottage belonged to State Senator Leroy Johnson, one of the key figures in Muhammad Ali's return to the ring. He had donated it to the champion's contingent for their training headquarters, and on this, the day of the Jerry Quarry fight, the interior was a shambles. The bedrooms, three of them, were crowded with unmade cots and half-filled suitcases. In the main room, where the curtains were drawn to provide a permanent gloom for TV and film watching, a stuffed kingfish had fallen off the wall and lay with its tail in the fireplace; beside it floated a half-deflated balloon with an inscription on it which read SOUL BROTHER. Scattered about the floor were newspapers and boxing journals, along with strips of film, soiled socks, upturned ashtrays, various items of athletic equipment, including a shuttlecock (there was a sagging badminton net out in the backyard), sweatpants, boots; above an unmade cot a bedsheet was tacked to the wall for a motion-picture screen; a long sofa was set along one wall, with a television console opposite with its screen showing an educational biology film entitled *Ponds.* A Miss Howells was talking earnestly, if almost soundlessly (the volume being turned far down), about a water lily she held lightly in one hand. In the corner of the dining alcove stood a big trunk marked MUHAMMAD ALI—THE KING. On it lay a yellow pad on which someone had written the words "Joy to the whole wide wide world a champion was born at 1121 W. Oak Street Louisville, KY it was . . ."—an unfinished document in the handwriting, it turned out, of Cassius Clay, Sr., the champion's father, apparently beginning a biography.

By contrast, the kitchen was neat—a woman's touch provided by a relative of the senator's who came in every day to provide meals for the camp. "I don't even dare look in those other rooms," she told me.

At noontime, Jim Jacobs, the former U.S. handball champion, who is a fight buff, arrived with a fight film he had recently completed on the career of the first black heavyweight champion, Jack Johnson, which he thought would particularly interest Muhammad Ali. The parallels between the two fighters are striking—both exiled from the sport, both in difficulty with legal authority, and both great showmen in and out of the ring. Ali lounged on the sofa, a telephone close at hand, and watched the film begin to flicker on the bedsheet. "Look at these advantages I have," he whispered. "Quarry. He don't have a machine and movies like this. He has nothing to look at today but the walls."

To Jacobs' despair, Ali's attention was constantly interrupted by the phone at his side. Instinctively he picked it up when it rang, invariably to find the caller someone trying to cadge a few tickets for the fight. Ali would announce himself, often to a startled squawk from the other end, and he would go on to say that buses were scheduled to leave the Regency Hotel an hour before the fight and he would arrange to see that those aboard got into the arena. Sometimes Ali knew the caller personally and he would call out, "Sidney Poitier, you're my *man!*" or "Whitney Young, my goodness." The prize guest he was taking to the fight was Mrs. Martin Luther King. When he announced from the sofa that she was coming with him, there were excited shouts, and Bundini, his trainer, called out exuberantly, "The King Mother . . . the King Mother comin' to see the champ rumble!"

Jacobs kept his film running throughout the interruptions. Ali paid as much attention as he could, lolling on the sofa, sucking on a blue plastic toothpick. Occasionally he rolled his shoulders to keep the muscles loose. "Jack Johnson," he said reverently. He mentioned that the old fighter's facial features looked a little like Babe Ruth's. The phone rang and he bent over the receiver, talking into it softly. He hung up the phone and the sight on the bedsheet screen of Jack Johnson chasing a chicken caught his fancy; he wondered aloud if running after a particularly lively chicken wouldn't be a valuable training exercise for a fighter. He thought he might hire some for his next fight. At one point in the film, the deep, simulated voice of Jack Johnson announced, just prior to the Jim Jeffries fight, "If I felt any better, I'd be *scared* of myself." Ali laughed, and one felt that he might have stored the line away for future use. He was interested that Johnson always insisted on being the first fighter to climb into the ring, a procedure so important to him that it was a stipulation written into his contracts. But the Johnson antics in the ring were what made Ali lean forward out of the sofa, and even if he was talking to someone on the phone, his voice would trail off. When Johnson grinned and appeared to taunt Tommy Burns in the early rounds of the fight in Australia that won him the heavyweight championship, Ali commented, "He's something else." He watched Johnson make a derisive gesture with his glove, waving good-bye to Burns as he turned for his corner at the end of a round. "Look at that," Ali said. "He's signifying,

'See you later, partner.' I believe I'll do that with Quarry to-night."

I noticed Angelo Dundee staring uneasily across the room. "Just like him to pick up some crazy notion from that film," he whispered to me. "Why doesn't the phone keep ringing?" Up on the bedsheet, scenes of the Jack Johnson–Stanley Ketchel fight were beginning. Ketchel was a middleweight fighting far over his class (the publicity movies of the signing for the fight show him in a long camel-hair coat and extra-high cowboy boots to disguise his relative lack of stature), and at one stage of the bout Johnson bulled him to the canvas, and then, almost apologetically, picked him up and set him on his feet as one would a child, so that, watching the film, I half expected Jack Johnson to dust him off. Ali was delighted. "Tonight," he said, "I'll just set Quarry down and pick him up." He rocked back and forth.

"Oh my," said Dundee. "At the bell, you never know what's going to happen with this fellow." He whispered to me that for the second Liston fight—the one that was scheduled for Boston and then postponed when the champion suffered a hernia—Ali was toying with the idea of hiding a muleta in his boxing trunks; he planned to produce the muleta in the first round and play Sonny Liston like a bull.

With the first reel of the film over, Ali suddenly stood up and announced that it was time for lunch. He sat down in the dining alcove to a meal of beets, greens, and lamb chops, which he ate with considerable gusto; his meal down, he announced he was going to "settle" it with a half-hour walk. He was accompanied on his stroll by reporters, a business advisor or two, a detective, and Jim Jacobs, who in turn was accompanied by a camera crew. Ali led this contingent off into the woods carrying a seven-foot stave, like a patriarch with his flock capering after him.

The cottage seemed extraordinarily quiet in his absence. Angelo Dundee remarked to me that he had not been surprised by the bedlam in the cottage—the shouting, the phones going. "It's always been like this," he said. "Since the very beginning. The kid's big concern on the day of a fight is to look out for his friends. When he fought Doug Jones in Madison Square Garden he arrived at the back entrance with a whole mob of people and he braced the door open and just passed these people through under his arm, one after the other. The matchmaker, who was Teddy Brennan, tried to stop him, and Ali said that if he couldn't get his friends in, well, that was that: he wasn't going to fight, and Brennan knew that he wasn't fooling. So that mob got in."

"Have you ever had another fighter who compares?" I asked.

Angelo shook his head. "No one like him," he said. "Not that you don't have to mother the lot of them." He went on to describe the fight-day habits of some of his other fighters. Willie Pastrano, for example, who searched zodiac signs and astrology charts for indications that he would do well. He fought Perralta when the stars were absolutely wrong and Angelo spent fight day pleading with him that the astrologers could have been in error, just this *once,* and Pastrano climbed gloomily into the ring, and, eventually, to everyone's surprise, his own especially, he knocked Perralta out.

And Alongi, the Argentine heavyweight. His trouble was that he began to develop a cold ten days before a fight, which intensified as the day approached, with additional symptoms developing, such as those of grippe and flu and malaria, until his spirits were as low as a whipped dog's. "I'm weak," he would tell Angelo. "I can't fight. I'm sick." Angelo would assure him that his problems were psychosomatic, that really ... "No, no, I'm sick," Alongi would tell him.

"For him, the biggest fight was leaving the dressing room," Angelo said. "It was like pushing a big piece of furniture to get him up into the ring. Even there, he'd keep insisting he was sick. This one time against George Chuvalo, he went out and had this great first round, punching heavy and good, and everything going right, and at the bell he came back to the corner to tell us that he was still sick with this terrible cold, that he was as weak as a kitten, and he thought he ought to go to bed and get himself tucked in with a hot-water bottle."

The coolest fighter of his stable, Angelo went on, and the one who reminded him most of Muhammad Ali, was the middleweight Luis Rodríguez. On the day of a fight he was serene and placid and he enjoyed people around him, particularly those who could play dominoes. He looked forward to a fight, not to get it over with, which was characteristic of so many fighters, but to provide himself with a showcase for his talents. A fight allowed him to display his artistry—his opponents simply a foil to his wizardry, just as the bull is to the superb matador—and Rodríguez' mood as he waited was one of pleasant anticipation. That was just like Muhammad Ali.

"Ali is an artist, and that's why he fights," Angelo said. "He loves it so much. Look at him. I never saw him out of shape. Maybe he got a bit fat and round when he went around and spoke at the colleges, but that's all trained off. Nobody loves boxing like he does. Everything a fighter does which begins to send him downhill—drinking, smoking, living around loose—he doesn't do, because he has such respect and love for the profession."

"What about Sugar Ray Robinson?" someone asked. "What did he do the day of the fight?"

Bundini, Ali's trainer, stirred himself on the other side of the room. He had spent some time in Robinson's corner in his earlier days. "Pee and chew ice," he said. "That's all he did."

Muhammad Ali's dressing room at the arena was small, not much wider than the length of the rubbing table set at one end, and only three or four paces long—hardly enough room, as Bundini said when he saw it, for Ali to "exercise up some sweat." Dressing tables were set against opposite walls, their mirrors outlined with light bulbs.

Ali arrived with an hour to go before the fight. Even before he got out of his streetclothes he was moving around the room, snapping out the jabs and staring at himself in the mirrors. "This room's too crowded," he said. "I want room to rest."

The room was cleared except for the entourage he would take to the ring, along with two interns assigned to the fight, and the Reverend Jesse Jackson. I was allowed to stay. I crouched in a corner with a notebook open. Ali stripped quickly. He pulled on a pair of white boxing trunks and turned slowly in front of the mirror. "I am the champ," he said softly. "He must fall." He tried out the Ali shuffle, his white gym shoes snapping against the floor.

"Angelo," he said. "I'm not wearing the foul-protector tonight."

Angelo looked up. He and Bundini were having words in the corner. In the days immediately before the fight there had been considerable argument about the regulation foul-proof belt. Ali wanted to wear a small tin cup rather than the leather device which bulked out his boxing trunks and made him look, at least to his eyes, fat. But Dundee had insisted on the regulation belt. He warned Ali that Quarry not only was a body puncher but had nothing to lose: he had been known to hit "south of the border," and it was just crazy to take chances.

Bundini had packed the equipment suitcase two days before and checked it out twice to see if everything was there, especially the foul-proof belt, which was red and had Ali's name on it. To his astonishment, the belt was missing when he opened the suitcase in the dressing room. So he and Dundee, who thought Bundini had simply forgotten it back at the cottage, had a low but harsh exchange. The champion, shadowboxing in the rear, gave no indication of being aware of what was going on: perhaps there was no need to, since the belt was found under his bed the next morning. Dundee opened the suitcase, which belonged to Rachaman—who had fought on the card earlier that evening—and produced *his* protector, a black model marked STANDARD. Ali looked at it warily. He turned to the mirrors and began some light shadowboxing, always exhaling sharply with each punch thrown—a hard, distinctive, explosive snuffle; after a minute or so he stopped and left the dressing room for the lavatory. There were forty minutes left to go. I went racing along with my notebook. On the way back Ali passed his opponent's dressing room, just a step down the corridor from his own. It had a hand-lettered notice, QUARRY, tacked to the door. Ali could not resist the temptation. He pushed the door open and peered in. Over his shoulder I could see Quarry sitting facing him, his knees jiggling.

"You, fellow," Ali said in a sepulchral voice, "you best be in good shape, because if you whup me, you've whupped the greatest fighter in the whole wide world."

He clicked the door shut before Quarry could come up with a reply, and back in his own dressing room he described what he had done with impish pleasure. It had been a ploy of the type which delighted him—the unexpected materialization. I remembered on one occasion, the year before, driving through Queens with a reporter, Ali had stopped the car and tiptoed up behind a truck driver who was changing a tire. "I hear you're talking around town that you can whup me," the fighter said. "Well, here I is."

The truck driver's ears had turned a quick red and he spun on his haunches to stand up; and then, seeing Muhammad, and recognizing him, his jaw dropped, and he froze in a curious half stoop, the tire iron clattering from his hand as the fighter grinned at him and stepped back for his car.

With a half hour to go a representative from Quarry's camp turned up in the dressing room to oversee the taping of Ali's hands. His name was Willie Ketcham, an older man, a towel over one shoulder of his jacket, and his jaws working evenly on a piece of gum. Ali's eyes sparkled. "Well, look who's here," he said. "You all in trouble tonight."

"Who's in trouble?" Ketcham said. He knew he was in for some badgering.

"Your man's in for a new experience," Ali said. "He's against the fastest heavyweight alive, quick and trim. Look at that." He slapped his belly. "Look how pretty and slim."

"You won't be when Jerry finishes," Ketcham said. "I know he's going to hit *you.*"

"How's he going to do that?" Ali looked genuinely surprised. "Angelo, how can he get away from the jab? How will he ever see it?"

Dundee shrugged. He motioned Ali to the rubbing table and began the taping of his hands.

Ketcham challenged him. "And if Jerry move in on you, throwing the big ones? Ho ho."

"He's going to get hit right in the banana," Ali said crisply. "He never seen a right like that."

"If you beat Quarry tonight, you are the greatest heavyweight who ever lived," Ketcham said. And he added with attempted sarcasm, "Yeh, and if that happens, I'll come in here and kiss you."

"Oh, my, no," said Ali. He looked at the taped hand Dundee had finished. "Hey," he said. "We will give you guys five hundred thousand dollars *cash* . . . if you let me put a horseshoe in my gloves."

Ketcham blinked. "Aw," he said.

Dundee finished the taping and Ketcham leaned over and crisscrossed the tape with pen strokes. When he stepped back, Ali stood up and moved close to stare into Ketcham's eyes. Ketcham is a tall man; standing, the two of them braced each other like fighters while getting instructions from the referee. "Look into my eyes," Ali said. "I'm the real heavyweight. I am the fastest heavyweight that ever lived."

Ketcham didn't back down. His jaw kept moving impassively.

"I won some money on you once," he said. "I bet fifty dollars at seven to one that you'd whup Sonny Liston."

Ali began to turn away. "We'll give them a good show tonight," he said. "I couldn't pick no better contender."

"Okay, pal," Ketcham said. He cuffed Ali affectionately alongside the head, and turned to go.

"Twenty minutes," someone said.

"We're going to warm up on the ropes," Ali said. "We're going out there and lay on the ropes. . . ."

"Don't say 'we' when you say that," Bundini said. "You stick him *fast,* you hear?"

"Who goes into the ring first?" Ali asked.

"Quarry," he was told.

He lay down on the rubbing table, his head to the wall. One of the young interns leaned forward and brashly asked Ali what he was thinking, just at that instant.

Ali began his litany. He said he was thinking about the people in Japan and Turkey and Russia, all over the world; how they were beginning to think about the fight, and about him; and the television sets being clicked on; and the traffic jams in front of the closed-circuit theaters; and how the big TV trucks out in back of the Atlanta arena, just by the stage door, were getting their machinery warmed up to send his image by satellite to all those people, and how he was going to dance for them—"I got to dance," he said—all this in the soft silky voice he uses when he does this sort of thing, almost the voice of a mother soothing her child to sleep with nursery rhymes.

"How about a verse?" the intern asked.

"Quarry/sorry," Ali said.

The intern was delighted. "Hey, that's pretty *short*," he said. "How about another?"

"I don't have time/to find a rhyme," Ali replied gently, and he went on with his thoughts, how finally he was thinking most of all of Allah, his God, the Almighty Allah, who had given him so many gifts. He began to enumerate them in his singsong voice—a long free-verse ode to carrot juice, to honey, to the things which grew in his garden and which he ate, never anything manmade that came in tin cans, none of that stuff, but only what came fresh from the gardens; and then the woods in which he would run "before the cars were up, and their poison"; and he talked about how he would face east and thank the Creator for all of this which had given him the strength to live right and to pray right. He said that thinking of all that the Creator had done made it simple for him to look at Quarry and see how little he was and how easy he could be whupped.

Ali swung his feet to the floor and stood up. Fifteen minutes were left. His corner man, Sazriah, applied a smear of Vaseline to the fighter's shoulders and started rubbing it into his torso. His body began to shine. A policeman stuck his head in and the crowd noise, roaring at the entrance of some celebrity, swept in for an instant and made the blood pound before it was shut off by the door.

"They're waiting for me to dance," Ali said. His feet were shuffling. Jesse Jackson put up a hand as a target and Ali popped a few jabs, snorting his sharp exhalations, and then he stopped and looked at himself in the mirror. "The Temptations are out there," he said. "The Supremes are out there; Sidney Poitier's out there."

He peered at himself closely.

"A hair comb, somebody." He held out his hand behind him blindly as he continued looking into the mirror, and it was filled by someone's slapping the comb into his palm as one might supply a busy surgeon.

He moved the comb through his short brush, flicking at some wayward tuft, until Dundee approached with the foul-protector and the boxing gloves, new and gum red from their packing case.

Ali balked. "I'm *not* wearing that thing," he said. A chorus of dismay rose from around the room.

"Just try it on and see," someone urged. Sulkily, Ali skinned out of his trunks and shimmied the protector up over his thighs. He pulled the trunks back up over them. A babble of voices rose.

"It looks just fine."

"Trim, man, beautiful. Trim."

Ali began some knee bends, hands out, and every time he came up above the level of the dressing tables he turned to look at himself in the mirrors. Then he stood up and slapped at his trunks disgustedly.

"Where are my brother's trunks?"

"Champ, those trunks look just *boss.*"

"Slim and trim, champ, slim and trim."

A pleading chorus rose from those around the room. Ali skinned off the trunks. Dundee opened up Rachaman's suitcase, and, rummaging through it, he produced a pair of white trunks with a black stripe down the side. Ali reached for them, put them on over the protector and turned slowly in front of the mirrors. Everybody stared at him.

"This is better," he said after a while. A quick chorus of approbation came from around the room.

"Right on, man."

"That's real trim."

"It brings your ass down just right."

Everyone was sweating.

"How much time?" someone asked.

"Ten minutes."

Ali began to shadowbox in earnest, throwing quick long jabs, flurries of combinations, and big hooks that seemed to shudder the air in that tiny room; the onlookers flattened themselves back against the wall to give him room. He stopped to tape his shoelaces against the top of his shoes so they wouldn't flop. "Too loose," he said. "In late rounds they can get soggy; and man, I want to dance."

The gloves were put on. He began another flurry of punches. Murmurs rose from those standing along the wall. "Hmmm, cook," called Bundini.

Hearing him, Ali stopped suddenly and turned to Bundini. "Now, I don't want you to be hollering in that corner, Bundini, and start to get all excited and shout things like 'cook' and all that. It takes my mind off things."

Bundini was furious. "What you expect?" he shouted. "You expect me to keep my mouth shut when the cake is put in the oven, when all the preparation and the mixing is done and it's time for the fire and you expect me to stand around with my hands on my hips? If'n you expect me to keep my mouth shut, you better kick me out of your corner and keep me in *here.*"

"All right, then, you stay out of the corner," Ali said. "You *stay* in here."

The two stared at each other, the enormity of what Ali had said beginning to hit. Bundini pressed his lips together and seemed on the edge of tears. "Aw come on," Ali said after an instant. "You can come on out," he said gently.

He started up his shadowboxing, once again concentrating on himself in the mirrors. Bundini wouldn't look at him for a while. "My goodness," he said. Sweat began to shine on Ali's body. "I'm warm now," he said, looking at Angelo.

The door burst open and Sidney Poitier, the actor, rushed in. The champion jumped for him and the two spun around the room in an embrace. "Sidney's here. I'm *really* ready to rumble!" Ali shouted. He held him off at arm's length and looked at the slim actor, elegantly got up in a tight form-fitting gray suit. "Man, you exercise?" he asked admiringly. "Hey," he said, "give me a rhyme to psych Quarry—when we're getting the referee's instructions." He held up an imaginary microphone. Poitier bent his head in thought; he had been caught by surprise. "You met your match, chump," he intoned in his soft voice. "Tonight you're falling in." He cast an arm desperately for a rhyme for "chump." "You're falling in *two*," he cried, giving up.

"That's terrible," Muhammad Ali said. "Man, you stick to acting and leave me the rhyming and the psyching."

Poitier wished him luck amidst the laughter, and disappeared.

Ali reached for a towel and began to rub off the Vaseline. "Is the ring nice?" he asked.

"Perfect," Dundee said.

"Is the closed-circuit system okay?"

"They say it is."

Outside, the voice of the crowd, impatient now, began to beat at the door. A big roar went up. "Quarry," someone said, "Quarry's gone."

Seconds to go. Ali stood immobile for a second, perhaps to pray, which is his habit, and Jesse Jackson hopped off the rubbing table and embraced him, almost trembling with emotion.

A knock sounded on the door. "It's time," a voice called. Muhammad Ali gave one last peek at himself in the mirrors and he went out into the corridor, his people packed around him.

14

Ali won the fight, of course, stopping Quarry with a punch that opened up his eye in the third round. Bundini was very lively in Ali's corner: "Jack Johnson's heah!" he kept shouting. "Ghost in the house! Ghost in the house!" I remember the jubilation in the auditorium and the big celebration afterward up on one of the floors of the Regency Hyatt House, where it was so crowded that one stood out on the parapetlike corridors of that tall cylindrical lobby with the elevators running up the sides, the whiskey glasses on the ledge, and looked over down that cool vast shaft to the main floor below, where the faces of the people, hearing all that uproar, kept looking up. Ali was there; it was impossible to get close to him.

But the celebration that kept coming back to my mind afterward was not Ali's but rather the one on the outskirts of town where the big holdup had taken place. I kept wondering about the circumstances of it—the gang that pulled it off, and their nerve, and all those hustlers stacked down there in the cellar, some of them the roughest racketeers Harlem had to offer, and what they were going to do about it once they got out of that basement. I was told that just the *concept* of the caper so entranced people that a few of the flashier sorts around Harlem dropped a couple of hints that *they* had a hand in masterminding it—just to make an impression standing around in a 125th Street bar, or in a pool room, or with a girl; just the barest of hints, maybe a knowing smile, and it made them feel pretty good to see the suspicion, or perhaps the awe, in the other people's eyes. But then they faced the horror of waking up the next morning, squinting their eyes against the pillow in despair as they realized that if anyone had *believed* them the night before, and started talking about it around town, the story might get to the wrong ears. The revenge arm of the mob could well be out to get them. What could one do in such a case? How did one go about disavowing a story already told? Perhaps it would be best to get out of town. But they'd come after you. The only hope was to have a phrase of explanation set to deliver, just bursting at the lips, so that at a sharp noise in an alley, or *anywhere,* a sudden knock at the door, a body could shoot his arms in the air and cry out, "Hey, cool it, man, I was just funnin'. . . . I ain't done nothing!" and hope that the sincerity in the voice was powerful enough to relax the trigger fingers.

Long after the actual event, my curiosity finally got the better of me. I called the Atlanta police department to start putting together some notes on the holdup. I was put in touch with one of the lieutenants who had worked on the case. He was now a warden at a correctional facility outside Atlanta.

He remembered the case well, but there was just the barest hitch in his soft Southern inflection to suggest his surprise at being questioned about it. "Frankly, we didn't get to know too much," he said. "A lot went on that I can't tell you about, not because I wouldn't want to—hear?—but because I just don't know. My potential witnesses were not very cooperative. They cleared out of town."

The warden started at the beginning. Ostensibly, the celebration was a two-day birthday party for a Harlem character named Tobe. The local host was an Atlanta hustler named William Gordon, alias the Chicken Man. It was his house that was given over to the festivities. But the true purpose of the affair was to cater a couple of days of gambling for the fast Harlem crowd that was coming down for the fight. A custom-built dice table was trucked in and they had it set up down in the cellar.

The hold-up gang had arrived at ten A.M., just about the first people there, carrying in their shotguns wrapped up; putting on their ski masks, just their eyes showing, they took over the place ... about seven of them. They left a man outside on the front lawn with a walkie-talkie and he would say into it to get ready, some *guests* were coming up the front path, and just as easy as standing on a city sidewalk and loading cases of soft drinks on a roller slide and sending them rattling down to the basement for storage, the newcomers were dispatched through the front door to that little greeting party with the shotguns and then hurried down the cellar stairs to the basement, where they were told to strip and to lie facedown on the cellar floor. Poor Mr. Tobe. The gunmen kept him sitting in a chair opposite the front door with a drink in his hand, greeting each guest with a ghastly smile on his face—just to keep the guests cool until they looked around into the nostrils of the sawed-off shotguns.

The warden talked about the scene with a sort of quiet relish— the guests arriving and the little greeting party, and what an outrageous sight they must have seen as they were ordered down the steps to the cellar, all those rows of people stacked up down there, and how the men in the ski masks motioned at them to strip, and then the business of these dudes stepping out of their fly-fly shoes, and the tight trousers, and the meerschaum pipes going out, and the foxes stepping out of what *they* were wearing—the sleek outfits which had dazzled the ringsiders at the auditorium—some of them doubtless without panties or under-wear so that the strange cordwoodlike heap must have been decorated with a number of bare bottoms; then the sound of the brooms sweeping the jewelry and the wallets and the watches into piles, which were scooped up and dropped into king-sized pillowcases. About a hundred people were packed in down there, some of them lying on top of one another because there wasn't room, and they were down there until four A.M., when the gunmen took two hostages and left. But it was the *sort* of people lying there, feeling the rough cement of the floor against their stomachs, and maybe some guy groaning under the weight of another, his nervous whiskeyed breath in his ear. Some of them were just about the roughest people in the world; that was the best part—that though all of them were probably thinking in their way how this indignity was going to be taken care of, for the moment these truly *bad people* were going through the most awful humiliation. I had the sense the warden enjoyed describing the scene.

"Who were the guys who did it?" I asked. "Was it a gang out of Detroit? Miami?"

"Oh, no," the warden said. "They were locals."

"Locals?"

He heard the surprise in my voice. "Professionals," he said, "would never dream to do such a job. It'd be suicide to fool with a crowd like that. It'd never cross their minds. These were local South Georgia boys; they hung around a pool hall down around Mason and Turner."

His theory was that one or two of them had been to the ranch house the night before the heist, the first night of the party, and had seen what a setup it was—all these gamblers, and the dice table going in the cellar, and the women with the jewelry. The next morning they sent a young junkie kid the police eventually pulled in as an accessory, though he wasn't in the holdup, to a number of pawn shops to buy the shotguns and the walkie-talkies and the pillowcases. They spent the afternoon sawing off the shotgun barrels.

He told me that the department had an idea that one of the seven people involved in the heist was a girl. Four or five of the witnesses who had been willing to testify had heard the clicking of a woman's heels on the floor of the basement where they had been herded. They thought her function was to search in the pants pockets as the clothes were handed to her.

"So there were witnesses willing to talk?"

"Very few," the warden said. "They surely weren't going to come in and tell us how much they had lost. That would have brought the Internal Revenue down on them. Just about all of them pulled out of Atlanta and as fast as they could."

"But you could piece it together."

"Of course, there were some theories that there was a master-mind," the warden said reflectively. "There was a Harlem hood named Emerson Dorsey, who had left New York up there ... came down here to Atlanta. He was shot in the head a couple of weeks after the robbery, and his girlfriend, she was killed, too, and it could have been a gangland thing because they killed her with knives and left them sticking out of her. Some people said he had masterminded the whole show—organized the boys and the rest of it—but I don't cotten to that idea."

"Could the girl have been the one in the cellar?" I asked.

"I don't reckon there's any connection."

"Just a bunch of local kids. Damn, what a lot of brass they had."

"I never could figure it different," the warden said. "But I think that halfway through that job these kids suddenly realized what they were doing, and that their lives weren't worth a plugged nickel. They must have seen a couple of guys looking up at them from the basement floor, and I don't care if they were wearing ski masks, they got to know they were in awful trouble. They'd like to drop their guns and go home if they could. They were South Georgia boys—pool-hall kids. They didn't belong in there holding shotguns on that crowd."

"Could you follow their trails afterward?"

"Afterward they *behaved* like kids," the warden said. "They left a trail a mile wide—down to Brunswick, Georgia, where we were able to find out they holed up in a motel for two or three days, pawing through those pillowcases, I suppose. They wouldn't let the cleaning ladies in the rooms, and they ordered meals left for them on trays outside the door. Then they went on a big spending spree down there—clothing, jewelry, and one or two cars—and then they did something I have never understood: they got into those cars and went up Interstate Ninety-five."

"Interstate Ninety-five?"

"That's the route north. They went right up there to the middle of the place where all these guys they'd robbed came from: Harlem."

"How much do you reckon they got away with in those pillowcases?" I asked.

"Well, there were four pillowcases, king-sized, and I reckon they were full; the people they took it from were in their finest—furs, stickpins, fancy jewelry, thousand-dollar watches—and there were some big bank rolls because the Chicken Man had everything set up so his guests could gamble. Of course, a lot they had in the pillowcases was worthless to them: no fence would have touched the stuff they had, that custom-made jewelry, knowing the sort of person it belonged to. Some estimations of the value got up as high as a million dollars."

"Think of that," I said. "One would like to think they got away with it."

"Well, they didn't," the warden said. "Word kept drifting into the department about it; we'd hear rumors out on the street. We were told, in so many words, don't worry about it. We'll get them. They were working harder on the case than we were. I let it out through the press that these guys who pulled the job would be better off coming in and giving themselves up; it'd be safer. But they took their chances. Finally someone called up police headquarters one day. Long distance. They said that three people had just been killed ... sitting in a Cadillac on Fulton Street in the Bronx. They'd been shot in there by some people leaning in the windows. They thought we would want to know. It was like they wanted to tell us that the file was being closed."

"So they got them all?"

"Well, we knew about those people. Two of them were funeralized down there in Robbins, Georgia. I reckon they got them all."

"Funeralized?"

"That's right," he said in his soft voice. "They never should have fooled around with that crowd."

I kept hoping to meet someone who had actually been at the affair. Bundini Brown finally helped me out. I was not surprised. His range of acquaintances was considerable. Walking down a street with him in Harlem was like being in the entourage of an emperor; people shouted at him from windows; he could not walk into a bar without producing a surge of people, though one of his detractors told me that most of them were gambling sorts to whom he owed money. So it was probable that he knew someone who had been in the Atlanta holdup. In fact, he knew more than one—and they would telephone very late at night: "Hey, man, Bundini tol' me to reach you."

The most knowledgeable of them turned out to be a man named Frank Molton. He was in jail when I talked to him. The government thought he was a top-flight racketeer; indeed, they had won a conviction against him for narcotics dealings and he had been sentenced to twenty-five years. He was in the new Federal Correction Center behind New York City's Foley Square. Bundini said that he would probably be willing to talk, since he had nothing much else to do in there.

That turned out to be the case. We exchanged letters, and I went down and received permission to see him. The prison facility is only three years old—split-level rooms with wall-to-wall carpets, tasteful primary colors for the decor, pool tables, and the *toc toc toc* of Ping-Pong balls over the low hum of men sitting around playing cards or chatting. One could well imagine oneself in a high-school recreation room—a student union—if it were not for the orange coveralls the prisoners wore, which were new and which shined like astronauts' gear, so that I had the fleeting image of the place being the ready room for some great space adventure.

Frank was very affable. He introduced me around the common room where we met. "Say hello to the Croatians," he said, and I found myself shaking hands rather formally with the group, sitting together around a table, who had hijacked a plane and had also been responsible for the death of a policeman who tried to defuse one of their homemade bombs.

Frank found us a corner up on the second level where it was quiet and we could talk above the murmur of men and the click of pool balls below.

"What have you heard about it?" Frank asked me.

"I talked to the police in Atlanta," I said. "What I keep

thinking about it is that these pool-hall kids actually pulled it off."

"What pool-hall kids? Who told you that?"

"That's what the Atlanta people seem to believe."

Frank looked at me and smiled.

"In fact," I went on uneasily, "I thought that's what made the case so ... umm ... glamorous—these kids hold up a party of big-time gamblers." (I was careful to use the word "gamblers" rather than some of the other descriptives I had heard applied to the company.) "Robin Hood sort of thing."

Frank shook his head. He was a strong-featured man, in his late fifties, I would have said, a noticeable scar on his chin; he had a gentle, very cultured manner of speaking. Bundini had told me over the phone that some people in Harlem called him the Black Godfather.

"Oh, no," he said. "The guys who thought it up were Cadillac Richard Wheeler, who was into dope dealing, and a friend of his named Fast Eddie Parker, who was Richard's enforcer and who was into killing and kidnapping. Nothing Robin Hoody about those two cats. They were rough. They took care of people who gave them trouble. Quite a long list. They killed a kid name of Bulletproof up on A Hundred Fourteenth Street."

" 'Bulletproof!' "

"That's what they called him," Frank said with a smile. "The name didn't help him. They not only got Bulletproof but in that particular shoot-out they killed a girl bystander by mistake."

He leaned back in his chair. "Of course, I didn't know it was them responsible for that thing in Atlanta until later. When I first arrived out there, I thought a police raid was going on. I drove to the party in a rented car with some friends. We stopped at the Lincoln Country Club on the way, and I suppose by the time we got there it was two A.M. I had been at the place the night before—big gambling party—and I noticed when we drove up that something was different: the shades and the curtains of the front room had been drawn. I joked with my friends: 'Look there, they don't want anybody to know what's going on. The police must be raiding the place.' That wouldn't have surprised me. Just about everyone in Atlanta must have known about the gambling. But I didn't expect a stickup. I knew as soon as I walked in the front door and saw the fellow smiling."

"Was that Tobe—the guy sitting in the chair?"

"No, it wasn't him," Frank said. "Tobe couldn't have worked up a smile on him if they'd put a shotgun under his nose. I heard tell he 'borrowed' all his wife's jewelry that night for his girlfriend to wear. It all went into a pillowcase. He was *sick*. No, it was some other guy. But I could tell from looking at him that the cowboys were there. Sure enough. They were wearing ski masks. I was aware of the sawed-off shotguns, and right inside the door someone holding a pistol with a long silencer on it. The guy with the pistol, he was the 'assassin'—to take care of anyone who got out of hand. You wouldn't want these big shotguns to be going off with all that noise, so the guns were just there for intimidation."

I whistled softly.

"Oh, yes, these guys knew their business. They sent us downstairs. In the cellar we got our instructions. 'Empty your pockets. Jewelry. Watches.' They meant it. They knocked one of the guys down the steps who wasn't moving fast enough for them. It was crowded down there. They were beginning to stack people on top of each other. It finally got out of hand; they couldn't handle the number of people being sent down. So they took two girls for hostages and closed up the shop. That was about four A.M."

I asked if he had heard the clicking of heels on the cellar floor and if a girl might have been one of the "cowboys."

"No," Frank said. "I would have remembered. It was quiet down there. Nothing to hear but the instructions 'Keep yo' head down, man.' And the sound of the walkie-talkies."

"Who were the hostages?"

"One of the hostages was the Chicken Man's old lady. The other was a kid from New York, a bargirl. I hear tell she didn't get over it for a couple of weeks ... really scared her."

"How did you know they'd gone?"

"We couldn't hear the radios no more. People slowly got up

and looked around. Then they tried to find their clothing; it lay there in a tall pile. I guess that would have to be pretty funny— to think of a body searching in that big pile, like a rummage sale, for his pants, and people calling out I got so-and-so's credit cards—but I don't remember much laughing. I recall that Chicken Man was wearing a pair of long underwear, and some- one came up and said that if he was wearing long underwear he must have *known* he was going to spend the night lying on a cellar floor. He was *prepared,* and man, that meant he was implicated."

"They accused the Chicken Man?"

"This one man did. He kept staring at the Chicken Man's long underwear. That solved the whole case for him."

"Well, who *were* the men in the ski masks?" I asked. "Were they all out of New York?"

"Fast Eddie came from Brunswick, Georgia, originally, and he had some of his old boys with him. But they were up in New York and all into killing and kidnapping ... they were hoods and real rough. They weren't guys just hanging around a local pool hall." He smiled. "I'm from Georgia. Yes, born in Thomasville, where all the great plantations are, and the bird shooting, and the mules pulling the wagons with the bird dogs in the cages in the back. I helped lay the grass for the polo field down there in Thomasville when I was a boy."

"Oh, yes."

"You been down there?"

"I know the plantations," I said. It was so incongruous think- ing of the elegant rituals of bird shooting in that area—the task forces of men on horses, and the mules, wagons, the dogs, and the sound of the whistles, and the trainers' soft call, "Daid, daid, daid," to the dogs crisscrossing in the underbrush for a downed bird that only weighed a few *ounces*—all that panoply ... so removed from those strange rec-hall surroundings with the Black Godfather sitting opposite in his orange jumpsuit.

He was speaking of himself as a cocoa distributor and said that the only justified beef the government had against him was that he was a gambler. "That's all I am," he said. "And a good bird shot." He had traveled widely, especially in Africa, and spoke of being on a first-name basis with a number of heads of state. His great love was hunting—especially wild boar in Spain. He had a number of boar heads mounted in his upstate home, but then his wife had a little hangup about the rows of heads peering at her as she went by, and in deference to her feelings he took them down and stored them. He was really more interested in bird shooting anyway—who wouldn't be, with that Thomasville background—particularly dove shooting up in northern Spain, near the huge mercury mines. He loved guns and had (until the government confiscated them) a considerable collection. He referred to his Purdy shotguns by the initials of their maker, J.C., an affectation of designation I had not heard before. If it weren't for the surroundings and his strange orange outfit, I could have been talking to a country squire.

"What sort of a gun was being held on you in the foyer?" I asked, to get him back to Atlanta.

"It was a Magnum, three-fifty-seven, by the quick look I had of it, with a silencer, of course. I always thought that was probably Eddie himself. He was the 'assassin'—just assigned himself that role."

"How did people begin to suspect Richard Wheeler and Eddie?" I asked.

Frank said, "Well, Richard Wheeler tried too hard to establish an alibi. He went down there to Georgia to set everything up (he knew about the party beforehand) and then he cleared out so he wouldn't be implicated. He flew up to New York on the day of the fight and went to the closed-circuit in Madison Square Garden that night, taking a big party with him; afterward he went to a number of night clubs and had some photographs taken—his arm around a couple of girls, that sort of thing. He thought people might think him capable of pulling the Atlanta job, so he wanted to be sure he was seen in New York."

"It didn't fool anybody?"

"Not really," Frank said. "His roommate at the Biltmore in Atlanta—who was one of the cohosts of the party—couldn't understand why Wheeler had suddenly gone to New York. His seat was empty at the fight. He got suspicious and began inquiring. And besides, Eddie, Wheeler's partner, told a couple of friends who were planning to go to the party that night that maybe it was a good idea if they *didn't* go. He didn't tell them why. So *that* got some people suspicious. Then a few of them who did go got their stuff back—friends of Eddie's."

"That doesn't sound very professional," I remarked. "What happened to the two of them?"

"Eddie's in jail somewhere," Frank said. "The police found him with a couple of hand grenades. But the others are all dead. Three or four of Eddie's boys were killed in the back of a car. That's what I hear tell, anyway."

"I heard that, too," I said. "The Atlanta police got tipped off that they were killed in the back of a Cadillac in the Bronx, and got themselves funeralized down in Brunswick, Georgia. Yes sir."

I felt very suave talking to the Black Godfather about killings in the Bronx. "Yup. They really got bopped," I said, leaning back in my chair.

"Bopped?"

"Well, they got nailed," I said desperately. "Whatever." I cleared my throat. "What happened to Richard Wheeler?"

"Fast Eddie and the kid who went around to the pawn shops buying up the shotguns are the only ones left. Richard was killed getting into a car; someone came up and shot him behind the ear."

"So they really took care of the business," I said.

"Well, people were upset. Their egos were involved. They had been pushed around. A guy got tumbled down the stairs. They got together. They were determined. So with everyone looking very diligently all day and night long, it wasn't surprising how it came out."

"Do you suppose there were meetings ... I mean to decide what was going to happen, and to coordinate things?" I asked.

"I don't know," Frank said. "It didn't mean much to me. I lost some credit cards. I'm a cocoa distributor."

*   *   *

Just by the most surprising stroke of luck I found myself in touch with Richard Wheeler's girl; she had been with him the last year of his life. She was an Italian girl—the ex-wife of the official in the New York correctional system with whom I had talked about making arrangements to see Frank Molton.

"You call her," her former husband had said. "She'll have a few things to tell you."

He seemed very much at ease suggesting it—finding her telephone number for me, and so forth—from which I could assume that he, a prison official, had somehow come to terms with the idea of his former wife's taking up with a top-rank black gangster.

Her name was Jackie. She worked in a restaurant in New Jersey. We talked over the phone. At first, I thought she was perhaps a vague acquaintance of Wheeler's who might give me a sense of what sort of man he was, and perhaps a few details, such as why he was called Cadillac Dick. Slowly I began to realize that the two had been lovers.

She told me that he was a good-looking man, tall, well over six feet, and a very powerful presence—he made an immediate impression when he walked into a room—but he was not a flashy man at all. "He had jewelry," she told me, "but it was very subtle jewelry. He drove around in Volkswagens. He had a couple of them, and an Oldsmobile." She did not know why he was called Cadillac, but she thought it was because he had driven one around in his earlier days in the rackets. She knew very little about the specifics of his career in crime—except that he was involved in the drug racket at a very exalted level. She had been trying hard to get him to try a legitimate business—a limousine service. "I really worked on him," she said.

Wheeler and Jackie had met in 1965 outside the building in which they both lived, at 165th Street and Gerard Avenue, in the Bronx. They were walking their dogs—Wheeler had a white Australian shepherd; Jackie, two poodles. Jackie's husband moved out five years later, leaving her with their three children. Richard, with one son (Jackie said that he had six children around the city, and a wife, who was a Jehovah's Witness and from whom he was separated), moved down three flights from his apartment to hers.

I asked, "Did you have any idea that he was a racketeer?"

"Well, I began to suspect," Jackie said. "There were large amounts of money around the house—under the bed, in the back of the closets."

"How much?"

"There was a quarter of a million dollars under the bed one time. I counted it out for him. I guess he was making a buy somewhere."

"A quarter of a million! Didn't that . . . er—?"

"I didn't ask questions," Jackie said. "I thought it was better not to. After he was killed, the police couldn't understand it, but I told them that since Richard didn't let me in on what he did, I didn't think it was my place to ask. Besides, the man out there on the street and the man I knew were entirely different. The man I knew loved the children; he helped them with their homework; you would have thought they were his children. The other man, the one out in the street, he was terribly feared; why, I don't know. I'd rather not know what he did out there."

I asked if her family was aware of what was going on.

"My mother never came to the apartment," Jackie said. "She's allergic to cats, and I had dozens of cats in the apartment. I like cats, but perhaps I don't like cats *that* much. I told my mother over the phone that my cats were all thriving."

"Did Richard take drugs himself?" I asked.

"He liked coke," Jackie said. "He went cuckoo with coke. He took so much—sniffing up pure crystals out of a bent match-box cover he used—that he went paranoid, which is what too much of that stuff does. He'd come in and start tearing up the furniture, looking for listening devices. Once, he ripped a switch off the back of my head—a small swatch of artificial hair that I'd braided on—and he began poking through it with his fingers looking for a little microphone. He'd wake me up late at night; I'd open my eyes and find him pointing a gun under my nose. I'd talk him down from these highs—hour after hour—and I'd get him to drink brandy and champagne, which helped. The re-frigerator was always full of little splits of Piper Heidsieck, but I always had to open them in front of him, or he'd think I'd dropped some poison in. It's a typical reaction if you take that much. He thought there was something under the couch."

"Did you know he was responsible for the Atlanta holdup?" I asked.

"It was the only part of his gangster life that he ever shared with me," she said. "You know why he did it? I think he did it for a lark."

"What?"

"That's right. A crazy lark. He didn't do it for the money. He was bored with the drug scene. I was trying to get him to go straight with the limousine service, and maybe that idea bored him. Or maybe it was a last big fling—a last hurrah—before he went legit. Whichever, it gave him a lot of pleasure to think back on what happened."

Remembering Frank Molton's description of Wheeler's establishing his alibi at the closed-circuit showing at Madison Square Garden, I asked Jackie if she had been with Richard that night. She remembered it well. "We went to this big fancy party at the Americana Hotel afterward," she said. "Richard had a lot of people at his table—I didn't know any of them. I remember the feds were there in the ballroom, and the plainclothes cops standing along the wall—they must have been tipped off that a lot of mob people were going to be there. When one of them came up with a flash camera, everybody at the table suddenly had a shoelace that needed fixing, or a spoon had fallen off the table so they were ducking down for it, or they wanted to whisper behind a hand to a guy next to them, so that when the flash went off, the camera didn't catch anyone but me, looking up into the lens with this big cheerful smile. I've wondered what the police department thought when they saw that developed photo, all these guys with their faces obscured behind hands, and hats, and looking down, and among them this bright silly cheerful face, just so innocent of the whole thing."

"How did you find out about Atlanta?" I asked.

"One day I heard him in the bedroom laughing. He had this

big dirty laugh ... it reverberated ... a laugh that got *you* laughing. I went in to see what was going on. Beside him on the bed was a newspaper which must have had some story in it about the holdup, probably some crazy lead someone in the police department was following, and it had got him laughing just fit to beat the band. It was then that he shared the story with me—enough of it so that I knew he had done it. It really made him laugh—thinking about everybody lying down there in the basement ... most of them people he knew."

"Did he share other things he did—?"

"Never. In the thirteen months I lived with him that was the only time."

"It makes sense," I said. "That explains why Fast Eddie got the money back to some of his friends—it was sort of a gag."

"Except that no one thought it was very funny," Jackie said. "Fast Eddie was the guy who killed Richard."

She heard my exclamation of surprise. "I thought they were partners in the caper," I said.

"That's right."

"What *was* their relationship?"

"He was ... well, Eddie was Richard's enforcer."

"He killed people for Richard?"

"That's right. He seemed to enjoy his work, and from what I heard on the street he was very good at it."

"But why Richard? Did they have a falling-out?"

"When guys who had been held up found out that Richard did it, they put a contract out on him," she said. "The original guy who was going to blow away Richard (and Fast Eddie too) was a hood named Blood, but he got killed in a shoot-out with the police. So they got Eddie to do it. I think Eddie made a deal. They came to him and said we know you were involved in the Atlanta holdup ... your only out is to blow Richard away for us. They didn't give him much of a choice. They said it's either you and him, or, if you do it for us, it's just him. So he accepted."

"Would it be easy for him to kill a partner?" I asked.

She chuckled. "He would not have thought about it twice, I'm telling you. He enjoyed his work."

"I know he blew away"—that was another word I could have thrown at Frank Molton—"a hood called Bulletproof. I heard that. And a girl got killed by mistake."

"He was a terrible man," Jackie said. "He was about thirty-six. He always wore black along with a short-brimmed hat. No glasses. Sometimes he wore a warmup suit, the kind that basketball and track stars use. He was a very trim man ... a physical-culture freak. He worked out all the time and he drank juice ... orange ... pineapple. He always had a black bag with him—an athletic bag, the kind you might put your equipment and your sneakers in."

"Did you ever look in it?" I asked.

"Oh my God! Are you kidding? Look in that bag? Oh my God, no! There could have been someone's *head* in there.... It wouldn't have surprised me, I'm telling you. I'll never forget him. I dream about him. He had a thin, chiseled face. His eyes! Oh, they looked right through you." Her voice sank almost to a whisper. "I met him only four or five times, including the day he killed Richard. He made your skin crawl. He came in a room and if you had your back turned you knew he was there. You'd turn around and there he'd be, holding that black bag. He was laconic—never said more than four or five sentences that I ever heard. It was eerie—the air around him seemed different. He was just old-fashioned creepy."

"What made you think that ... er ..."

"He blew Richard away on February third, 1972. Richard was being helped into a car. He had got into trouble with the police a month before and they had bounced him around. He was recuperating, spending a lot of time in bed. But that morning, he was going down to the limousine service on an errand. Just as he was going out, the front doorbell rang and it was Eddie. He saw Richard and he said, 'Want me to help you?' I remember his face. Always it was totally inexpressive—like a robot's—but this time it was *alive.* Richard said, 'Sure.' He was wearing his suit over his pajamas. He was just going out on a short errand. He wasn't ready."

"Ready?"

"He wasn't packing a gun. Always Richard was very prepared and alert. But not this time. There were three of them, counting Eddie. I think Eddie shot him from the back just as he was leaning down to get into the car. The chauffeur, Stefan, got the car moving, but one of the others shot him; they blew him away at the corner and his foot jammed down on the accelerator and stuck there; and, a dead man, he drove the car into a drugstore across the street. The killers ran around the corner. The getaway car was a green Oldsmobile—people saw three men jumping into it. Richard had given Fast Eddie one just the week before. That's a strong connection."

"You must have heard all the commotion," I said.

"I was upstairs," Jackie said. "I had never heard shots before. Little pings."

"Pings?"

"That's it—a ping. Not even enough to get me to look, but then I heard the crash of Stefan's car—a big noise, the crash of glass, and then everything very quiet out there—and I ran to the window and saw the car across the street half in the drugstore. I thought maybe Richard was in there. I couldn't see anyone in the street. It was raining hard. I ran down to the corner. I didn't dare look. In five minutes the street was full of people, the rain pouring down their faces because folks rushed out without looking for a hat or an umbrella. I called out, 'Where's Richard?' and someone nodded his head down the street, and he was lying there by a parked car where I couldn't see him from the window."

Her voice rose. "They left him *three* hours out in the rain. It was a human being lying there, but they treated him like garbage. It was ten-thirty-five in the morning when he was shot and it was around two in the afternoon when he was gone. Oh God, he was just going down to the limousine office on an errand. He was coming right back and going to bed. You could see his pajama bottoms sticking out of his trouser legs as he lay there in the rain."

"I'm sorry," I said. "Did the police pick up Fast Eddie?"

"Not for that," Jackie said. "They couldn't pin it on him. But the next August a cabby happened to look in his rearview mirror and he saw the butt of a gun sticking out of this guy's coat. He was a gutsy driver. He took his cab right up to a precinct station and the police leaned in and it was Fast Eddie they grabbed. He didn't put up any fuss at all. He went very meekly. I'm told they found a couple of grenades in that black bag. He'll never get out. He's what they call a 'persistent criminal'—just the longest string of jobs up and down the East Coast from Georgia to New York."

"Maybe he feels safer in the penitentiary," I suggested. "He's probably the only one actually in the house for the Atlanta holdup who's left ... and whatever deals were made, he can't feel very secure."

"I wouldn't be one to weep if they got him," Jackie said.

"It was a pretty expensive joke of Richard's, wasn't it?" I said. "I mean, all those people dead. I mean, apparently there wasn't much laughter."

"I'll tell you one thing," Jackie said. "Richard's friends, very likely the guys who'd decided to kill him, gave him one terrific send-off. I had never known to what extent he was into the rackets and who his acquaintances were until that funeral. There were two miles of limousines waiting. The whole church was full of people I had never seen before and I looked and they were all hoods—just rows of them. These huge floral arrangements were everywhere in the church, great massive things it took two or three men to carry, and they were shaped like cocktail glasses and naked girls. All those characters sent things."

"What did you ... er ..."

"The children and I did a little booklet—we wrote nice things to him—and it was in the casket. It had some tiny rosebuds between the pages."

"Why do you suppose so many people came to the funeral?" I asked.

Jackie thought for a while. "Well, he was a sort of Santa Claus out on the street ... handouts, he'd help guys, and of course he was a provider of the stuff a lot of them were hooked on. So some came because he was so important to them. Some came in disbelief. They couldn't believe he had gone. He gave you the sense that he was invincible, that nothing could touch him. I know I've never had such a sense of security with any man. He was like a mantle enfolding you."

"I suppose some of his enemies were there. . . ."

"Oh, I guess so," Jackie said. "Everyone was there to give him a big send-off. The street has a strange code. I remember getting this terrible telegram the day after he died. It was signed by five dead people . . . and it was welcoming him . . . the implication being that Richard had killed them. I remember two of the names: Jacky White and a guy called Moustache Bobby."

"Did you sit down in the front of the church?"

"I stayed in the back," Jackie said. "I wore a very simple black dress, a mink hat, and a mink coat he'd given me the night before he was shot. And I wore sunglasses. It was a lovely service—not too much of a eulogy," she admitted with a laugh. "The reverend tried, but he could not be that hypocritical to start eulogizing a street hustler. So the service was short. There were fifty limousines waiting out there in the street."

"Did everyone go to the burial?"

"It was a double funeral—Stefan's, too, the guy who drove the car into the pharmacy—but just about everyone drove a half hour upstate to where they buried Richard, even Stefan's sister. She was one of Richard's women. I thought it was pretty tacky that she didn't go to her own brother's burial, out on Long Island. But it shows you the power Richard had over people. When he was gone, his power went. I stood there—a scared Italian girl—and I thought for the first time since I'd known him, 'Oh, my God, what have I done . . . what could have come over me . . . what would my *mother* think?' And I knew I was beginning to think like a normal Italian girl is supposed to. It was when I thought of my mother that I knew that part of my life was over."

I kept thinking that a near-vigilante process had wiped the slate clean—all of them gone except a man tucked away in a penitentiary.

"Those people really take care of things," I said.

"Oh, my God," she said. "You're telling me?"

15

worry very much about the fellow who is going to lose, which is neither sophisticated nor practical. Sports journalists are supposed to be inured to defeat (after all, every event they cover has its losers), and in their postperformance interviews their concern is to find out *why* a man lost—what did he do wrong?—a technical consideration of his performance—not how he was going to be affected by losing, or how he was going to get through the next couple of days.

Losing a prizefight has always seemed to me the ultimate disaster for an athlete—with no one to blame but himself, a nose or brow ridge often damaged in the bargain, his dignity shot, while across the ring his opponent capers about with his arms aloft, his features split in a manic grin, as he prepares to come across to envelop his victim in a sweaty embrace, which in itself must be an ugly indignity. It surprises me that a prizefighter does not take out his disappointment more—perhaps a low chop during that embrace; or, when he gets back in his corner, a knockout blow of frustration at the wizened little man who carries the water bucket; or even assaulting the referee with a quick combination.

But he doesn't. The loser works up a ghastly grin for his opponent during the embrace; he accepts having his hair tousled with the heel of the other fellow's glove. A.J. Liebling once offered an interesting explanation for this behavior: that the fighter, whatever the outcome, always "felt good" after it was over: "A fighter's hostilities are not turned inward, like a Sunday tennis player's or a lady MP's ... they come out naturally with his sweat, and when his job is done he feels good because he has expressed himself."

Dave Anderson, of the New York *Times,* once told me that George Chuvalo, after his loss to Ali in Vancouver—quite badly nicked up and his face beginning to balloon—looked out at the press people in his locker room and began his interview session by saying, "Gentlemen, I enjoyed the fight..." which would seem to substantiate what Liebling had to say.

Still, it is no fun to lose, however "good" you feel afterward, and my own suspicion is that the nonchalance one watches in a losing fighter is often a desperate posture of bravado to try to show that he truly has not been affected. A fighter named Joe Grim, a second-rate boxer in the early part of the century whose forte was the ability to take punishment, would totter to the ropes at the end of a fight, whatever his state, and call out to the crowd, "I am Joe Grim! I fear no man on earth!" Great panache! In 1903 he was matched against Bob Fitzsimmons, the inventor of the solar-plexus punch, and though beaten and absolutely pulverized by the sixth round, Grim managed to pull himself up at the bell and get himself to the ropes where he mournfully murmured down, "I am Joe Grim. . . . I fear no man on earth."

One of the reasons it must be so hard for a fighter, especially a champion, to accept defeat is the complete change of social status that immediately occurs—as if one had been striken with a virulent and very noticeable disease. Rocky Graziano once told me, "They look at you different. How soon they forget. It's no longer 'Hiya, champ!' It's 'Hello.' After I got belted out by Tony Zale it was a very difficult feeling. Yourself, you feel funny. You feel self-conscious. You go to the old places, the old joints, and you walk in and it's completely different. Everybody is very uneasy."

Of course, the fighter most affected by this sort of thing was Floyd Patterson. No old joints for him. Following his defeat by Ingemar Johansson, he spent two weeks locked in his house in Rockville Centre, Long Island. He slept fitfully, perhaps for an hour at a time, relentlessly refighting the bout in his mind. His wife kept begging him to take her out. He finally agreed to take her to a film—as long as it was at night, so no one could recognize him; she had to agree to go into the theater after the house lights were down and the picture was underway so that there was complete darkness inside. It was worked out, but then the two of them came around a corner, and there on the marquee of the local theater was the announcement that as a special feature the management was showing films of the Patterson-Johannson fight! Patterson wheeled his wife around as if he'd seen a bunch of muggers down the street and took her, protesting, back home. He locked himself back in. His wife despaired, but Patterson was very proud of his feelings, trusting them and indeed attributing his success to them. Because he *felt* like hiding from the world, he finally found a makeup man from Poughkeepsie who made him a whole series of disguises so he *could* go out. He described them to me with the pride of a collector, say, of Toby jugs: various types of beards, semi-Vandykes, a muttonchop special, mustaches of all shapes, and wigs. His best was an old man's disguise which was supplemented with a cane. He wore it to watch Jose Torres fight in Madison Square Garden, hobbling into the arena in an old man's walk he had perfected out in the woods. The disguise worked. It gave him an odd sense of confidence not to be discovered. Imagine what it would have done to him if someone had looked into that beard and said, "Well, hi ho, Floyd. You're looking just grand."

Patterson was an extreme case. Some fighters accept defeat with equanimity, without trying to kid themselves, or anyone else, for that matter. My favorite of these was Kid McCoy. When he was knocked out by Joe Gans and later recovered in his dressing room, he said thoughtfully, to someone who came along and asked him how he felt, "I'm not a fighter. I'm a lover."

Of course, losing was something that Muhammad Ali did not know anything about until, working his way back from the suspension, after his big success against Quarry in Atlanta, he fought Joe Frazier in Madison Square Garden in what was billed as the Fight of the Century.

Sports Illustrated asked me to cover the postfight activities—how the winner would spend the evening—which I expected would involve following Muhammad Ali around on a hectic evening of celebration; he had looked so strong against Jerry Quarry that I had an idea he would prevail against an opponent who was shorter and, however busy with his fists, was easy to hit and would succumb to a great jab and a lot of footwork.

Of course, that is not what happened at all.

What destroyed Ali's evening plans was what happened to him in the fifteenth round—being decked by Joe Frazier's big left hook, which was the best punch in the business. Ernest Hemingway once wrote, "If you fight a good left hooker, sooner or later he will knock you on your deletion. He will get the left out where you can't see it, and in it comes like a brick. Life is the greatest left hooker so far, although many say it was Charley White of Chicago. . . ."

Well, the left hook is what happened to Ali. Actually, he said later that he had seen the punch coming; he told the doctor that he couldn't get away from it. Exhaustion had set him up for it. He couldn't move.

The punch knocked him off his feet, so that rather than sagging to the canvas he fell splay-legged like a man off a girder. Bundini, seeing him down, reached in one instinctive motion for his water bucket and sent an arc of spray in the direction of his fighter—an act for which he was subsequently suspended by the New York State Athletic Commission. "I was just trying to revive my soldier," he told me later. "My, you'd think I'd climbed into the ring to get Frazier with a baseball bat."

The more immediate consequence of the left hook was that

Bundini knew Ali was going to lose the fight. "That punch blew out all the candles on the cake," he remembered thinking, and when the round was over, he hurried to the side of his fighter to help shepherd him through his first defeat. Bundini had always said that there were seven or eight sides of the man that he had to tend to, but here was one with which he had had no experience. He kept looking at Ali as if a new personage had suddenly materialized in the ring. At the announcement of Frazier's victory, the jubilation starting up in the opposing corner, Bundini burst into tears and grabbed for Ali. "Don't worry, champ," he yelled over the crowd noise. "You fought like a champ. You got nothing to be ashamed of."

Ali twisted away from him wearily. "Don't hold me, Bundini. Damn. I'm sore. I'm sore in the neck. I'm sore in the ribs."

Bundini kept at it. I could catch some of it from the ring apron, across which I was leaning, at shoe level, trying to hear through the bedlam. "Don't feel down!" Bundini was shouting. "Look at Frazier! He's more messed! He's sitting on his stool. He looks like the Hunchback of Notre Dame!"

"Let's go," the fighter said. I could read his lips. "Let's get out of here. Let's go home."

They started for the corner steps. Behind them, clear through the racket, Joe Frazier's exhausted voice was calling, "Good fight." He had come across the ring. "You're a real tough man."

Ali turned and said, "You are, too. You're the champ." He turned back. Bundini told me Ali kept half whispering at him, "Come on, let's go home. Home." Dutifully Bundini began to push again toward the corner and the steps leading down to the arena floor.

By now, the press of people in the ring was considerable, with more coming up the steps, trying to get to the fighters. I stood alongside the steps, waiting for them to come down. But most of the movement was from people moving and jostling up. Among them was the Reverend Ralph Abernathy, head of the Southern Christian Leadership Conference, dressed in his familiar proletarian outfit of worker's overalls. Tears streaming down his cheeks in his grief, reaching arms outstretched for Ali, he created

such a weird, demented figure on the steps that one of Ali's
bodyguards, a tall ex-Muslim, hit him with a left hook and
toppled him backward off the steps into the lap of Edward
Bennett Willliams, the famous Washington trial lawyer, who was
sitting ringside. We watched stunned. Someone at my ear was
acute enough, even in the turmoil of the moment, to whisper
that if the Reverend wished to initiate a lawsuit for being
slugged, certainly he was in the proper hands.

I don't know if Ali noticed, or if at that point he would have
cared about, his friend being bopped. He began to come down
the steps. We stared at his right jaw, swollen to enormous
proportions from the tremendous left hook *he* had received. He
seemed hardly aware of the heaving and pushing; he let himself
be buoyed back and forth by his supporters, half carried down
the steps, and once on the arena floor he was hurried along, his
hips now beginning to stiffen on him, through the tunnel of faces
toward his dressing room. He looked terribly tired. I was just in
front of him, looking back from time to time as we were jostled
along. I could see his lips moving. Bundini told me later he was
saying, "I got things to do. I got a family to raise. I got money to
collect. Let's go home."

That seemed a typical reaction from a defeated fighter—the
thought of home—that with his professional world so abruptly
toppled, he grasped at the thought of any available security.
When Jess Willard was led stumbling down the ring steps after
his destruction at the fists of Jack Dempsey, half blind, his ribs
broken, some of his teeth knocked out (there had been a
scramble for them at ringside), the young Chicago reporter
Charles MacArthur (who went on to team with Ben Hecht as a
famous dramatist) overheard him muttering through the cheers
for Dempsey, "I have a hundred thousand dollars and a farm in
Kansas. I have a hundred thousand dollars and a farm in
Kansas . . ."

When they got to the dressing room, Ali was brought over to a
rubbing table. He sat on it first, and then turned over and lay on
his side, his feet drawn up because the table was short for him,
so that his position was nearly fetal. I watched Bundini cut the

laces of his red-tassled shoes with a scissors and draw them off. He skinned off the socks, the red boxing trunks and the protective cup; he wrapped a towel around the fighter's waist. A pillow was fashioned for him out of towels.

Ali's eyes were closed.

Bundini whispered in his ear, "You fought one of the great fights ever fought in history."

I could see Bundini's chin trembling. He looked around frantically and then leaned over his champion. "You're not going to quit?" It was a question—however odd its timing— Bundini could not help asking, since his own future so depended on the reply.

Ali opened his eyes and looked at him. "Bundini, we're going to set traps for big game." His voice was very tired. We could barely hear him, but I remember the quick shine of relief on Bundini's face before he began bustling around officiously. Now he had more than a relic to tend after.

Ali's mother and father were let into the dressing room. The Muslim guards held the door fast against the straining crowd out in the corridor. One quick view of heads craning.

"How are you, Gee?" his mother asked.

"There's Bird," Ali said softly.

They were using their terms of endearment for each other.

"How's my baby, Gee?" his mother asked.

"I'm all right, Bird," Ali said. He remained motionless, his head pillowed on the towel.

I don't know where "Bird" comes from, because Ali's mother is a very earthbound person, quite large, more of a balloon than a bird, with a large pleasant face, curiously strawberry in complexion, on which it is impossible to map concern. Ali's father is more birdlike, bird-boned. He shouted, "They robbed us!" His anger shook him; he is a small dapper man who often sports saddle shoes which give him the appearance of wearing spats—a 1920s dancing man, really, more than a bird, and his slight body beset with trembling seemed to suggest that he was about to pop into a buck-and-wing; he looked this way and that; he speaks in a quicksilver rush of words that is difficult to understand, though on this night he was very explicit. "Robbed!" he called out bitterly. "That is the question, truly!"

It has always surprised me that boxers have their families around for their fights; the thought of being beaten up in front of Mom is appalling. It never would have occurred to me to invite my mother around to see my struggle with Archie Moore; it was bad enough having Father there, inspecting me gravely through his round steel spectacles. But professional fighters seem to have their families around as a matter of course. Jerry Quarry had not only his wife but also his young son at his fight with Ali in Atlanta, and the two of them broke into tears when Quarry began to be carved up—very depressing to see something like that if you were at ringside.

Actually, an even more vociferous family group than Ali's during that era was the Emile Griffith clan. What a great Mom figure she was! She would arrive in Madison Square Garden along with the middleweight's brother and a cousin, and they constituted a ringside claque that pulverized the general area with the vehemence of their support. She, like Mrs. Clay, was a large woman, colorfully got up in her native Virgin Island regalia: bandana, bright print dress that fell to her ankles, and an armful of bracelets that rang when she shook her fist at an unbeliever. Her voice was enormous. The Garden officials seemed to move her a few rows back every time her son fought— out of sight, out of mind, perhaps—a plan which backfired since Madame Griffith simply increased the volume of her voice to compensate for the distance she was away from the ring. I had a fancy that by degrees she would be moved farther and farther back, up into the high third-balcony reaches of the Garden, from where she would yodel down her support, and then finally she'd be banished into the corridors outside ... but still that gargantuan voice blatting through an entryway into the arena as if out of the bell of a French horn.

I remember the night when, heavily favored at 13-5, Griffith lost his middleweight title to Nino Benvenuti in a Garden awash with Italian flags. His mother's voice pierced through the bedlam like a Klaxon. Afterward Griffith paced around his dressing room furious about the fight, bewailing how it was going to affect his mother, complaining in the high singsong vocal style of the Caribbean that seemed so unlike a fighter's. Finally, he got out of his boxing trunks and into the shower. "They've stolen my title," he said, the water streaming down his face. "I feel naked without my crown." He was so preoccupied that he failed to notice he was still wearing his socks.

Actually I don't remember that Griffith's mother was in the locker room. It would be Ali—typically—who would institute a sort of family-parlor atmosphere in a fighter's dressing room ... after victory, or, as it turned out, even defeat. I kept watching Mr. Clay strutting around the dressing room. He was behaving with a vehemence that bore comparison to Madame Griffith's. Now he was hollering that Rachaman, Ali's brother, who had fought a preliminary against a tough English brawler not unlike Frazier in style, had also been "robbed." He hopped up and down in his anguish. In fact, Rachaman had been lucky to escape without being knocked out; his face was covered with little strips of adhesive tape to cover his bruises. "Robbed!" his father shouted. People stared at him curiously. The room was filling up. The Muslim guard was having his problems at the door. Out in the corridor, people looked so anguished that he let them in assuming that anyone looking so bereaved ought to be able to practice it closer at hand. Gordon Parks turned up, of all the photographers on assignment that night perhaps the most distinguished—a Pulitzer Prize-winner. In the pockets of his trench coat he carried two Nikon cameras. He told me a touching thing later. He said about his cameras, "The guns were loaded." But he looked at Ali—the puffed face, the curious fetal position on the rubbing table, his people and his family standing around—and his compassion for Ali overcame his professional instincts. Only once before in his professional career, Parks told me, had he refused to take a picture he recognized as the sort which the picture editor outlines in red crayon on the developed contact sheets and calls out, "Double truck!"—meaning he will spread it across two pages of his magazine. On Stromboli, leaving the island by motor launch for the last time, Parks,

standing on the pier, happened to look back and see the actress
Ingrid Bergman and her director, Roberto Rossellini, in a torrid
embrace in the shadows of a movie set. The temptation to take
advantage of that instant, considering the worldwide interest, the
rumors about the pair, must have been considerable. But the
privacy of the moment was such that Parks turned back on the
dock, his cameras untouched, and stepped down into the launch.
It was the same with Ali, he said.

We went over to the rubbing table. Parks stood looking down,
hunching his shoulders. Just then, Jerry Perenchio, the en-
trepreneur who had promoted the bout, came through the crowd
and joined us. He fingered his bow tie as he stared down at the
motionless fighter. Ali opened his eyes and looked up at him.
"You're the one who went and got me whupped," he said. His
voice was resigned. "We got whupped," he said a number of
times, almost as if it were a foreign phrase he had to learn to get
along in a strange country. His protest was mild when Angelo
Dundee and Dr. Ferdie Pacheco, the doctor in his corner,
insisted that he be taken to the hospital for a check of his
swollen jaw. He did not have the strength to dress himself.
Bundini fitted socks over his feet. Then he lifted Ali's legs and
tried to insert them into the trouser legs. "Come on, Champ."
He pulled the trousers up to the thighs and discovered he had
put them on backward. The towel fell away from Ali's waist.
"Keep that towel on him," somebody called. "We got women in
the room."

"Oh my," Bundini said in a half whisper. "His *mother*. She
gonna fall over in a dead faint!"

A protective cordon of men stood in front of the rubbing table
as the naked fighter, almost a deadweight, was lifted and
jockeyed into his clothes. Bundini zipped up his trousers.

"Go home, Bird," Ali said, "I'll be home soon."

I hung around the periphery of all this trying to figure out
how I was going to stick with them and get a firsthand account—
the ride through New York, what happened in the hospital
(whichever one they went to), where he spent the night, and so
forth. Was he going to say anything more than "we got

whupped." It seemed very important. I went up and down on my toes trying to attract Bundini Brown's attention.

He shook his head. But he whispered the name of the hospital—Flower and Fifth, up on 106th Street. They crowded around him and began to jimmy him out the dressing-room door, like carrying a grandfather clock. I followed them down to the street to the limousine where they set him into the backseat. It was crowded out there with people trying to find a place to wind down after the fight.

They came running. They flung themselves around the car, peering in. What could they have seen—the tip of a nose, the dark shoulder of a man leaning toward the fighter to minister to him in some way, a chauffeur's mouth ajar as he shouted soundlessly within the hermetically sealed interior for them to clear out of the way? The crowd was as curious as I was—aching for some sign, some indication of what it had been like to go through that evening.

The limousine pulled out past them, drawing away from the onlookers and finally uptown. I followed them in a cab. Through the rear window I could see Dundee's profile in the streetlights, looking down at his fighter beside him. They ran a light and my cab driver lost them.

They reconstructed it for me afterward. There had been very little conversation on the way up to the hospital; they drove up through Central Park. Angelo, staring out the window at the trees glistening in a light rain, told me afterward that he could not keep his mind off the contradictions of the fight. The whole plan, he kept thinking, had been to keep the other guy moving, to turn him, never to face him head on, never to stay in the line of fire. And never to trade hooks. Suicide, that—to trade hooks with a hooker. And there his man was, hooking to beat the band, lolling on the ropes—completely taboo, that was. He'd shouted at him between the rounds. Ali would flop down on the stool. "How'd I do?" was always his first question. Angelo would shout, "You blew the round."

Still, for all of it, Dundee believed that his fighter had won—a biased view, he would be the first to admit, but the other fellow had taken tremendous punishment. He doubted that Frazier would be celebrating that night either. Not a chance, unless he was watching the festivities from a soft chair. Angelo sat in the dark limousine and thought about what might have been, running the fight like a motion picture through his mind but with Muhammad working at Frazier in a different way. A melancholy exercise, he remembered thinking, but he couldn't stop it. The tick of the windshield wipers lolled his mind into running it again.

Ferdie Pacheco was also in the limousine. He kept shaking his head in awe at what he had seen, punches of such power that in Ali's case, when he had examined him in the dressing room, he found that the hip joints were swollen, the first time he had ever seen such a thing in his years of examining fighters. When had such a thing ever happened before? The hip joints, the toughest joints in the human carcass. Why, they hold up the whole body; they can withstand anything. And yet Ali's were swollen, almost paralyzing him. The esthetics, even the legality, of the low hip punches from Frazier did not disturb the doctor in the least. It was inevitable that a bobbing, crouching, hook-style fighter was going to hit low, particularly against a standup fighter like Ali. No, it was the power.

Ali sprawled in the backseat of the limousine, stirred and said, "Must have been a helluva fight 'cause I'm sure tired." The voice was very slow, and the doctor could see the fighter had slipped back into a state that reminded him of a diabetic coma. The fighter's jaw was enormous in the dim illumination of the passing streetlights. The doctor told me that the ride was the longest of his life. A gynecologist friend of his, Dr. Gus Moreno, had made the arrangements at Flower Hospital, seventy-odd blocks up the spine of Manhattan from the Garden, and Dr. Pacheco kept thinking of the available hospitals they were passing, any one of which, if his fighter had neurological damage, they should have turned into. He kept thinking of the power of the punches he'd seen.

They reached the hospital about ten minutes before me. I could not get in. I walked around the block to see if there was a side entrance where I could talk my way in. By then, every guard in the hospital knew that Muhammad Ali was in the place; the security was very tight. Because it was after midnight, it was hard to cook up a reasonable excuse for wanting to visit a patient at that hour. I thought of bluffing myself in, but the dialogue of subterfuge worked up in the head came to an abrupt halt. ("My aunt ... my sick aunt ... I got a phone call!" *"Oh yes, and what's her name?"* "What? Oh well. Mercy, I think I must be in the wrong hospital.")

But I stayed around. It seemed important to follow the thing to a conclusion, not as a reporter but almost as if there were a compulsion to share in Ali's defeat. I walked along the wet avenue thinking of our commitments to him, and how little effect they had had ... a half-finished letter to a U. S. senator! Logically, I supposed, the redress of wrongs was one he would have to do himself in the ring—that was the dramatic way, winning back his title with his boxing skills. But he hadn't. His future now seemed very uncertain. Perhaps if we had worked harder we could have forced the issue earlier, given him a chance to right things two or three years ago.

About two in the morning I was allowed in. Ali had left without my being aware—spirited out of some side entrance. The X-ray technician, Booker T. Hardy, showed me around. Earlier that evening, he had received a call on his "bleeper"—the radio device that doctors carry in their pockets—that a patient was coming in for a mandible. "I knew about the fight, but I never made the connection," Hardy told me, "until he came in, draped across the shoulders of his people."

The examining doctors agreed that Ali should spend the night in the hospital. They were making arrangements to check him into a room. But Ali, apparently asleep on the graphite table, suddenly roused himself, the heads all turning as they heard his voice, and he announced softly that he did not want to stay.

"Okay," said Dundee.

"Make it look like Joe Frazier put me in the hospital, and that's not true."

"Right," said Dundee. "Okay."

"Take me back to the hotel."

They heaved him up off the table and began to support him out to the elevator through a staring crowd of interns and nurses. As the elevator door closed, Hardy heard him call, "The Greatest is gone."

Hardy let me lie down on his X-ray table. I looked up and saw the same apparatus Ali himself must have seen an hour or so ago, the pipelike lens above my head, the shutter closed and the color of slate. I took notes. The machine's brand name was Eureka. Hardy had taken four pictures of the fighter's jaw.

"You are sure into this," Hardy said.

I admitted that I was a little surprised at myself; it had not been an ordinary evening.

Two days later Hardy called me at home and told me that considering my absorption in the matter, he thought I'd want to know about a curious thing that had happened the night after the fight. A man had been mugged on the West Side. Small and slightly rotund, he had put up a stout struggle. But there had been a number of assailants and he had been beaten up very badly—both eyes almost entirely shut, his face grotesquely swollen. When the police found him, he persuaded them to take him to Flower Hospital. That was where Ali had gone the night before, he told them, and that was where he wanted to go if they didn't mind. He could barely speak through his bloated lips. The police shrugged, and they took him to the hospital he wanted. He was X-rayed on the same table as Ali had been the night before. "Is this the table? Is this the machine?" he kept asking.

Odd. There was a coincidence that caught on the edge of my mind; finally I remembered what it was. Two weeks after Manolete, the greatest of the Spanish bullfighters, was killed at the little country bullring at Linares by a Miura bull named Islero (every Spanish kid knows the name of that gray mottled animal), a Mexican bullfighter named José López (known as Carniceríto de Mexico) was gored in the Portuguese bullring of Vila Viçosa. His *cornado,* high on the right leg—severing the femoral artery—was exactly the same as Manolete's, and somehow the idea lodged in his mind (as it did in Dr. Hardy's mugging victim's) that his chosen function was to relive Manolete's last minutes exactly as they had been described in the nation's newspapers two weeks before.

From the infirmary cot he looked up at his doctor and repeated Manolete's deathbed phrases: "I can't feel anything in my legs, Don Luis."

His doctor—who was called José, or Pedro, or perhaps Jorge—blinked and realized that his dying patient was referring to Luis Guinea, Manolete's physician.

Next, his patient murmured, "I can't see you, Don Luis." A perfect reading! Then came a slight departure in which López made sure everyone standing around his cot was sure what he was up to. "Watch me," he whispered. "I am dying like Manolete," and he then proceeded to do so.

The coincidence of this and Dr. Hardy's mugged patient overwhelmed me. I went around talking about it. A girl I knew said, "Can't you get off this business about losers. Guys getting beaten up and sounding off on their deathbeds. It's going to infect you," she warned.

"It's important," I said.

She wasn't listening. "But I like your story about Kid McCoy," she was saying. "I like him."

"Who?"

"The guy who got himself beaten up and in his locker room he said, 'I'm not a fighter. I'm a lover.' I can take that story."

"Oh, him," I said.

16

It *had* been a traumatic evening. Before the Frazier fight, I had some idea that in trying to rectify the episode of his banishment Ali would be invincible, his skills exalted by the situation. The passage of years would not make any difference; nonetheless, though his skills were there, he had been beaten anyway. It was an agony to witness. I recalled what Hemingway had once written of El Gallo, the great bullfighter of the twenties, and I went and looked it up: he had played the gray Concha y Sierra bulls "as delicately as a spinet" and yet it was something that endured so that "you knew that if a bull should ever gore and kill him, and you should see it, you would know better than to go to any more bullfights."

Perhaps that is what Ali meant when he said that if he were ever beaten, it would be the finish of boxing. *Sports Illustrated* wanted me to keep to the story—go on out and check him in Cherry Hill to see if he *was* finished. Some of the people in the office seemed to think he would be.

Before I went I called Dr. Pacheco.

"You're going to be surprised out there," he told me. "Everyone is brainwashed. They assume a loudmouth like Ali is going to react to being beaten by wincing and moaning and carrying on like a child. But they forget that over the past three years he's had to go through a number of very severe confrontations—socially, religiously, politically, monetarily—in each of which he's been raked over the coals. Socially, he's learned what it is to be despised by his countrymen for refusing to join the army. He was tossed out of a religious organization he feels very strongly about. His politics got him into such trouble that jail continues to be a possibility. His money-making potential was taken away by the boxing commissions. Well, all this hurting must help when it comes to facing losing a fight."

I asked Dr. Pacheco if he thought fighters had an easier time accepting losing than team players do. I mentioned the deep gloom that pervaded the locker rooms of losing football and baseball teams—especially baseball players who sat on their little stools and peered into the backs of their lockers for a suitable length of time even if their contribution to the game had been limited to sitting in the bullpen. Perhaps it was a tradition to which they felt they had to apply themselves ("Oh, God, now I have to go in and *mourn* for a while.")

"Well, maybe fighters do have it easier," he said. "After all, it's just you and the other guy. If you lose, you've got only yourself to blame. If you fight to your capacity, and the other guy wins, you can be very stoical about it. If you get knocked out, well, how can you argue about that? Grim resignation, that's about all."

"Still, it can't be easy."

"No, sir."

Ali's house, set back about fifty yards from a curve in the road in Cherry Hill, New Jersey, was hard to miss—cars parked for a mile along the road. I passed people carrying banners; they came shyly down the short, steep driveway, perhaps put off by large lettered signs on both the back and front doors of the house that read, in a variety of spellings, NO VISITORS, HOUSE UNDER CONSTRUCTION. But Ali was out in the driveway urging them in, calling out to the children, hoisting them up and nuzzling them, putting them down to sign autographs, rough-housing with dogs, their tails beating against his legs; he waved at the girls standing in giggling groups at the top of the driveway, his hand occasionally drifting up to touch his jaw.

"Kennedy!" he called out. He was about to take a group of sightseers on a tour of his house. I joined them. We stared at the NO VISITORS sign as we trooped through the doorway. We passed through a room in which his wife, Belinda, was sitting on the floor, sullenly staring into a television set, ignoring us as we pulled up in a tight museum-tour group to listen to Ali. He told us that he was handling the interior decoration himself. He pointed out the chandeliers ... hard to miss since each room had one, often two, each with its own rheostat so that the light, reflected and shining off the pendants like the sparkle of a dance hall, could be adjusted to best effect. He showed us. He turned the rheostat knob and the room blazed into light. Then he brought the light low, and blazed it up to full power to try to extract a gasp from us. "I like pretty things," he said. When he turned the light low, the rectangle of blue TV light shone on his wife's angry face. Ali was telling us he had bought the chandeliers in Miami; they hung everywhere in the house, a variety of sizes and shapes, delicate rather than massive, though one of them reached halfway to the floor; our group stepped gingerly around it, the pendants clicking musically from the slight drift of air from our passage by.

Except for the lighting, none of the rooms had been completed. A large oil painting of Elijah Muhammad, the Muslim leader, sat on the floor of one room, propped up against the wall. An occasional chair stood abandoned, as if someone had set it down to go off somewhere and answer a phone. I noticed a bouquet of flowers with a card from the singer Aretha Franklin on the floor next to the painting.

Ali shepherded us into the master bedroom. The room was dark with wrapping paper taped across the windows for curtains. He clicked on the chandelier. "There!" The room was entirely done in bright red, close to hot pink, with wall-to-wall crimson, flamingo-red carpeting. We gasped. The bed, a large round model, had a red coverlet. Ali led us to the bathroom door, pounding on it and calling out to make sure no one was within, and we crowded in to see it—the vermilion walls, the black marble basins, the sunken Roman bath at one end with gold faucets and a little bouquet of flowers set on a shelf. A small chandelier hung from the ceiling.

During the tour there was no talk about the fight. The visitors chatted about the house. Ali picked up the small children and whispered in their ears. The older ones stared at him.

"Why don't you say something?" a mother asked, shaking her child. "You talk so much around the house. You haven't said a word."

Ali poked him in the shoulder. The youngster backed away.

"Thank him, Irwin," the mother said crossly. "Where are your manners? You can tell all your friends in school that you've been punched by Muhammad Ali."

"Aw, Mum," the boy said.

After the tour had been led out, Ali and I had our interview. I shared his time with two boys from a neighboring high school who were doing their interview for their school paper. Ali ushered us to a living room fenced off by a guard rope; we were allowed to step over it only after removing our shoes.

Of the two high-school reporters, the taller was more professional and less intimidated. He unpacked his tape recorder, a small inexpensive model, and plugged in a microphone extension that he handed to Ali, who was lolling on the sofa. The other boy had a Polaroid camera, which he carried awkwardly, hefting it up and down as if he wished to put it down somewhere. Perhaps he was abashed by having revealed, when he took off his shoes, that he was wearing socks that did not match. He stared at Ali. Finally he lifted his camera for a snapshot, clicking it rather wildly as if to get his assignment done without being caught at it; the flashbulb failed to go off.

"Tom, give me that thing." The other boy clucked his tongue and reached for the camera. He angled himself into position in front of Ali, down on one knee, one leg stretched out, very tense and professional, as if he were taking a dramatic shot through a line of police holding back a straining crowd. The bulb went off.

"What are you going to do with the picture?" Ali asked as we waited for the photograph to develop.

"It'll be on the school bulletin board," the boy said. He pulled the developed picture out of the camera and handed the negative paper to Tom, who fumbled with it before finally stuffing it in his pocket.

"The jaw shows real well, don't it," said Ali, looking at the photograph.

The boy reporter produced a paper from his jacket. I could see that he had a long list of questions. He sat on the edge of the sofa and cleared his throat.

"Is the machine working?" asked Ali. "Got to always check it out." He mumbled a few words into the microphone. The reporter bent over his equipment.

"When is this going to appear?" asked Ali. "What's the name of the paper?"

The Sentinel," the reporter said. "It's mimeographed. We can't print the photographs in the paper, so that's why we have them on the bulletin board. The students can look at them on their way to classes."

"Oh, yes," Ali said.

Ali started by telling us that the evening before he had gone with ten of his associates to watch a twenty-five-minute condensation of the Ali-Frazier fight showing at the neighborhood theater in Cherry Hill. The most memorable moment on the screen was the way Frazier came for him after clubbing him with the big left hook in the eleventh round—quick little purposeful steps, but he had such a distance to go to reach Ali that he dropped his hands as he came, so that the camera could have been focused on a man hurrying down the street for a bus.

Ali put down the microphone and got up to demonstrate.

"Here's me," he said, snapping his head to one side from the imaginary hook, then taking big backward steps, his head gracefully dodging the chandelier, his black-stockinged feet picking up green fluff from the carpet. "He really tagged me, so I have to stay away from him and clear my head.

"Now here's Frazier coming after me." He strode across the

room, turned, and went into a little strutting walk, hands down, which brought him back to the sofa on which he flopped, laughing. "That long long walk of Frazier's. Oh, my, we were laughing at that."

While Ali was going through his performance, the reporter on the sofa pointed the sticklike microphone at him to pick up what he could. He checked his machine to see how his tape was holding out.

"What is the main thing you think back on, remembering the fight?" he asked.

"Weli, I think back on that left hook," Ali said. "All through the fight I kept thinking, 'My, I just got hit with the left hook *again.*'" Ali shook his head, once again his hand grazing up over his bruise. "Now, I don't get hit with left hooks, you understan', but he was doing it, and they was hard and accurate, to the head and to the hips. The first two left hooks he hit me with, well, I thought he'd got some lucky ones in; but he kept them coming. . . ."

The young photographer, who had remained standing, staring at Ali, suddenly asked, "How . . . I mean, what was wrong?"

Ali demonstrated, a hand up alongside his head. "Here's how you're supposed to do it. I had my hands too low."

"Couldn't you bring them up?" the boy blurted.

"That sounds simple, don't it," Ali said.

The interviewer on the sofa rattled his paper impatiently. Ali turned to him. "What was your battle plan?" the boy asked.

"I had one," Ali said. "Every fighter must, but in the third or fourth round I saw I had to change it. A good fighter must learn how to do this. If something's wrong, he must adjust. That's what happened to Jimmy Ellis when he fought Frazier. He kept doing the same thing he was doing, which got him into trouble."

"What did you do?" asked the photographer. "I mean . . . what?"

"Tom, can't you keep quiet," the reporter said. "You're wasting tape." He cleared his throat and looked at his paper.

Ali went on, unperturbed. "After I saw he took my best shots—lefts, uppercuts, hooks, right-hand leads, good shots—and he kept coming, I knew the fight was going to be long and that there was no way I could dance for fifteen rounds with that man and not get tired 'long about the tenth or eleventh round. So I knew I must come down off my toes and plan to outpoint him. Then I lost a couple of rounds—I played around in them—that I could have took."

The reporter smoothed out his list. "What is your honest opinion of Joe Frazier?"

"We both have respect for the other, more than when we started," Ali said. "But Frazier do one thing he should not do if he expect to keep fighting. He accepts too many punches to get in. It messes up your face too much, takes too much out of you. He looks much worse than me after the fight. I hit him three times what he hit me. Of course, that left hook of his leave a swole"—his hand stole up to his cheek—"but nothing else. When that swole go down, I won't have a mark, not a bruise. . . ."

The boy again looked down at his list. "Was it," he asked, "your opinion that Joe Frazier was easy to hit with a punch?"

"Yes," Ali said.

The fighter touched his cheek again.

Suddenly the photographer interrupted again. "But what do you *look* at? I mean when you fight. Do you look at his *nose?*"

"You look at his head," Ali said calmly. "He moves his head better than any fighter I know. But still I got in maybe eight out of the ten punches that I throw."

The tape machine clicked. The tape had apparently run out. The reporter gave a petulant sigh and looked at his photographer.

"Could I ask you something?" the photographer said. I noticed he was wearing a field jacket that read BEARS on the back. "What is it like to . . . lose . . . I mean."

The boy on the sofa said, "Oh, Tom," the way one might be embarrassed for a younger brother. I wondered if the two were related.

Ali shifted easily on the sofa. "Oh, they all said"—he glanced over at me—"that if he ever lose, he'll shoot himself, he'll die; but I'm human. I've lost one fight out of thirty-two, and it was a decision that could have gone another way. If I'd gone down three times and got up and was beat real bad, really whupped, and the other fighter was so superior, then I'd look at myself and say I'm washed up. That is what is sad. The fellow who's through who's got nothing left . . ."

"Will you be able to . . . ah . . . forget it?" the boy asked, almost in anguish, it seemed to me. "Don't you keep remembering?"

"Not as much as I thought I would," Ali answered. "For me now, fighting is more a business than the glory of who won. After all, when the praise is over"—and he shifted into the low singsong voice that he uses for rhetoric and poetry—"when all the fanfare is done, all that counts is what you have to show for it. All the bleeding, the world still turns. I was so tired. I lost it. But I didn't shed one tear. I got to keep living. I'm not ashamed."

The two had put on their shoes. "We'll send you a copy of *The Sentinel,*" the reporter said.

"Yeah?" Ali lolled back, working his toes in his stockings. I had the sense he was working up a sigh of boredom; he didn't want to be asked much more about the fight.

When the kids had gone, I asked, "Why didn't you sue those people who took your title away? They're the ones who took it."

The yawn arrived. "Aw, they did what they thought was right," he said.

I shuffled my notebook. "We didn't do much of a job for you."

"Who done expected you to? The title was taken away from *me*. I'm the one who got to get it back."

17

On those occasions when *Sports Illustrated* sends me off to cover a topical event such as a championship fight, I think they do so bemused, and with certain trepidation. The editors know that I prefer to write leisurely, longish efforts about static, nontopical subjects such as bicycle polo. When they want a history of baseball bullpens and the social activity that goes on in them, they call me up and I am let loose. I am asked to do postfight stories, such as Ali's state of mind following his defeat by Frazier. But the deadline story, the telex machine, an hour "to file," the editor waiting at some distant desk drumming his fingers while I sit there aghast in some press box, my inadequacies emphasized by a pro like Red Smith or Dave Anderson flailing at his typewriter next door in his cocoon of concentration—all of this fills me with a powerful sense of despair.

Prizefights are the most forbidding to cover—especially a championship bout. To begin with, the focus of so much attention is directed at a small area, so that the unnerved reporter is aware that those who make up his immediate competition, as many as two hundred correspondents from around the world, are staring at a space measuring only twenty by twenty feet and containing, forgetting the referee, only two men. What can he see that they will not? Worst of all, a fight can be over in a few seconds, which still means, however, that a couple of thousand words must be constructed out of an act which very likely took place when the reporter was looking down and fiddling with the ribbon of his typewriter. I remember a writer from a Richmond, Virginia, paper, covering a big fight in Madison Square Garden, who was looking up, his pencil poised, when the fellow in front of him hunched forward suddenly. When the fellow sat back, one leg of his metal folding chair came down on my reporter friend's foot, just behind the toe. It caused him such substantial pain that after wrestling the chair up again, he was gazing forlornly at his foot when the knockout occurred in the ring. He saw nothing of it. Neither did the fellow in front, who twisted around to apologize and turned out to be the photographer from the same paper, which meant that Richmond, Virginia, readers were not treated the next morning to the best of eyewitness reports.

Still, *Sports Illustrated* tests me with a fight from time to time and I accept the assignment perhaps out of the vanity that a writer should be able to cover such stories. The ones they send me to are invariably overseas, because the resident fight expert at *Sports Illustrated,* Mark Kram, cannot abide flying in airplanes. He will travel long distances on trains, but when it comes to transoceanic hops, he shakes his head sadly. His resolve finally broke down when the third Frazier-Ali fight was scheduled for Manila. He is a great student of fights, a superb reporter, and the rubber match of that rivalry was irresistible. He flew to the Philippines in the same plane with Ali, which he felt might help him survive, considering the benedictive powers of Allah, but it was a traumatic flight; his friends said that all that was left of him to unload in Manila were a few flakes of dandruff.

The first championship fight the magazine sent me to cover as an official assignment—that is, to provide the story of the fight itself—was the George Foreman–Joe Frazier fight in Jamaica. I went down with Bundini, who designated himself Ali's unofficial representative—he told me he was going to make sure that neither Foreman or Frazier forgot who was waiting in the wings to challenge the winner . . . or the loser, for that matter.

The hotel in Kingston where we stayed was packed. I could look down from my eighth-floor room and see the crowds standing six deep around the poolside bars, pushing forward as if at a trough. The drum-throbs from the bongos drifted up, thumping incessantly. The other predictable sound was the distant crash of crockery and glass. Sometimes the crash was a solitary glass, just discernible, perhaps someone sweeping it off a poolside table with a swipe of the elbow; but more often, it seemed, it was a huge cascade of sound, as if the floor had dropped out from beneath the hotel kitchen. I remarked on it to Bud Shrake, a fellow writer, and he said he had noticed it, too. "I think the Jamaicans break glass the way we clear throats," he said. "Periodically."

Shrake was also from *Sports Illustrated.* In fact, there were four writers down on a busman's holiday (I was informed), but it was difficult to rid myself of the notion that they were actually on hand to back me up on my first fight story if things went awkwardly.

Almost as soon as I arrived, I went to see Archie Moore, who was one of George Foreman's advisors. "Hello, Roger," he said. He had a small corner room in the Skyline Hotel. On his bureau was a red rubber mouse, the type that squeaks when pressed. "George Foreman and I play Ping-Pong," Moore explained, "and at certain points during the game we play for the mouse. The loser of the point has to pick up the mouse right there at the table and squeak it. That's right. Man or mouse. It's a good mental exercise. Every fighter must have a belief that he can do anything he wants. The mouse is helping." Moore picked it up and squeaked it. "I like the man who puts priorities in perspective. I like a man who wants to win the championship of the world."

He took me and Bundini to watch George Foreman in his last workout. We watched him take the challenger's hands for his workout on the heavy bag. Bundini had never seen so much protective tape and gauze and bandage used.

"I think maybe his hands is broken," he whispered to me.

He and Dick Sadler, Foreman's head trainer, began talking about the hardest punches they had ever seen thrown. Both of them agreed that one of them was Rocky Marciano's hit on Ezzard Charles in their last fight—a blow, as Bundini described it, that landed under "the goozle pipe . . . which swole up so the neck and chin became the same." Throughout this, Foreman remained quiet, watching Moore put on the tape.

We went out in the gym, where the heavy bag was hanging from its chains. Old women in green smocks mopped the floor, heads down; I never saw one glance up at the concussive sound of Foreman hitting the heavy bag. Dick Sadler held it for him, both arms clasped around the smooth leather like a sailor clutching the mainmast in a hurricane, leaning into it; and when Foreman landed his enormous socking punches, Sadler was jolted back and his white hat, a jaunty yachting variety, bounced slightly on his head. He wore a look of considerable foreboding as he held the bag, as if the force hitting it was ultimately unearthly and uncontainable.

Bundini was scornful. "What good is that? He's hitting something that don't move. They should let the bag swing free. Frazier's not going to stand still for him. They're depending on his power alone. It's like a kid using a gun without a sight. He don't know what to hit. He'll hit the ropes, the referee." He shook his head. "But my goodness I can see why they bandage up those hands. That man can punch."

There were a few other Foreman supporters. Joe Louis was one, though that was probably because the promoters had asked him; his support of the underdog would hype interest in the fight. I met him at a garden party, with a semicircle of people around him; his coat was fastened across his middle by a large gold button, and a full plate of food sat on a camp chair in front of him. Did he know either fighter? Not really, and to truly enjoy the fights, he said, it *was* important to have a friend involved. He had not had a close friend in boxing since the days of Sugar Ray Robinson. "They pay me to come here, of course," he said, looking slowly around at the people, with the cocktail glasses glinting in their hands.

"You'd rather be out on the golf course?"

"Oh, sure," he said. Just the name of the sport seemed to stir him. "For three hours you can go out there and forget about just everything," he said.

People would not let up on him. They asked him about Foreman. He tapped his chest. "Heart," he said. "It's going to be a question of heart. It's easy to quit in boxing. 'Heart' is where you don't give up. Tony Farr had it. Billy Conn had too much of it."

Howard Cosell was a Foreman supporter as well. He was in Kingston to do the television broadcast for ABC's *Wide World of Sports.* I went up to the Stony Hill Hotel on a ridge above Kingston to have a drink with him. A group of us sat on the terrace and watched the lights of the town come on far below in the valley. Cosell was wearing a pair of Bermuda shorts. He stretched his legs. "Take a gander at these limbs," he said. "At the PSAL championship held in 1931 at the Hundred sixty-eighth Street Armory in Manhattan, these legs carried me to a second-place finish in the standing broad jump. My wife wears the silver medal on her charm bracelet. Don't you, Emi?"

She nodded.

Cosell began talking about Foreman. "I have been with George since the 1968 Olympics in Mexico City when he took out the Russian, Ionis Chepulis, on a TKO in the second round," he announced in the darkness, intoning the name, place, and date with his customary relish. "Tomorrow night, there are going to be some shocked people in the world."

One of the guests asked Cosell about the worst fight he had ever seen.

"The Fullmer-Benvenuti fight on December fourteenth, 1968, in a San Remo theater. I said at the time, and over the air, and I would say it again anytime, anyplace, that what the fight fan was watching was a silent Italian movie."

He leaned out of his chair. "Isn't this great up here? You're staying downtown in the Sheraton, George? What sort of slob thing is that to do? Look at this," he said, sweeping a hand at the opulent setting—wicker bird cages hanging among the palm fronds, wooden statues standing in the shadows, everywhere the splash of the fountains. "How inelegant and pedestrian to be staying elsewhere. Emi and I are living in the Errol Flynn suite where, I have been told by the proprietor of this hostelry, Flynn watched Beverly Aadland dance in the nude. We have a pet lizard that comes in from time to time. I have named him Roscoe."

"Why Roscoe?"

"Because he *is* Roscoe," Cosell said. "What other name is possible?"

Just about everyone else in Kingston thought Frazier was going to stomp Foreman. The seventh-ranked heavyweight, Ken Norton, who has the muscles of a bodybuilder and seemed to spend his afternoons posing his way around the edge of the Sheraton-Kingston pool, was plumb scornful: "He stinks." (Foreman subsequently destroyed him in the second round in a Venezuela bout.) "He's going to need a bunch of luck. He's got a hard jab, but he misses it and goes off balance. And it's so hard that he can't do anything off it, like hook. As for his big punches, you can pack a lunch before they get there."

"If you're wrong," said a Frazier supporter who was standing next to him, "I'm eating beans."

As for Joe Frazier, he was truly contemptuous of Foreman. I went calling on him in his villa on the grounds of the Sheraton-Kingston. He was lying on his bed wearing a pair of boxing trunks and a T-shirt. He looked over at me and asked, "How're you feeling? How're you feeling?" (He has the habit of repeating his sentences.)

"Fine. Fine," I said in spite of myself.

It was hard to get him to talk about Foreman. I had my notebook open. He seemed to shrug his challenger off. His manager, Yank Durham, had announced, utilizing the manager's traditional use of the first-person singular, "I'm going to take him in the first round." I asked Frazier if that was right . . . the first round?

"You better believe it. You better believe it."

Had he watched Foreman fight? Had he studied films of him? Wasn't that important? Frazier shook his head. "What help is it to scout another man? You understand? What help is it?"

"I don't know," I said.

"Even sparring partners don't work your opponent in a fight. So I work on *my* strengths. Let the other guy do the best he can." He folded his arms on his stomach. They had the heft of a large constrictor snake. "I met George in New York. He said he was ready. In Omaha. He said he was ready. Saw him last Monday. He said he was ready. Well, *I'm* ready. You better believe it."

His villa room was filled with the paraphernalia of boxing—a small medicine ball, gloves for the light bag, sweatsuits. Wires snaked from a small transformer on the floor to a cassette player. A Bible lay next to him on the bed.

"When the fight comes, I hate everyone," he was saying. "It's the eight weeks of training that does it. You *hate* the man for making you spend the length of time it takes to whup him."

I remembered what Archie Moore had once told me—running in his rubber suit through the rocks, seeing his man materialize through the hot haze . . . and the hate generating . . .

"It's the roadwork that you dislike?" I asked Frazier.

"That's part of it," he said. He smiled. "But that can be nice. Cool. We run at five in the morning—all the fighters. It's black and quiet then, except for the dogs. A few people are going to work. A bus goes by. Maybe a cab. We can look over the hedge and see lights shining in a few of the houses where folks are getting up. The moon be up, very high. Sometimes we come around a corner, a whole bunch of fighters, running with towels on our heads, and maybe a woman is waiting on a bus. She looks up and sees us, you know, and *she* don't know, seeing all these men running, if we're running *away* from something, or maybe running *at* her, and she can get nervous."

It was hot in the room, the sweat beads standing above his eyebrows. He blew the sweat off his upper lip. "I'm telling you, it's nice out there. The guy in the car following us plays tapes, so we have music to listen to when we run. Al Green's group—'I'm

Still in Love with You,' 'Pretty Woman,' 'Love and Happiness.' "

I thought of the pack of hooded men running along the street, and the gentle music accompanying them under the trees. I said, "They don't sound like the kind of titles to pump up a fighter."

"It's the beat," he said. "You know what I mean? They got a good beat."

"You ever run into George Foreman out there?"

"Naw, he runs at six-thirty. In Detroit, once, we catch up to Bob Foster and pass him when he's doing his roadwork. We didn't say nothing. We just went right on by." He grinned.

"So you're ready."

"You better believe it."

I liked what Frazier had said about roadwork in the morning— about the woman looking up to see the men running along the road and about the lights in one or two windows—and I asked him if I could run with him. Perhaps I could get a paragraph or so for my piece. He shrugged his shoulders. He told me that if I was of a mind to run six miles in the early morning, why, that was entirely up to *me,* not him.

The next morning at five A.M. I got up to run. The hotel elevators were not working. After a long wait, I heard a vacuum cleaner whining far down the shaft; presumably the elevators were being cleaned. I ran down eight flights. Out by the pool, as I raced by, thinking I was going to be late, twenty or thirty people were still out there with glasses in their hands. Perhaps they were waiting for the vacuums to get out of the elevators.

In Frazier's suite the fighters had collected. They looked up as I came in already puffing from my run down the stairs and past the pool. The greetings were perfunctory. The only sparring partner's name that stuck was Willie Munroe. His nickname was Worm. "Meet the Worm." There was hardly any conversation. I was reminded of the subdued, somewhat grumpy atmosphere of duck hunters in someone's kitchen before going out in the predawn.

We drove into the country in two cars. The night air was very dry. I was acutely conscious of how far we were going. After about ten minutes, we stopped and piled out. The cars led the way back, their rear lights as bright as flares ahead. The music thumped. I dropped back almost immediately. My fear was that if I ran with the pack, one of them might want to make conversation, just to be polite. "What magazine do you work for, man?" And then I, holding my side to contain a stitch, the breath working hard in my throat, mouth ajar, tongue thick, would have to make the vast physical effort of saying, "*Sp-Sp-Sports Ill-Ill-Ill-Illus...*" which would probably tire me so much I'd have to drop down in the roadside grass for a rest.

So I pegged along by myself. Up in front the fighters trotted easily, sometimes one of them turning and backstepping for a fifty-yard stretch at a time, his knees lifting to the music beat. The sound of us going down the road woke up the dogs, and by the time I ran by, they had come out now under the shanty porches and down through the truck gardens and put their muzzles through the iron gates, and I could see their teeth shine in the moonlight. Sometimes the gate bore a crude hand-lettered sign: VERY BAD DOG. One gate had a sign DO NOT KNOCK. DOG VERY VERY BAD. For a while I ran along speculating how friends ever managed to call at *that* particular house. Did they call nervously out across the fence or perhaps peg stones until one of them fetched up against the corrugated roof and alerted the people inside? DO NOT KNOCK. That was certainly putting it bluntly.

After a while the cars stopped and we climbed in and drove back to Kingston. I thanked Frazier and went somewhat gloomily up to my room. The experience had not been especially illuminating. My feet were sore, since I had borrowed a pair of ill-fitting sneakers to run in. I began to worry about my assignment. I looked over my notes in my room, unnerved by their paucity and by how little substantial material I'd collected since I'd arrived in Kingston—material I'd need to fall back on if the fight ended quickly.... *Mouse that squeaks ... goozle pipe ... Cosell's lizard named Roscoe ... "How're you feeling? How're you feeling?"* ... and now the new addition—DO NOT KNOCK. DOG VERY VERY BAD.

I paced around. I had heard there was a fighter over in the

Skyline Hotel who had actually been in the ring with George
Foreman. Perhaps there was something there. Later that day I
took my notebook and went to find him. He was a Jamaican
heavyweight known as the Big Bamboo, a sobriquet invented by
a group of stockbrokers from Toronto, Canada, who first discovered him. His real name was Stanford Antonarias, and
almost everyone around called him Harris, or Two-O-Two,
which is his weight, and I was told he was very popular among
the cab drivers standing out in front of the hotels because he was
a local fighter and had been in there with George. That was
where I found him, gossiping with the cab drivers. He had a
round face, the size of a small pumpkin, with a few of his front
teeth missing, and he had obviously suffered in the boxing wars.

"I fought Chuvalo in a main event up in Alberta and got
stopped in four," he said quite cheerfully. "I fought Jerry Quarry
and got cut in six. I went against George Foreman and got
knocked out in the third."

"It was the fourth," a bystander said.

"Oh, yah, it was the fourth," the Big Bamboo said gratefully.
"To be in there with George Foreman and get away from his
shots is very difficult. His hands are very fast. He punches . . ."
He paused. "Oh, mon," he said in his natural island lilt, which
sounds almost Scottish. "To box with George you must get low
and very close. He's dangerous at far range. If I ever fight him
again, I'd fight him much closer." He looked very dubious about
the possibility. "Yah," he suddenly said brightly. "It *was* the
fourth round. Sure, mon, it was." He seemed quite pleased with
himself.

The night of the fight, I sat next to Tex Maule, one of those
Sports Illustrated star writers I suspected was in Jamaica to be on
hand to supply the story in case I collapsed on the assignment
and could not set down what I had seen.

I did not mind at all. I was quite relieved. The night was
warm. We chatted. He said that the most arduous companion to
be seated beside at a boxing match, or indeed any sort of athletic
contest, had been Jimmy Cannon, the great columnist for the
Scripps-Howard chain. The trouble with Cannon was that he

never seemed to have his mind on what was going on; he was always grumbling about the Vietnam War, or some political boondoggling, or the trading policies of the New York Yankees, or the state of food at Toots Shor's, grimacing and shaking his head; and when a big punch was thrown up in the ring, or a sixty-yard pass completed down on the field for a touchdown, Cannon would touch Maule on the arm and ask, "Hey, what happened?"

This occurred so often that finally Maule stipulated to the authorities that he wanted to be seated elsewhere in the press box; it was hard enough to collect his own thoughts about a climactic moment without having to help out Cannon, acting (as Maule put it) like a "sort of vocal seeing-eye dog."

Howard Cosell came by, his Jamaica sunburn shining as pink as cotton candy in the ring lights. He motioned back at the huge crowd in the darkness behind him. "Boyle's Acres," he said mysteriously. "Jack Dempsey versus Carpentier. July, 1921. But you *knew* that. You were there." A cackle of laughter and he disappeared around the corner of the ring.

"What was the point of that?" I asked.

"Who knows," Maule said. "There's no recourse. The next time you see him, jab your finger at him and say, 'June fourteenth, 1938, Polo Grounds. What about it, Howard?' "

"What happened back then?" I asked innocently.

"How do I know?" Maule said. "Maybe nothing. But you've got to throw those guys like Cosell—keep them off balance."

I asked Maule about the fight.

"Frazier's absolutely going to kill him. I'm telling you, I hope they have a stretcher ready, because Foreman's going to be carried off on it. No doubt about it. Sooner rather than later."

I thought about the horror of a thirty-second fight—the typewriter and the pile of foolscap (what an appropriate word) back in the hotel room. I applied myself diligently to the legal pad in front of me. As the moment of the main event crept up, I kept notes frantically. I wrote down that a large insect with a discernibly big red head had flown over, its wings a perfectly circular blur in the ring lights. I described the tropic heat, and I wrote notes on the fighters in the first event on the card—one of them named Carlos Baker, a squat fighter who had the same name as the Hemingway scholar at Princeton University and who confused matters by wearing the name Bill down the side of his trunks. "A literary obfuscation," observed Red Smith, of the *Times,* turning and grinning at me over his shoulder. I wrote notes about the ring announcer, whose name was Dwight "Nightingale" Whytie, a local radio personality—a stout gentleman, formally attired, with a beard swept out from his chin like a New England sea captain's; he spoke gentle admonitions out at the crowd as if directing guests at a cotillion: "Please, please, please. Sit down for me." His gentle voice reverberated in the night. He was very precise when it came time to introduce the main event. He referred to the "northwestern" corner of the ring (where Joe Frazier was sitting) and the "southeastern" corner opposite. Eddie Fisher came up into the ring; he took his sunglasses off, much as a citizen removes his hat, and he sang "The Star-Spangled Banner."

Of course, what happened then was that George Foreman, to my horror, dismantled Joe Frazier in some four minutes. I sat there and stared at Foreman in despair. One of the odd phenomena of a fight is that the boxer who gains the upper hand seems to become so physically huge in the ring, right before one's eyes, as if success ballooned him with air; the other fighter deflates. Sonny Liston, sitting on his stool after the sixth round of his title loss, seemed as small and dejected as a schoolboy sent to a corner, whereas Ali, leaping with his limbs askew in his triumph like a beserk pterodactyl, suddenly became a mammoth presence in the ring. In Jamaica it had been the same—Frazier, in his misery, had been transmogrified from his original state of enormity ("My God, he looks like a tank!") into someone rather "tubby" and "foolish" (words I wrote on my pad), his gloves, which had green thumbs, hanging down like children's mittens, while across the way on his stool, with his handlers adoring around him, Foreman looked vast and wise and, with his somewhat Mandarin features, not unlike a sumo wrestler sitting on a throne.

In Foreman's dressing room I looked for Archie Moore; he showed me one of Foreman's gloves with a little chip out of it which he said had been made by one of Joe Frazier's teeth. "Talk about big punching," he said with a shake of his head. He said he never had seen anything like that before.

I rushed over to Frazier's dressing room; it was steaming hot, like a jungle undergrowth. When I got in only one writer was still holding out, his shirt plastered flat against his back, and he was pressing Yank Durham, Frazier's manager, to find out what had happened. Frazier wasn't there. Durham was dressing as he answered, wrenching his belt tight in a gesture of petulance. "What a stupid bunch of questions. What happened? He got hit. Didn't we all see the same fight? He got hit and he fell down. What happened to Marciano when he got hit? He fell down. What happened to Joe Louis? He fell down. It's no mystery."

The dressing-room door opened, I had a quick glimpse of policemen outside, and the last fighter on the night's card came back from the ring—Willie "the Worm" Munroe.

Yank Durham looked up. "How'd you do, Worm?"

"Left hook. Took him with the left hook."

"That's good, Worm. When?"

"First round."

"Good work, Worm."

The fighter, wearing a green-trimmed robe, sat on the edge of the rubbing table. He wanted to exult, but the mood of the room was oppressive.

I asked, "Worm, did you happen to watch the main event?" posing the question as much to use his odd nickname as to hear his answer.

"Not really," he said. "I was in here. I heard the hollering, and I ran out to the top of the runway and peeked, and I saw Joe down—the second time, I guess, he went down in that first round. I took one look and run back in here. I didn't want to get my mind messed up. I didn't want to see no more. I couldn't believe my eyes."

I rushed around and talked to the new champion the morning

after. He was sitting out on the terrace of his tenth-floor suite, high above the countryside with a direct view to the high hills inland from Kingston. His people had been throwing flyers with his picture off the balcony, which fluttered down into the street below for almost an hour, and across onto the tennis courts. I saw a man bat at one furiously which had sailed into his line of sight just as he was about to serve.

Foreman lolled back in his chair—a portrait of contentment, master of all he surveyed. He talked about his three advisors. "Archie Moore was necessary—all business. He balanced Dick Sadler, who knows me best, but is lighthearted about some things. Sandy Saddler was one of the most cold-blooded fighters ever, and he kept that idea around. The team was right."

What instant of the night before would he remember above all others?

"The next-to-last knockdown," he said. "I knew just then that I was going to be the new champion, that there was no way Frazier was going to get up and come back. I knew because I looked and I saw on his face that he was staring around for help."

I remembered that, too—a great surge of sympathy for Frazier, his glance sailing by mine, and I wondered if he saw his peculiar doom reflected in how we stared back at him—our mouths ajar, aghast . . .

Foreman was saying, "He was telling me at the weigh-in, 'I'm going to smoke you out after the bell rings, and that's the end of you.'"

"Oh yes."

"He was trying to get his courage up saying that, but he lost it when he looked away. I was within him."

I asked how much rage and hate had to do with his devastating power the night before.

"Oh, I like Joe Frazier. I pray for him. I always pray for him. I pray twice a day, and I pray for people I am conscious of. I've been conscious of Frazier for a couple of months. So I prayed for him."

I went back to my hotel room very nervous indeed. I had two

days to provide the magazine with my story. But I had no line of direction. I couldn't write about Foreman praying. I dawdled around the room and looked out the window, which had a view of the distant stadium, the tall standards around it still on, even in the daytime, so that the structure seemed to glow in a huge pool of bright light. I kept thinking of the little nip in the glove which Archie Moore had shown me. Could I use it in some way?

I gazed at my legal pad of notes. (See page 223.)

The thought struck me that perhaps I could use the helter-skelter of words to illustrate my story, deciphering each sentence at a time—a device which might make the fight seem more immediate to the reader. It would be a question of persuading the editors to publish the page.

The first notations are relatively easy. Red Smith was sitting just in front of me in the press section, and just before the fight started, a moth landed on the back of his seersucker jacket, on the right shoulder blade. I noted it, thinking if the fight were dull I could keep an eye on the moth to see how many rounds it stayed around on Mr. Smith's coat. I did not think to look for it again. The allusion to the nightingale getting out of the ring referred to the Jamaican ring announcer, Dwight "Nightingale" Whylie, who at the moment the referee waved the two fighters together to commence hostilities was standing inside the ring, leaning nonchalantly on the top rope, smiling; seemingly he didn't know what was going on behind him. Perhaps the tremor of the ring under those first quick steps of the fighters alerted him—I don't know; but the smile froze on his face, and without daring to look around, he ducked down through the ropes.

The next notation is "huge right hand," which I set down because Foreman led with it, one of his first punches, which was a surprise because such a punch would have opened him up for a counter by Frazier's most fearsome weapon, his left hook. Schoolboys are taught not to lead with the right hand ... *bang!* you get clobbered. But Foreman got away with it. Indeed, "F. down" refers to the first Frazier knockdown, and "Keeps his mouth shut ... Mandarin" was to remind me of Foreman's composure at that time—aloof, cool, in such contrast to his opponent, who was stumbling across the ring, a puzzled look on his face, as if he'd put something down which he couldn't find, the glazed smooth white of his mouthpiece showing. Frazier seemed to move toward his opponent in a sort of hideous tiptoe, tilted forward as if only his weight, off balance, kept him moving into that savage peppering.

"Tex??" was to remind me to ask Tex Maule what on earth was going on. He had told me, after all, that Foreman was going to be removed from the ring on a stretcher.

The next block of scribbling describes the second round. "F. down" is, of course, a reference to another Frazier knockdown. What one can decipher of the next sentence alludes to the terrible something or other "we heard in the gym"—that Frazier was being subjected to the same awesome thunking blows we'd seen Foreman deliver to the big punching bag. The question marks that follow "left" and "F.'s left" probably refer to the inability of Frazier to do anything with his famous left hook. I remember watching it in that second round, and seeing it flail a few times, but it was done in the throes of his dilemma, like a dying lizard's tail flopping over, and after the fight Foreman was reported to have said of the punch, "You mean *that* thing was his hook?"

The next fragment, "Sadler gestures uppercut," recalled a vivid picture—the little manager on the steps in his corner, his face contorted, his arms pumping up, and then Foreman, looking directly at him, almost *nodding,* and then turning to produce the uppercut that sent Frazier down for the last time. It was at this stage that Foreman looked into the Frazier corner and began shouting, emphasizing what he was saying with a little shake of his head. He was shouting at Yank Durham, unheard in all that tumult: I read his lips as saying, "I'm not going to kill him! I'm not going to kill him!" Apparently I had got it wrong. Afterward, he declared he had said, "Stop it, or I'm going to kill him."

The kissing referred to was done by Archie Moore, of course, who, in his blue wool ski cap, clambered through the ropes when the fight was stopped and kissed his pupil on the cheek.

moth on Red Smith's shoulder-blade
Nightingale almost not out of ring

HUGE RIGHT HAND

F. Down

Keeps his mouth shut... Mandarin

Tex??

F. Down
Terrible chunking sound we heard in gym

left? F's left???

Sadler gestures vehement from corner

I'm not going to kill him
"   "   "   "   "   "

Archie kisses him

No pumpkins

melancholy

That word "melancholy" was jotted down not because of dashed support for the beaten man but because what we had seen was so quick and devastating, so one-sided, that it had none of the esthetic niceties of, say, the psychodramas of the Ali-Frazier fights, which could be studied like a good piece of theater. After it was over we stood there for a long time, looking up at the ring, not sure how to accept it. We had been witnesses not to a fight but to an execution.

I haven't the slightest idea what "no pumpkins" refers to. Later, staring at the legal pad from time to time, I strode around the hotel room pressing my temples to remember. I was not really surprised. My notebooks are studded with obscure notations and "things to remember" which make little sense. The other day a piece of paper fell out of my wallet. It read, "Remember Jake's story about the hat." Utterly foreign to me. I don't remember the story, or even Jake.

Sports Illustrated finally published the story along with a doctored version of the fight notes. There was grumbling about its form. The editor, André LaGuerre, was not a proponent of what he scornfully called "personalized journalism." He was a dour, though brilliant, editor. My nickname for him was Heavy Water. "Has Heavy Water read it yet?"

"*Um,* yes. He doesn't much, *er,* like that paper. He calls it that 'goddamn Plimpton papyrus.' "

"Oh."

I had assumed the "papyrus" would take up at least a third of a page in the magazine, so readers could refer to it. Heavy Water cut it down to about a square inch—the notations on it barely visible. He took out "no pumpkins" and also "Tex??" to protect the infallibility of his star writer.

18

The result of that fight in Jamaica, and of Ali's beating Frazier in the second act of their trilogy, set up the confrontation between Foreman, now the heavyweight champion, and Muhammad Ali, the affair to take place in Kinshasa, Zaire, Africa. A huge stake was guaranteed for the fighters to do this—$10,000,000—a sum possibly only a country could raise, in this case through the decree of a ruler, President Mobutu Sese Seko, who felt that the publicity attendant to such an event would show how his country, formerly the Congo, was recovering from the throes of freeing itself from Belgian domination.

Once again, Mark Kram, the palindromic *Sports Illustrated* fight expert, decided not to risk an airplane trip; besides, no one at the magazine felt that Muhammad Ali had much of a chance; it was going to be very sad. They were not alone in their opinion. "A big name and not much to defend it," one columnist described him. Jimmy Cannon wrote, "We all know he passed our way. No athlete ever stirred up more excitement. But you can't dance to a dirge." Dick Young, of the New York *Daily News,* went so far as to criticize the face that Ali once said should be a "natural resource—the Secretary of the Interior should appropriate money to preserve it." The columnist took a discerning look and wrote, "Even the facial beauty is departing."

The people in the fight game were unanimous that his career was done. Jerry Quarry said simply, "Ali's had it. He's at road's end." Dick Sadler, Foreman's ebullient manager, announced sadly, "I hate to be the one to do it, but Ali's gonna go. He has been a great contribution to boxing. But like all great men, there's got to be an end, and I'm going to provide it."

George Foreman himself, who had scored twenty-four consecutive knockouts, saw himself as a sort of lordly bestower of an anesthetic. "I don't like fights," he said. "I just land the right punch and everything is over. Nobody gets hurt and nobody gets killed"—this said with such dispassionate conviction that Ali's ripostes ("My African friends will put you in a pot") seemed shrill and silly by comparison.

Still, I was very grateful to be sent by the magazine. After the fruitless efforts on Ali's behalf, it seemed incumbent upon me to be a witness at his attempt to get back the championship which we always reckoned was his. So I packed my bag and went.

The center of everything in Kinshasa was the Hotel Inter-Continental—a fairly new establishment up on a hill, with a steep ramp leading up to the front entrance; down beyond the balustrade was a parking lot in which bands collected daily with Calypso-like steel drums and, with great perseverance, bombarded the facade of the hotel with their music. Inside, it was quieter: the lobby was spacious and quite elegant. Deep wicker sedan chairs were placed about, like sentry boxes, and when one sat inside them, the noise of the lobby was shut off: one looked out like a spy. Fans turned in the ceiling. From time to time a bellboy carried a blackboard sign past with two Buddhist temple bells tinkling attention to whatever name was requested for a message: "Martin Bormann" was carried by a few times, and "Judge Craven" (these were requested by Hunter Thompson, representing *Rolling Stone* magazine), and Dick Sadler, of Foreman's camp, got them to carry aloft a black expression for the lower tract of the alimentary canal (which I have forgotten) that got all the knees slapping and the guffawing emerging from the depths of the wicker sedan chairs.

The lobby of the hotel was called "the living room of Kinshasa" by the manager, a Belgian named Jacques, and it was an accurate enough designation: there was such a clash of dress, deportment, languages, that at times the lobby seemed the set of an exotic Baghdad movie set.

At times a cripple appeared among the crowd—the worst condition I had ever seen—his legs long, stick-thin, and bent off at a useless angle, so that he moved by jacking himself up on his fingertips and scuttling along on his hands. I don't think he was a beggar. He wore a constant enormous smile, and occasionally I saw people bending to talk to him. Perhaps he was a local dignitary. I know that later he turned up at the fight, sitting in one of the $200 seats with his legs hauled up so that he peered out between his kneecaps with that grand beatific smile on his face.

Most of the writers sent to cover the fight were quartered in the Inter-Continental, and if they were not, they spent a lot of time devising ways they could be. The other hotel in which the writers were barracked was the Memling. Located downtown, near the open-air ivory market, it was named after a Belgian explorer and its name, surprisingly, had remained intact despite the shift in power. Once, it had been the grand hotel in town—the Rialto of West Africa. In the bar the Belgian restaurateur who ran the place had installed a large wire cage in which hundreds of parakeets fluttered about and shrieked—activity which was preliminary, according to old Congo hands, to the act of copulation. "Monkeys are pikers compared to parakeets when it comes to public fornication," one of them told me. "Hell, man, sometimes half the cage was at it. It was rather dismaying, and it was best to sit with one's back to them." He said you could hear the uproar of the birds out on the street.

Now the cage had gone, and the hotel had run down. The writers even snarled about their accommodations in the copy sent to their home offices (one of them wrote that its cockroaches could play in the front wall of the Green Bay Packers)—comments which got blue-penciled by the government officials censoring the teletyped copy being sent out.

Almost all of them spent their day up at the Inter-Continental. There they sat in the wicker sedan chairs and had quantities of tea. They "consulted" one another as the Chinese consult their dead ancestors. They invented rumors to see how long it took for them to return full circle, usually told to them, glazed-eyed, by the person originally confided in.

The day I got there, there was considerable excitement. George Foreman's brow ridge had been sliced in a sparring session, and the whole costly affair was postponed until the cut healed. It was thought it would take a month before the two fighters were in the ring against each other.

At the news of Foreman's cut there had been some splendid rhetoric in the lobby. Don King, the omniscient promoter, a large man whose hair starts up from his head as if he had put his thumb in an electric-light socket (a number of writers came to the same image independently), tried to calm a group of reporters frantic to hear about the effect of a postponement. He offered some quotations about adversity. He had memorized a considerable list while serving time on a manslaughter charge in Cleveland, where he ran a numbers racket. " 'Though He slay me, yet I love Him'—that's Job talking to the Lord," he said in a booming voice. "We must look on the bright side of things." He held out his hands. "Adversity is ugly and venemous like a toad, yet wears a precious jewel in her head," he cried. The press shifted uneasily. "Shakespeare," he said. How lucky it was, he went on less dramatically, to their relief, that the accident had happened a week before the fight, and not the day before. There was time for everyone to adjust, and now there was an additional month in which to promote interest. The fight would move from the "colossal" level to the "supercolossal." "We are turning lemon into lemonade!" he shouted as he rushed away.

Just about everyone else who had a stake in the fight was worried stiff. They gathered in small worried groups, heads nodding, and one could tell from overhearing snatches of conversation how frantic they were.

"We got to send Ali out. He's our only hope to hang on to the public interest. Maybe we can send him out to see some tribal chiefs."

"Yeah."

"Maybe we can get him photographed out there in the bush wearing one of those tall tribal masks and shaking hands with a black emperor. Maybe we can get him down on his knees to box a pygmy. Something is bound to come of that."

"Yeah."

"He's got to say some provocative things. Didn't he say he'd promise not to hit Foreman in his bad eye? That's very provocative. Let's get him to say that a few more times."

"Yeah."

"Maybe he should disappear. How about that? The guys look in his room and there's no one there. His bed hasn't been slept in. No note. He's just plumb disappeared. Out in the bush. Maybe the lions have got him ... search parties out there ... camel trains ... maybe he's gone native...."

"Yeah."

"... renounced everything, and he's discovered, in some God-forsaken place with a jumble of huts, being a witch doctor."

As a matter of fact, just about everyone thought that the fighters were going to skip the country. Reports circulated in the lobby that Foreman was off to Paris—he wanted to walk his big German shepherd in the gardens there. Ali himself said that Foreman was leaving the country for quite a different reason— that he was scared to death of him and wasn't coming back. "I see fear in the eyes of all his followers," he shouted at the end of a workout. "Watch everything. Watch all strange boats slipping out into the river. Watch the buses. Watch the elephant caravans. Watch everything. The man has troubles. He wants out. Check all luggage big enough for a man to crawl into!"

No one was that sure about Ali either. A rumor was about that he was going stir crazy up at N'Sele, the presidential com-

pound twenty miles up the river where the challenger was training, with the huge silent river flowing by outside his villa, and
his people sitting in the big armchairs with their legs straight out,
sleeping. The persistent story was that since the authorities were
on guard at the road crossings and the airports, he was planning
to heist a fisherman's pirogue and paddle across the Zaire—an
appalling choice not only of conveyance, since the things were
tippy, but also of destination, the People's Republic of the
Ccngo on the other side being at odds with just about everyone,
especially the U.S., and quite likely to fling the challenger into
the nearest jail.

So when I arrived, nobody seemed to think the fight would
ever be held in Kinshasa. The project, with Foreman's cut eye,
seemed doomed. My favorite rumor drifting around the lobby of
the Inter-Continental was that the fight was eventually going to
be held aboard the French ocean liner *France,* which had been
seized by its crew a few months before in protest against the
French government's decision to take her out of service. The
liner was moored off Le Havre. The passengers had been sent
ashore full of champagne and sympathy for the crew staying
behind who intended to stick it out—a small enclave of French-
men on a ship they now thought of as being without a country.
They were their own masters: why not the heavyweight championship in the grand ballroom, far at sea, under the great
crystal chandelier, perhaps in a heavy sea, with Angelo Dundee
looking a little green in one corner, and the fighters working up
the slant of the canvas, and then down again? . . .

As soon as I arrived, I went out to try to see Foreman. His
press agent, a likeable fellow named Bill Caplan, drove me out
to N'Sele, where both fighters had their training quarters. It was
dusk when we left Kinshasa.

"I don't think we're going to get to see him," Bill told me.
"Hell, I'm his press agent and I rarely get to. In fact, he won't
speak to me, and he won't let me speak to him."

"And you're his press agent?" I remarked in surprise. "How
do the two of you communicate?"

"I write him notes," Caplan said. "Apparently he likes to get things in writing."

"How does it work?" I asked.

"Well, I write a note and it says on it, 'Be at the Hotel Inter-Continental at nine A.M. for press conference. Signed. Your press agent.' When I see him I reach out, a little like a quarterback handing off the ball, and sometimes he takes it and sometimes he doesn't. Sometimes he takes it and drops it on the floor without looking at it."

"That's the only communication you have?"

"We play Ping-Pong. At the Inter-Continental Hotel. He points at the table down by the swimming pool and we go down there and play. I'm a good player and I beat him to pieces, perhaps out of frustration. He never says anything. I even keep the score. I don't really think he knows that I am his press agent. He probably thinks that I'm carried on his rolls as a Ping-Pong player. He thinks the notes I try to pass him are old scores."

We got to N'Sele. The road turning up a dark hill toward Foreman's camp—a small cluster of lights in the distance—was blocked by two sets of gates and a pillbox with a conical straw roof. We argued with the soldiers.

One of them allowed me to use a field-box telephone. I turned the handle on it briskly. To my surprise George Foreman came on the other end.

"Champ, I'd like to come and see you."

I hoped he would get someone to say something to the guards so they would let us up, but he said the authorities around him were very protective. No one was allowed through the gate except official members of his party.

"I could hide in the trunk of Bill Caplan's car," I said. "They'll let *him* through the gate."

"Who?"

"Bill Caplan. He's your press agent."

"Oh, yes?"

Foreman sounded worried at the other end. He said there were a lot of people with guns around his camp, and they sure would be tempted to start shooting if they saw someone crawling out of the trunk of a car. He said he'd see me some other time, and I heard the click of the receiver being put down.

So Caplan and I drove back to Kinshasa.

"You're right," I said.

"What about?" Bill asked.

"That he doesn't know who his press agent is."

Finally Foreman made it easier for us by moving from N'Sele to Kinshasa—indeed, into the Hotel Inter-Continental. The word was that he had awakened one morning to find a lizard on the ceiling above his bed—he couldn't believe the lizard could hang on up there; he was going to have to make a great head move to keep from being slapped in the face when the lizard fell. The soldiers and the security bothered him, too, the sound of their rifle butts on the floor in the next room, and the click of beer cans being opened.

John Vinacour of the Associated Press wrote a fine story about his boredom out there and how seemingly difficult it was for the champion to fill his life. He talked about his wealth making things happen too quickly and efficiently. He had wanted some kennels built for his dogs in Houston; the word was given, and the kennels had been completed with such speed that there wasn't time to engross himself in their design or construction: an army of carpenters arrived and after a furious day of hammering and sawing they backed away, and there the kennels were ... standing ready for a coat of paint and occupancy. Vinacour told me that Foreman was very nervous as he told him this—as if a part of life was simply escaping him—and he described the fighter's hands as reaching out on occasion and snatching at "imaginary flies."

Foreman was not much easier to see when he moved into the hotel. His guards kept everyone at bay. The most forbidding of them was his brother "Sunny" Foreman, who was invariably at his shoulder, dressed in denim or sometimes in leather outfits, the length of him from an engineer's cap on down to his flared trouser cuffs studded with brass and copper eyelets, so that he seemed to catch and hold the light in the hotel lobby like a line of reflectors along a highway. A huge man, he seemed more prepossessing than his brother, and probably was often mistaken for him. I never saw him smile; he glowered. Indeed, if one met George Foreman in a back alley, just coming on him suddenly, he was not a frightening figure. But if it were Sunny Foreman coming around a corner, just innocently, carrying a Bloomingdale's shopping bag with the head of a toy giraffe sticking out, and a giant box of Fanny Farmer chocolates under the other arm, the sight of him would still give one a considerable start.

When the Foreman entourage emerged from the lobby elevators, everyone gathered around to stare. Sometimes if a reporter was there a question would be thrown at him, but he always ignored it. We stood silently and looked over the circle of heads at the bandage over his eye; we looked down at his big dog. Once, I watched him standing in a corner of the lobby's gift shop, reading a comic book. On the cover, Superman was shown throwing a villain off a rocket ship; the villain's fedora remained firmly affixed to his head. "Superman's gone mad!" the man was shouting as he spread-eagled into space. "Instead of arresting me, he's killing me!" Foreman peered into the magazine's contents, his face as composed as a deacon's, as, all around, people jostled to peer at him.

"What's going on? What's going on?"

"The champ's reading," I heard someone say.

We solemnly watched Foreman pick up another comic book. This one was in French. Its cover showed a green monster coming out of a window of the Union Hotel, shouting, "Bientôt, je serai le maître du monde!"

One day a writer managed to get close enough to Foreman, and for some reason—probably he was so flustered that he had the chance—he asked him what he had been dreaming about. Foreman creased his brow and volunteered that a night or so before he'd had a rather complicated dream in which he was teaching a dog how to ice skate. In the lobby we all settled back in our wicker chairs to consider this. "Teaching a dog how to ice skate. *Hmmm.* A gin rickey, please." The most persuasive interpretation, offered by Larry Merchant, of the New York *Post,* was that it was a "grace envy" dream—that Foreman, manifesting his desire to be more like Ali and less of a bludgeoner, saw himself as an instructor in the art of being graceful.

"But why a dog? Why put ice skates on a dog?"

"Well, why not? Foreman's damn hung up on dogs. He communes with dogs. He looks into their eyes. Look at that damn wolf that pads along beside him. He's not going to dream about putting ice skates on his mother, for Chrissakes, or something like a sheep."

It turned out to be easier to talk to members of Foreman's entourage—at least to the people directly involved in preparing him for the fight: Dick Sadler, his peppery little manager, was always there in the lobby, perched up on an end table, his legs swinging back and forth, and carrying on with anyone who'd stop by. "I'm an indoor man. Barrelhouse piano man. You don't catch me messin' around with the outdoors. Elephants? You seen one elephant, you seen 'em all."

Archie Moore, my old friend, was there, to my delight. He and Sandy Saddler, the former welterweight champion, formed with Dick Sadler the same triumvirate which had guided Foreman to the crown in Jamaica. Moore moving through the lobby looked very wise and unflappable. Despite the African heat, he wore a heavy woolen cap with *Jamaica* stitched across it, and often a fireman's belt around his waist with an enormous steel belaying ring attached. Down by the swimming pool he played a very good if somewhat nonchalant brand of Ping-Pong, often the thumb of his free hand hooked in the suspenders of his bib overalls. He often played Foreman, giggling when he made a good shot and fanning himself with the paddle, which had a zebra decal stuck on the rubber. With him he carried a picnic basket—of the hamper variety, with a top that squeaked open on hinges. He would not let anyone look in his basket, which got everyone wondering what he *did* have in there; he was not fessing up. "I abstain from duffel bags," he told me. He went on to hint that he carried his "writing materials" in the basket. He *had*, I knew, produced some excellent prose from Africa about the upcoming fight. On Foreman's power: "Foreman has TNT in his mitts, and nuclearology as well. Even if he misses, the whoosh of air will lower the 90 degree temperature in Zaire very considerably." On Ali's palaver: "It had become time-worn, an act as thin as a Baltimore pimp's patent leather shoes." He produced a poem:

> Foreman's left will make you dance
> Turkey in the straw
> When his right connects with your mandible
> Goodbye jaw!

One of the more fanciful rumors was that he carried around raw meat in his hamper for Foreman to chew on—cuts from wild animals—buffalo, lion. "Not at all true," Moore told me one afternoon. "It is not as important to eat wild-animal meat as it is to watch them fight."

I asked him what he meant.

"To study tactics," Archie went on, "a man should always watch an animal fight. I'd love to see wild dogs—great fighters—take on a lion who could take out a couple of them with a single swipe of his paw and see how those dogs handle him. Every fighter should, once in his life, watch a pit-bull fight. I had a pit-bull once called KO and someone came around once and said they had a dog who was better. They said, 'Let's put the two dogs down in the basement of Mallory's liquor store and let the winner come out.' I said, 'No, let's put them in the yard so's we can watch.' My dog went for the other's leg, the elbow, the other dog for my dog's throat ... for three seconds we could hear the gritting of bone and then my dog went from the elbow to the other's throat. Big scream and that was the end of the business."

He saw me looking a little squeamish and he said, "A pit-bull'll only fight another dog. Don't like horses much. They love children."

As for Muhammad Ali, he stayed up in N'Sele during the

postponement, but occasionally he put in an appearance at the Inter-Continental, usually for a press conference. They were always well attended. He had two translators on hand to put his words into French for the local press. The two men worked in relays. At the first conference I attended I noticed them wrestling over the microphone as Ali began talking, struggling over it as if competing for the honor of putting his words into French—a dubious wish since the quick spurts of rhetoric, hyperbole, verse, hosannahs, would tax the most expert of the United Nations translating staff. One of them finally wrested the microphone from the other, who stood off to one side and listened with a bemused expression until his companion had disgraced himself sufficiently for him to snatch the microphone and try it himself, starting with great relish and enthusiasm which, however, subsided into tentative smiles of bewilderment.

Ali's rhetoric was up to snuff, though I noticed that the officials had apparently persuaded him that "a rumble in the jungle"—a hype phrase he had been using back in the U.S.—was not in the best promotional interests of a country on the move; he had been asked to drop it, along with his threat that his African friends were going to put Foreman in a pot. But there was much else—his vocal performance studded with fine flights of hyperbole: he had taken a quantum leap from his familiar "I am the greatest" on to "I am an era!" and splendidly on to "I am an *epoch!*" He looked out at us and told the Zairian translators to tell everyone that he was so fast that the night before, when he cut the light switch on the wall, he was in bed before the room was dark. He said that if he got any better, he'd be scared of himself. (That line he had remembered from Jack Johnson, apparently.) There were others: "I'm so fast, I hit before God got the news." "'Gainst me, I'd druther take a chance on shaving a wild lion with a dull razor." The French translators struggled manfully.

Of course, Bundini was at hand, always at his side at the conference, nodding, and calling out "Right!" or "That's tellin' 'em, Champ!" He had brought his wife with him to Africa. He

had married a second time—an attractive white girl he called
Mama. Sometimes when she was off shopping in the ivory
market he would have some rum drinks at the hotel. He carried
on. "The oldest thing in the world," he shouted at me one
afternoon down by the swimming pool, "is Africa, a hound dog,
and either a black man or a Chinaman. One time I saw a
Chinaman and I was curious about who was the oldest in the
world. So I went up to him and I leaned down—he wasn't one of
your big Chinamen—and I said, 'China-man! Am I *your* daddy,
or are you *my* daddy?' "

There was a pause, and I asked, "Well, what did he say,
Bundini?"

But he was off on another tack. "Daddy greased me in
Vaseline and he looked at the muscles of my stomach and he
said, 'Before you die you'll go all over the world and you'll be
rich.' I been called many names—Black Gator when I was a
small boy in Sanford, Florida, runnin' round in the white dust in
the backyards; and then Sailorboy in the Navy; and Fast Black
on the Harlem street. But now I'm the Black Prince, the
Archangel himself"—he pronounced it "art angel"—"and there
are only seven of us on the planet!"

I said that almost everyone in Kinshasa thought of him as a
witch doctor.

"I always was a witch doctor. You know that!" He was
incensed for some reason. "Goddamn, you *knew* that." His
nostrils flared and I thought he was about to break into tears.

He ordered a drink. His wife appeared at the far end of the
swimming pool. She saw his somewhat flamboyant condition and
turned away.

"Family and flies surround me," Bundini cried out.

Mrs. Clay, Ali's mother, was sitting with us. "Cut the noise
down, Bundini. It's a big racket."

"I'm ready to die now. Pin me to the cross," he ordered us
loudly. He threw his arms wide. "I am prepared to die. My
bones are hurting. You show no respect. That's why we have
hurricanes and storms and lightning cuts the houses to two and

the floods drown the cows and cover the fields and the fence posts—because you show no respect, because you disrespect your mother and daddy. *I* am your mother and daddy.

"You is no such thing, Lawd's sake, Bundini," Mrs. Clay said, rattling her bracelets. "You git along with you."

"Then I am Solomon!" Bundini cried out as people looked up from their deck chairs around the pool.

Bundini's counterpart in the Foreman camp was a tall black sparring partner of the champion's named Elmo Harrison, who was announced in the sparring sessions as the "Heavyweight Champion of Texas." Whenever Bundini would shout, "Float like a butterfly, sting like a bee!" or "Rumble, young man, rumble!" or "Ali, *boma yé!*"—the latter a rallying cry Ali had initiated, from the local Lingala dialect meaning "Ali, kill!"— Elmo Harrison would bestir himself and follow Bundini around the hotel, shouting through a white megaphone, "George the Eagle will fly/ Ali the Butterfly will die." In the final stages of the competition between the two (which the Foreman side won hands down by means of sheer volume) Harrison got himself a bullhorn to bellow through, a sudden and deafening noise in the hotel lobby, though in fact he kept at it so persistently, shouting, "Foreman, *boma yé!*" or "The flea will fall in three," with the hotel children following him around and repeating the cries after him, that the ruckus became acceptable after a while—as much a background noise to the premises as the ringing of the concierge's bell on his counter, or the pleasant tinkling of the temple-bell chimes as the message board was carried by.

Harrison's efforts notwithstanding, Muhammad Ali was obviously the more popular of the two fighters, not only around the hotel lobby but out in the country. Some felt that Foreman's big shepherd dog had something to do with his lack of favor; the Belgians had kept such dogs during their time in the Congo—as watchdogs at the end—and, driving around Kinshasa, I rarely saw even a mongrel.

But then suddenly Foreman made a big hit with the public at a huge ceremony at the Twentieth of May Stadium where the two were scheduled to fight, at which the facility was being dedicated to the Youth of the Nation. It was the sort of occasion usually made to order for Ali—the great oval packed with people aching to cheer Ali on and waiting to be led in his *boma yé* chant, perhaps including President Mobutu himself, who was on hand flanked by his general staff dressed in camouflage khaki.

About ten minutes into Mobutu's speech, which he delivered in French, the leader called the fighters down from their seats—first Foreman, who received a decent-enough cheer when he arrived at the president's chair and shook hands. Then Ali. He came shadowboxing his way down the aisle and when he reached Mobutu he leaned over his outstretched hand and kissed him, French style, on both cheeks. Pandemonium! A strange, high yell went up from around the stadium. Some people in the stands probably missed it and jogged their neighbor's elbow.

"What happened. D'ja see it?"

"Hell, he kissed Mobutu Sese Seko. Hell, *yes,* I saw it!"

During this Foreman stood off to one side of the president and looked glum. Could he have been inwardly kicking himself for not having thought of this kissing business first? Probably not. Foreman does not strike one as being concerned with that sort of gesture. But he must have decided that some action on his part was called for, because when Mobutu sent both fighters down to the track to take a triumphant tour of the stadium, Foreman was suddenly inspired to remove his brown jacket and reveal his bare chest.

A great roar went up. Foreman flexed his enormous muscles and held them aloft. Another roar. His chest shone in the heat. He began his tour. Foreman's public-relations man, Bill Caplan, was beside himself—his client, who had been as phlegmatic and as difficult to promote as a three-toed sloth, suddenly now as audience-conscious as a song-and-dance man: he paraded around the circular running track with his arms up, and every time he pumped his fists into the air, the roars came down from the seats, the people standing and shouting "Fore*man!* Fore-*man!*" and Caplan, running backward in front of the bare-chested fighter, kept calling out to him, "Beautiful, beautiful, George, give it to them!"

Ali, up in his seat, took all this in—the effect of it, everyone craning to see, and the cheering—and realizing he could do no worse himself, he stood up abruptly from his seat and began to remove *his* shirt. But the theatricality of the gesture was considerably blunted not only by the timing (being second to Foreman) but by the annoyance of a shirt button at the wrist which he could not get undone: his shirt half off, his chest muscles shining in the sun, he tugged at the shirtsleeve busily; someone reached a hand in and tried to unbutton it for him; he swayed back and forth; from afar he seemed to be struggling with a spectator who had picked this curious moment to challenge him at arm wrestling.

Afterward I rode back to N'Sele in Muhammad Ali's bus. He was petulant, not so much because he was upstaged by Foreman's tour around the stadium but because during President Mobutu's subsequent speech someone had been holding a black umbrella over Foreman's head to protect him from the sun. Ali had an umbrella, too, but he was holding it himself, which he apparently felt demeaned him.

"Do you think anyone noticed?" he asked.

His camp was confused. "What's that, Champ?"

"The umbrella. That business with the umbrellas. Why wasn't someone holding *my* umbrella?"

He looked around and saw the puzzled looks on his people.

"You was asleep," someone said.

"Only for a time," Ali protested.

I had not seen it, but apparently Ali, along with his umbrella, had swayed alarmingly forward onto the back of the man seated in front of him.

Ali yawned enormously, like a child, as if remembering the heat and the slow drone of the words he could not understand and how sleepy it made him. The thought of Foreman, though, continued to bother him. "Foreman, *boma yé,*" he said softly. "Foreman, *boma yé* . . . no, it doesn't sound right. It don't sound right at all," he said, brightening up. "The people are still for Ali."

*   *   *

The next day, the American ambassador came to the hotel and he was asked where *he* stood.

"Who do you like in the fight, Mr. Ambassador?"

The American ambassador knit his brows. "You may quote me as saying that a fine black American will win the fight."

The reporters poised their pencils above their pads and stared at him.

"That's right," he said.

A journalist I took to be from one of the European countries leaned forward and asked, "Aren't you sorry for sentencing Ali to jail for those three years?"

The ambassador looked confused. "Who . . . me?" he asked.

19

Some of the correspondents had stayed on through the postponement—the "old hands"—and the experience seemed to affect them as it might Conradian characters bogged down too long in a strange culture. They stalked about like colonial planters, their khaki clothes, bought so long ago at Abercrombie and Fitch, hanging off them in folds. Their conversation tended to be abrupt, as if to concentrate on a whole sentence or a complete thought were too difficult, or perhaps boring, so that listeners were stuck with a few cryptic sentences, an occasional Lingala word thrown in, often punctuated with a sharp, disconcerting guffaw. Hunter Thompson had a theory that collectively these correspondents had found a grand Medicine Man who kept them supplied with various pills and concoctions. One of them was Bill Cardoza, who was in Zaire for *New Times;* he had stayed through the postponement. He was certainly a pepped-up character. "There are great stories here," he shouted at me. "I'm told there's a house somewhere in town that's full of pygmies. I don't want to go in there. I just want to lie in front of the house and watch them go in and out." He scarcely paused for breath.

"Yesterday I heard about a cobra in town. Not far away. He lives near a sewer and from time to time he puts his head up and looks around. I'm thinking of including a good look at him as one of the requirements in an Easter-egg scavenger hunt we're going to have. I'll give a hint. There are twenty-eight zones in this city and he is in Zone Limba! Right. M'Bele!"

Cardoza and Thompson talked in an odd pidgin English they had developed: "He very m'Bele. He okay. Very, very m'Bele." Cardoza said that his English had disintegrated, since his arrival back in September, into an amalgam of Lingala, French, and English, plus a little Portuguese in deference to his own blood (he has a sharp face with a mole on one cheek), and his and Thompson's behavior around town was almost as puzzling as their language. In the bars Hunter signed a number of his checks "Martin Bormann" and Cardoza signed his "Pottstown Batal Bogas"—a name he had made up for an imaginary football team. Occasionally, Cardoza would lean forward and grasp two black miniature hands hanging from a thin gold chain around Hunter's neck and shake them at people in the bars. He introduced Thompson as Chief N'Doke from the Foreman camp—"Big Doctore." Thompson let himself be pushed around by his small, agile friend, his necklace shaken at people; he seemed very abstracted. It was often apparent he had Martin Bormann on his mind. He felt the Nazi criminal was hiding in Brazzaville, across the river; he talked of renting a plane to fly over there and roust him out.

The true sportswriters hung around the lobby. Some of them did not like the assignment at all. Dick Young, the columnist from the New York *Daily News*—well, if you get within earshot of him he would be saying, "Johnny Bench hit two home runs and knocked in six" … information he had picked up from a three-day-old *Paris Herald* box score, or maybe from a phone call to the States, just plain homesick he was and not liking anything about Kinshasa, and I had the sense of him hanging around the lobby wearing his snappy hat with its shaving-brush decoration, wishing he were in the Pfister Hotel in Milwaukee with a couple of hours to spend before the visiting Yankees left the hotel for batting practice. When he got back to the U.S. from Zaire, he wrote in his column that he "kissed the ground" to be where such things as Johnny Bench's run-producing feats were going on. The complaints were constant. The most interesting one I heard was that one reporter, from the UPI, had filed his story to his home office over a Teletype only to discover that it had been received by the Teletype machine in the Pan-American Plastics Corporation, in Forest Hills, New York.

The sportswriters' corps was expanded by a number of war correspondents—far more controlled about things—from various countries. Perhaps their home offices felt that a wild place like Zaire required that sort of representation. The war correspondents were bored. They sat together at the café tables. They went together in the cars going out to the stadium, where they sat in a row and watched the Zairians working on the rain canopy over the ring. They gossiped in the sun. What one sensed about them was their self-sufficiency, the assumption that nothing would happen which would surprise them very much; they talked about Cam Ne and Da Nang and Khe Sanh and Phu Bai, and the other Southeast Asian places, with nostalgia and with a certain anticipation about the redoubts in the Sinai, where most of them felt they were going to spend a considerable time in the coming decade. The place names of these war zones were dropped with a suburbanite's ease—familiar spots just down the road and around the corner. By and by, their stories became touched with violence and the grisly things they had seen—and here too there was a sense of smugness and disassociation, perhaps because as observers they were never able to step in and stop what was going on, or even caption their photographs or write dispatches which suggested their feelings: thus they assumed a somewhat lofty attitude, as if they were Sunday visitors at a zoo, looking in on odd comportments behind the bars.

They also talked about Angola, to the south. It was possible that their next theater of excitement would be there. The situation was beginning to get serious. Indeed, Kinshasa was reputed to be a marshaling place for mercenaries being infiltrated across Angola's northern border. There were rumors about

Mad Mike Hoare ... that the legendary mercenary leader who had fought in Zaire for the Belgians was about to come out of retirement and leave his home in a place called Kloof, South Africa, and lead a mercenary band in Angola.

One of the correspondents told a story about Hoare—that on one occasion he had been asked to sit with three other officers in judgment of a white mercenary who had raped and murdered a Congolese girl. The soldier had shot her on the end of a dock leading out into the Congo, and then dropped her in. The prisoner was brought before the officers. The evidence was irrefutable. The mercenary's only defense was that he was a family man and a good citizen back in Germany, where he had been a professional soccer player.... *That* was what he was truly best at and wanted to get back to. He didn't like the look of his judges and he was led from the room crying.

With his admission of guilt the four officers' only function was to determine what penalty he should receive. They decided that each officer should write down his suggested sentence on a sheet of paper; the proposer of whatever sentence was agreed upon would then be responsible for carrying it out. The officers worked on their papers, and then handed them in to Hoare as if finishing an examination at school. He opened them. The first paper recommended that the prisoner be removed to the same dock where he had taken the girl, then shot and dropped into the Congo, just as he had done with his victim. The second suggested that a few lashes with a cat-o'-nine-tails would suffice, along with a dishonorable discharge.

The third officer (as the war correspondent pointed out) told more about himself than about the penalty he recommended. He too thought the prisoner should be executed, but he refused to have anything to do with carrying out the sentence: not conscionable to shoot another white man in Africa. No, he recommended that the prisoner be given a pistol with one bullet and "told to commit suicide." He himself would sit out on the veranda of the Hôtel des Chutes (one imagined) having tea and waiting for the pop of some distant gun. "Ah, *there* we are."

The last paper was Mike Hoare's own. In it he suggested a

"punishment worse than death"—which was to take the prisoner down to the river and shoot the big toe off each foot, thus immobilizing him as a soccer player.

His fellow officers on the tribunal heard him read this and looked at him with astonishment: "Splendid. Jolly good. Bully for you, Michael!"

They took the prisoner down to the dock and Hoare did the deed with his Colt pistol. Later on, actually, a higher providence prevailed—the war correspondent remembered—when the victim was killed in the crash of an airplane carrying mercenaries out of the bush.

The absolute champion at this sort of lugubrious story-telling was Horst Faas, a Pulitzer Prize-winning Associated Press war photographer. He had a round, somewhat cherubic face, and whatever dire horror he was offering, it came accompanied by a boyish smile. He reminded me of the man of "indeterminate nationality" who attempts to make conversation with Rosemary in the first pages of *Tender Is the Night:* "I say—they have sharks out behind the raft. . . . Yesterday they devoured two British sailors from the flotte at Golfe Juan." Faas' stories were similarly appalling, but he was at his happiest telling them. At the café table he would lean forward, cough slightly, and remark, "Say, that reminds me . . ." and we would wince slightly, knowing that we were in for it. Perhaps he was inured to such horrors because he had seen these things through the lens of a camera and was removed from them by his apparatus. They were no more actual to him than the images on a screen in a theater. But what he had seen through his viewfinder was certainly fresh and vivid in his mind, described with the relish of a teenager recounting the best parts of a horror film. He told us about his Pulitzer Prize photographs of the Bangladesh killings—four young Bengalis just picked out of the prison yards where they had been put for being drunk and insulting a girl on the day the Pakistanis had fled. They could not have imagined for a minute what was going to happen to them—oh, perhaps a bit of pummeling for their indiscretions as they were hurried out to a dusty soccer field outside of town, a lot of people standing around, and they were thrown down, hands tied; oh, perhaps a little lashing at their backsides, pants at their knees, and they'd be let go, hopping off, pulling their pants up, and everybody hee-hawing behind them; even when it started, the four never truly believed it, even when one looked over and saw another lose an ear to a knife; they kept jabbering away and telling their torturers that they were truly sorry, it was just high spirits and the girl ... and a nose would go, and a cigarette in an eye; and then finally after an hour and a half of this chipping away, an officer with a bayonet on the end of a gun stood over them one by one and slid his weapon in, the crowd cheering each time, as if a good punch were being thrown in a prizefight ... all of this described by Faas with a somewhat sly grin, as if what was being disclosed was a schoolboy prank.

I remember his photographs—hard to forget if you ever saw them ... the arch of a dying man into the bayonet blade, so that the page of the magazine itself (they appeared in *Life)* seemed to give off just the most infinitesimal squeak of sound ... which I had the sense that if magnified would expand into that frightful miasma of sound from the soccer field.

It took very little to trigger reminiscences of this sort from Faas. One evening a group of us were sitting in the street café of the Palace Hotel, a big ramshackle structure down on the river with only its restaurant functioning. We were talking about crowds (most of us having spent the afternoon with Ali and having seen the great press of people for him, the marketplace stalls going over and spilling the tribal masks out into the crowd, a wood crate of chickens broken open) and I found myself telling how in Miami for the Ali-Liston fight I had been pushed by a big band of teenage girls against the side of a large Cadillac limousine which had the four Beatles inside. It was at the height of the group's popularity; many of the girls trying to push past me to see were carrying drumsticks to honor Ringo Starr. They leaned over me and beat them in a furious *rat-tat-tat* salute on the roof of the limousine. Inside, it must have sounded like a hailstorm. I was shoved up flat against the car, my nose pressed against the glass window. I couldn't budge. Inside I could see the four Beatles. Two of them were sitting up on jump seats. Because of the press of bodies blocking out the noontime light, it was quite dark in there. Just then the limousine started to inch forward and the rear tire ran slowly over my foot. I opened up my mouth and let out a considerable squawk of pain and dismay. I kept it up. The car moved so slowly that I thought they had parked it on me. I was only two inches away from Paul McCartney, just the glass between us, his face slowly beginning to slide by again, and I remember the slightly puzzled look—quite possibly so for looking out at the sight of a grown man with his mouth murderously ajar, the pain showing in his eyes—and yet he could have had no idea what was wrong, what was going on below, with the tire on my foot. He could only have assumed that I was an inordinately possessed Beatles' fan. I told this, and the people at the table laughed.

Faas cleared his throat. We all looked down the table at him aghast. He began talking about Nehru's funeral, in New Delhi in 1964—the huge crush of people trying to get close to the leader's house, so grief-stricken that a day or so later, when they finally had cleared away, they had left two hundred corpses up against the fences and the concertina wire. Whew!

Well, that left my foot story pretty small potatoes. It was like Faas to do that.

He wasn't finished. "That reminds me . . ." he said. We all cringed and squeaked our chairs. "In Saigon they had the execution of a Chinese businessman. He had gouged the public . . . pushed up the price of rice . . . and so to make an example of him they tied him up to a post in downtown Saigon surrounded by a ring of concertina barbed wire. I covered it for the Associated Press. He was dressed up in a dark suit and a tie. He was to be eliminated at four A.M. Somehow the authorities thought it would be a nice gesture if they brought his children around to see him off. There were nine of them!—and they hopped down off the truck that collected them and they ran for their father in that dim light *smack* into that concertina wire . . . and they got stuck in it, yelling and carrying on, while the preparations were being carried out."

He leaned back with his gentle smile.

"Lord Almighty, Horst."

He arched his eyebrows as if surprised at our reactions. Sometimes his stories had a type of piquant beauty to them—his description of the SAMS rising up over the Israeli desert, the thin quick trails behind the rockets, the planes diving straight down to avoid them, perhaps through a whole raft of SAMS going up, and it was grand to watch, Horst said, because it was all so clear against the desert sky and easy to understand. He had a writer's eye for the appeal of contrast. He talked about the columnist Joe Alsop sitting in the bucket seat of a helicopter in Vietnam during a particularly heavy engagement, the aircraft buffeting about, and reading a book in Chinese on Oriental vases. Or how right here in Zaire in 1967 they hanged four tribal chiefs in Kinshasa's Place de la Révolution—a dereliction of the Bantu (which is what they call the tribal code)—so that everyone involved was scared of what they were doing, especially when a small tornado came through town and picked up a spiral of bright red bougainvillea flowers, a column high up over the houses, and everyone thought it was a sign, however striking, of the worst sort.

But then after this sort of black lyricism he would clear his throat and he would tell us about the people in Yemen getting their hands or arms chopped off on a block for various crimes, making very little noise about it until the cauterizing took place with the red-hot irons, and someone would say, "Oh, for God's sake, Horst."

I guess he didn't surprise the war correspondents. His little bureau in Saigon was noted for the blowups, stuck on the walls of his office, of photographs too gruesome to be accepted by the home offices—heads floating down the Mekong, pictures of the Chinaman in his suit and tie and the children yelling on the wire, and things like that. He had made a remark in his broken English then (it is now perfect) which they all knew and quoted: "Oh, the war, I like it, *boom boom!*"

I hopped in his car when he was driving out to N'Sele. "Do you want some company?" He would nod. I was never much company. I listened. I looked back and stared at his cameras resting on the backseat, thinking of the images that the shutter had opened up to let in—these perfectly outlined rectangular *guignols.*

At dinner I'd sneak a look at his eyes. I always expected to see something there. Once, I asked him, "Did you ... *er, ah* ... ever try to intercede ... I mean to try to *stop* any of those things?" (I suppose I was thinking once again of my vague guilt at not having helped Ali enough.)

He said, "My function is not to make judgments. I am there for the Associated Press. Or for Magnum."

He did not have much to do in Kinshasa. But when George Foreman got gashed above the eye by his sparring partner's brow, Faas was there, right on hand for as much gore as he could expect out of such a relatively peaceful assignment; it must have seemed like "ol' home week" (as someone said laconically).

I occasionally spotted Faas moving swiftly through a hotel lobby with loosely wrapped packages under his arms. He was spending his spare time cornering the market on tribal voodoo dolls, which didn't really surprise anyone. He was very assiduous about his collection, scouring the market stalls for them, and his room in the Memling Hotel was stiff with them; the dolls crowded the corner, and they lay in stacks under his bed. A woman photographer on assignment for an Italian magazine went up there for a drink and said that though she and Horst were alone in the room, she had the sense—all those wooden fetish figurines staring out into the room from cowrie-shell eyes—of being at a bizarre cocktail party: she found herself speaking abnormally loudly.

Faas was very courtly. He didn't tell her any horror stories. His only reference to the Indochinese battle zones, she told us, was to tell her how often he had seen huge butterflies there.

The most idiosyncratic journalist on hand in Kinshasa was Hunter Thompson, who had been on hand to cover the fight for *Rolling Stone.* I had always felt a close relationship with Thompson, for though he was called a "gonzo" journalist for his personalized reportage *(Fear and Loathing in Las Vegas)* I had always thought of him as a participatory journalist, especially for his extraordinary book *Hell's Angels,* in which he joined a motorcycle clan, much in the spirit with which I had joined the Detroit Lions, except that the motorcyclists turned out to be extremely disagreeable company, beating him up, finally, and quite severely.

I had met him on the plane coming down from Europe. He had arrived on board at Frankfurt—a big, loose-limbed figure wearing a pair of dark aviator sunglasses, a purple and strawberry Acapulco shirt, bluejeans, and a pair of Chuck Taylor All-Star basketball sneakers that seemed too large for his feet, as if he had snatched them from the back of a Los Angeles Laker's locker. They took him this way and that, sashaying him around so that he bumped into people a lot. With him he carried a large leather flight bag with a *Rolling Stone* identification decal and a badge which read PRESS; he referred to it sometimes as his "purse" and often as his "kit"—full of pills and phials and bottles, judging from the way it clinked when he moved it. He carried a very expensive tape recorder, and also a portable radio set, a German model which he had bought on impulse the day before—military onyx, very fancy—and which he said could receive twenty-seven stations including WBSP in Spokane, Washington. "I can tell you a white sale is going on in Liberty's or some such shop down on Green Street—big news in Spokane," he said to me. "It came through clear as a bell. It's going on tomorrow, Tuesday, if you want to do anything about it."

He sat with me during the flight. He said he was trying to recover from a humiliating evening back in the States a few nights before when, lecturing at Duke University, he had been given the hook for being outlandishly drunk on Wild Turkey bourbon and making a fool of himself in front of a large and muttering audience. The representative who met him at the airport had offered him some hashish. He had taken it. Back in the motel he felt the day begin to slip away. He poured himself a couple of shots of Wild Turkey. He kept his audience waiting for forty-five minutes. When he walked out with his glass in front of a large velvet curtain in the university auditorium, he got himself in a further state of belligerency with the crowd by starting off, "I'm very happy to be here at the alma mater of Richard Nixon."

"That did not exactly put them in my pocket," Thompson told me. "He went to the law school there, which they were either trying to forget or were proud of, and my telling them that truly stiffened them up. The questions began. They asked me if I thought Terry Sanford was going to run for the presidency in 1976. I said that he had been party to the stop-McGovern movement and that he was a worthless pig-fucker. I didn't realize that he was the president of Duke. Not long after I was given the 'hook.' "

The "hook" had been a small blond girl sent out by the head of the lecture committee; when Thompson saw her coming, he tossed the Wild Turkey, along with the ice cubes, high in the air, a fountain of resignation, and he walked off with her. He said that the booze had fetched up against the velvet curtain behind his head and left a noticeable stain that he hoped was still there . . . to backdrop future speakers as they leaned solemnly against the lectern. Especially when Terry Sanford spoke to the student body. He asked me if I thought he was going to get paid.

"I don't know," I said. I asked how long had he been out there on the stage before the hook arrived? He couldn't remember. "Did I say it was Duke?" he asked.

"Yes," I said.

"Well, I *think* it was Duke."

He said that after his removal he had gone out into the parking lot and had talked to a circle of students in a pool of light under a neon standard, but he wondered if that was sufficient representation of his role as a lecturer. He usually read his lecture contracts very carefully. On one occasion he had been asked to lecture in Miami, but he noticed that proviso number seven of the contract stipulated that if the lecturer was under the influence of alcohol, all agreements were off. Hunter told me that he had not gone to Miami.

In Kinshasa I rarely saw Thompson. He never turned up at the press conferences or sparring sessions. But he always seemed very busy—mysterious missions, looking this way and that through his big aviator glasses as he rushed through the lobby of the Hotel Inter-Continental, and one half expected him to raise a finger to his lips to warn us to keep mum. He walked along with his toes cocked out at an angle, moving along at a jack-rabbity, somewhat zig-zag clip, not unlike the bouncy lope of Jacques Tati, the French comedian of *Monsieur Hulot* distinction. He seemed incapable of taking a small step, so that if he happened to come up to say hello, he would take one last big sideways step to keep from crashing into you. Walking somewhere with him was difficult—his feet carrying him off at the oblique one minute, *bang* into you the next—and it was quite easy to trip over him. Since he wore sneakers, all this backing and filling and sashaying and bobbing and weaving was carried on in cat-burglar silence—which lent considerably to the conspiratorial aura which he affected.

His focus of interest was never on the upcoming fight, so far as I could see; and almost out of perversity he scorned those single-minded reporters who talked shop and gossiped about what had happened that day in the two fighters' camps. "They're blind," he said. He told me that he had "tested" one small group standing in the lobby of the Inter-Continental by leaning into their conversation and telling them he had uncovered a tremendous *news* story—to hell with the fight. He told them that he had snuck into the Republic of the Congo, across the Zaire, the night before and had discovered that the Congolese were working on some huge device down by the water, a sort of *torpedo,* he thought it was, damn near half the length of a football field, and it was his opinion that they were going to point this thing at Zaire and *put-put* it across the river and blow a great hole in the waterfront section of Kinshasa. "They turned away, mumbling," Thompson said of the group he had buttonholed.

"No kidding," I said.

Then he would be gone, rushing off on some strange self-imposed quest.

Any time spent with Hunter Thompson seemed to generate its

own carnival lunacy, especially when he was with Ralph Steadman, his cartoonist cohort who was with him in Zaire and who
served to pep things up and inspire a corporate rather than an
individual madness. Once, I got Hunter seated and reminiscing
(God knows where Steadman was!) at the outside bar of the
Inter-Continental (he sat under a sun-sheltering thatched roof
drinking Planter's Punch, which he thought appropriate to the
colonial atmosphere of the hotel), and he began telling me about
the time he and Steadman were sent to cover the America's Cup
yacht races at Newport, Rhode Island, the year the Australian
twelve-meter *Gretel* raced against *Intrepid*—I can't imagine what
sort of report their editor expected to come out of it—and the
decorum and dignity of that occasion with the blazers with the
yacht club insignias and the gray flannels and the pipes and so
forth prompted a flagrant counterreaction on the part of Thompson and Steadman. The two of them "borrowed" a rowboat and
with Hunter at the oars set out across the harbor late at night
toward the *Gretel* at her berth. Aboard they had an aerosol can
of black paint. Their intent was to range up along the *Gretel* and
paint "Fuck the Pope" on her sides.

"We planned it quite carefully," Hunter told me. "We were
truly inspired by the thought of that yacht setting out the next
morning for the trials without anyone noticing, so that it would
appear in Narragansett Bay in front of the vast spectator fleet
with those terrible words brandished like a seagoing advertisement, for Chrissakes, and these little yachts would dart out of
the spectator fleet, and the skippers' faces red with rage under
their braided yachting caps, and they'd point and sputter, and
yell against the wind, before falling away as if they were too
affronted by the message to stay close. The great thing," Hunter
continued, "was that being up on the deck, *no one on board the
Gretel would know what the hell the matter was.* They would look
at each other, knowing that something was wrong, and they'd
check the rigging, and someone would say, 'Do you suppose it's
the spinnaker pole *lift,* or something, they're trying to tell us
about?' and they'd check *it* out, and there'd be a lot of shrugging
of shoulders under the wet-weather gear while all the time those

awful three words were being carried along through the seas on the sides of that long white knife. . . ."

"Well, of course," I said. "But what—"

"We were truly prepared," Hunter told me. "In the rowboat that night I even had these parachute flares along—cost me six dollars apiece—to shoot up and create a diversion if we needed one. Our idea was that if something went wrong, we'd shoot off a flare and the guys on board the *Gretel*'d look up; 'Jesus, what the hell's going on, *look* at that thing!' and in the confusion we'd finish painting our message and clear off."

The adventure turned out to be traumatic from the start. Thompson was not especially adept with oars, and on the way to the *Gretel*, ahead in the darkness, they spun around a bit in the harbor, everything deathly still out there, the black water with not a ripple on it, so that the oarlocks, the crack of oars against the hull as Thompson caught a crab, the "whoop" from Steadman as the rowboat lurched under him echoed (Thompson said) across the bay "like gunshots."

Somehow they got to the lee of the *Gretel*, shipping oars and gliding up to her as she lay alongside the wharf. Hunter was entranced by the great white expanse of the twelve-meter's flanks in front of him—"I felt like Gully Jimson." He reached for the aerosol can and handed it to Steadman, who was, after all, the artist of the two.

"Well, right from the start we had our troubles," Hunter told me. "First of all, those aerosol cans have these steel ball bearings in there to stir up the paint, and they clatter when you shake the can up to get it operative. Not only that, but it makes a kind of hissing sound when the plunger is pressed down to apply the paint. Well, as soon as Ralph shook the can, things began to happen. Maybe they knew we were coming ... overheard our planning, which we had done in a number of bars quite loudly that week. All around lights went on. A couple of jeeps parked on the wharf turned on their headlights. Guys with flashlights began to move around on the deck of the *Gretel*. Time for a diversion. I set off a parachute flare. It went right up past the nose of the guy who'd just happened to peek over the rail and look down at us ... *whoosh*, within a foot of him going up, and then it popped open above the *Gretel* and began swaying. It lit up the whole scene. There was enough illumination, what with the flare and the jeep headlights and the rest of it, to read the instructions on the damn aerosol can. We had to pull out. I don't remember that Steadman ever got even an *F* of his slogan on the side of the *Gretel*. He was very badly upset—the frustrated artist, spaced out and all, and the excitement made a heavy reaction on the both of us. We abandoned the rowboat and fled along the streets. One of us left a pair of shoes in the boat. We had to get out of that town. We couldn't even go back to the hotel to get our stuff. We argued about the shoes—Steadman said they were his. I suggested he buy a pair the next day. He said it was Sunday. Then I told him I had an important appointment in New York the next morning, which was true, and it was more important for me to wear the shoes than him. Besides, I told him with great sincerity that many New Yorkers went barefoot in the summer, no one would notice when he got there, even in the evening, if he wanted to go out to the theater, or the Empire Room at the Plaza. It was quite common to see guys who were shoeless. How would he know? He was English. I told him the fastidious ones wore black socks. Perhaps he didn't believe me, but by that time I had the shoes on my feet. He couldn't dispute that. He didn't even ask for *one*. He gave up."

Thompson finished off his Planter's Punch with a noisy pull on the straw. He stood up and walked out by the pool, where he gazed up at a small biplane, barely moving against a wind coming down from the north across the Zaire; it was towing a long sign sweeping behind it which read ASHIMA, advertising, apparently, a local travel agency. Thompson gazed at the sight with longing. "I wonder," he mused when he came back to the table, "if I could get a sign made. Some local guy. Quick-order job." He told us that the message he wished to have hauled across the skies of Kinshasa was to read: BLACK IS WEIRD.

Norman Mailer talked about Hunter Thompson somewhat disparagingly. He felt the Thompson constituency was too easy to please. It was like playing tennis without a net. Thompson's readers were not interested in the event at all—whether it was the Super Bowl, or politics, or a championship fight in Zaire—but only in how the event affected their author. So, in fact, the only reporting Thompson had to do was about himself: the more he disdained the fight and stayed around poolside bombed and absorbed by his own peculiar paranoias (as long as he could remember them and get them down on paper), the better his readers liked it.

Mailer was in Kinshasa to cover the story in his more straightforward, if inimitable, style. I could never see him in town, covering the same event as I, without wanting to snap the top back on my felt pen and flop my notebook shut. I glanced at his notebook (often we sat together at the press conferences or the sparring sessions), which had the most childlike, illegible scrawl helter-skelter on the pages, little pips and whirls, as messy as the smudge of a thumb, page after page, because he worked very hard on these assignments, and with an intensity that I felt was stoked by his knowing two hundred other journalists were on hand challenging him.

His competitiveness! I had known him for years and marveled at it. It consumed him. The oddest and most touching instance of it—at least that I ever saw—had happened in a venue in startling contrast to central Africa: at a country party arranged by Drue Heinz for her husband, Jack, the head of the Heinz empire, for his fifty-seventh birthday on a chilly spring night in Bedford Village, New York. To honor the parity of her husband's years and the number of varieties of Heinz products, his wife had gone to considerable trouble. Everyone was supposed to come in costume appropriate to the year the host was born. A lot of people wore boaters and white flannels. I remember how cold and clear the night was. Down on the lawn among the apple and dogwood trees behind the house, the midway of a fair had been set up—a merry-go-round with a bandstand in the middle, and a ferris wheel, and a row of concession booths lit with lanterns, where guests could have their palms read or throw baseballs at wooden milk bottles, and there was even a shimmy dancer "from Egypt" and a stage with a red velvet curtain for her to go behind. The concession that particularly attracted Mailer was a strength-testing machine—a tall column rising up twenty-five feet or so, lit by an overhead light, so that the length of it glowed in the night, and it was worked by banging a big mallet-headed sledgehammer against a flat trigger device which sent a plunger up its runners toward a fire-alarm bell at the top. Levels were marked off to indicate how strong the wielder of the hammer was—a perfect blow would send the disc roaring up past MR. PIPSQUEAK, MR. HEN PECKED, MR. AVERAGE, MR. BIG SHOT, MR. MUSCLES, on up to SUPERMAN! which was synonymous with hitting the alarm bell. *Clang!* Very satisfying indeed. Many of the guests tried it. I remember Charles Addams, the *New Yorker* cartoonist, rang the alarm bell with his first swipe, and everyone clapped. Then Mailer stepped up. I've forgotten what Addams was wearing for a costume, but Mailer had got himself up in a frock coat, pantaloons, and shoes with silver buckles on them; he wore a pair of small spectacles with square rims and it was apparent that he wished to be taken for Benjamin Franklin. He hadn't realized he was supposed to dress circa 1910. He looked very benign. He hefted the sledgehammer. With a little grunt of effort he brought it down on the trigger pan; the disc flew up three quarters of the length and stopped just a bit above MR. AVERAGE MAN and quite a bit below MR. BIG SHOT; the little crowd went, "Oh."

Mailer toiled at the machine most of the night, trying to clang the bell—going off to rest after a while, but then irresistibly drawn to it once again, a curious sight in his Ben Franklin specs, and the black prayer-meeting frock coat, his body swaying back, the hammer poised, then down, and the disc would fly up just about to the spot where it had when he had first tried it. Sometimes a knot of people would collect behind him in their strange costumes, one a girl in a hen's head with russet feathers, and encourage him; he had become one of the more or less permanent sights on the midway, along with the shimmy lady "from Egypt"; but they left him, sad because the disc would never seem to get any higher, and indeed as the night wore on and he got tired, it began to sag toward MR. HEN PECKED. Most of the time I remember him alone, the frock coat off sometimes, and he swung the mallet in a fancy ruffled white shirt that shone in the light like a moth's wings; you could see him through the trees and hear the thunk of the hammer.

Since that time much had happened to him, trauma on trauma, but in Africa I had never seen Mailer in such a relaxed mood and at ease with himself, which always meant that he was splendid company. I remember being slightly surprised because he had spoken of the country as Hemingway's territory, which was going to require him to be on his mettle.

I could never think of the two writers without thinking of the competitive streak in both which was so apparent, and without wondering, with a certain amount of despair, if such intensity was a necessary adjunct to one's craft. They had never met, though it had been close. I remember once when Hemingway was passing through New York, he called up and asked if I would like to join their party for dinner; Miss Mary and George Brown would be there, and A. E. Hotchner, and Antonio Ordoñez, the great bullfighter who was seeing the U.S. for the first time, and Hemingway said they were going to begin by showing him the Colony restaurant, which was perhaps not a genuine U. S. landmark but a good enough place to start from.

I said that I had arranged a dinner with a girl named Joan that evening and he broke in and said, "Fine, fine, bring her along." He sounded in great form. Yes, that would be fine indeed. I never had a chance to explain that we were supposed to meet Mailer later.

But I brought it up when we met before dinner at Willie Hearst's pied-à-terre at the top of a brownstone on Sixty-third Street off Fifth Avenue. Hemingway stood in front of a big marble fireplace, looking at Joan, the girl I'd brought, perhaps deciding whether to call her "Daughter," which was his particular term of affection for girls he liked. I said that Mailer was in town; I knew he'd always wanted to meet Hemingway ... perhaps this would be a good time. "He'd be delighted to join us. He's expecting to hear."

Hemingway was interested. "Well, yes. You call him." But Hotchner—who perhaps then was beginning to note the suggestions of paranoia, the dips of the decline, that would eventually appear in *Papa Hemingway*—had overheard. He came up and shook his head; apparently he felt the mix wouldn't work, and he was quite solemn and rather worried about it. "Well, I'm not sure, Papa," he said. He sounded like someone counseling against having another drink. "No, really, I don't think so."

"Oh, well, forget it."

But Hemingway kept bringing up Mailer's name throughout the evening. We arrived at the Colony carrying our own wine in brown paper bags because it was election night and the bars were shut down until the polls closed. In deference to the Colony's rule about coats and ties, Hemingway wore a sportcoat, a pair of khaki safari trousers, and I remember a plain woolen tie knotted hugely at his throat. There was a lot of excitement at the door; the management was honored. Hemingway picked out a table in the back of the restaurant next to the swinging doors to the kitchen, and he settled himself with his back up against the wall so he could look out at what was going on: a "good *querencia*," as he put it—the bullfight term for the area in the ring the bull repairs to, and fights best out of—and besides, he said he felt comfortable with the waiters coming by, and the clatter of the kitchen so close at hand. It was in fact the worst spot in the house and there was quite a lot of fluttery concern on the part of the captain who seated us there. Tables had to be pushed together; extra chairs had to be provided. Joan was settled in on Hemingway's right; I sat on his left. The waiters stared at Hemingway from under the weight of their dishes, as they went by, and the chefs, in their hats, peered at him through the diamond-shaped panes in the swinging doors.

Almost immediately he began asking about Mailer. I found myself telling him about the "contests" that Mailer at that time seemed to engage in with near manic intensity; there was hardly a social occasion at which he did not challenge someone to a confrontation of some sort. With females, he involved them in a staring contest—in which he and the person opposite stared into each other's eyes until one or the other gave way. Mailer always seemed to win, the girls never knowing quite how to react, usually glancing away out of embarrassment, or because they were bored and wanted a fruit punch, or more often simply from giggling. As for Norman, I supposed he did it to establish his dominance, like Mowgli staring down Shere Khan, and he apparently got a lot of satisfaction out of it. At cocktail parties it was not an uncommon tableau to see his somewhat chunky figure, legs slightly akimbo, a drink in one hand, swaying slightly as he engaged in this sort of ocular showdown with the girl opposite.

"For Chrissakes," Hemingway said.

With males, I went on quickly, the confrontation was much more spectacular. The most physically awesome was a knock-the-heads contest, in which he and his opponent stood opposite, perhaps five feet apart and, at a signal, came together like a pair of rams fighting during the rutting season, bopping each other with the crown of the skull—harmless, apparently, but producing a booming sound, like a pair of gourds *thonked* together—an alarming sound to hear at a cocktail party, especially if one of them had been knocked to the floor among the chair legs. Big banging sound, and then a groan.

"Hmmm," Hemingway said. He reached down and pulled the wine bottle from the paper sack by his chair.

The one who had been knocked down would get up, shake his head, and the two of them—absolutely oblivious of what was going on around them—would go at it again. In fact, the guests got rather accustomed to it—as if what they had in the midst of their party was a bizarre piece of sculpture by Tinguely that had parts, and a motor to work them, so that if people arrived late and saw the two of them coming together with the *thonk* of the heads, and asked, "My God, what's that?" the response could indeed be, "What? Oh, that ... well, that's our . . ."—you know, very blasé about it.

Of course, not many people played this game with Mailer. I had been asked, but declined. Of course, there were other contests, quite a bit of arm wrestling, but Mailer's favorite *mano a mano* at the time of my dinner with Hemingway was thumb wrestling—in which the contestant grasped the other's hand so that the two thumbs faced each other on top of the two interlocked fists; the idea at the word *go* was to try to pin the other thumb down for three seconds. The thumbs wave around a lot like snails' antennae. Mailer was pretty good at it. There was a period of time when he got his friends doing little else, sitting around bars or after dinner, and one woke up in the morning with the thumb so sore from exercise that it was hard to handle a fork at breakfast.

"How do you do it?" Hemingway suddenly asked. "What do you have to do?"

I showed him—our hands clasped over the tablecloth, elbows between the wineglasses, and his thumb began to weave back and forth. But it moved very slowly and awkwardly, and I could see that he was going to be bad at it; someone told me later that his hand had been crippled in some long-past accident.

So Hemingway, who himself could see that his thumb was outclassed and was mumbling under his breath about it, swiftly changed the rules of the game, simplifying it considerably to a purer test of strength: now let's just see who can squeeze the other's hand hardest. All of this was done without explanation: he simply began to apply pressure. His grip was enormous, quite belying the relative passivity of that thumb of his. I could feel his nails bite into the palm of my hand. His arm trembled from the force flowing through it, and I could see his face begin to mottle under the white of his whiskers. I looked at him blankly, quite terrified. There was nothing I could do: I could not detach myself from Hemingway's grip.

Then under the table George Brown began to kick at my shins. He told me later that he had seen what was going on and was trying to get me to stop—Hemingway was no person to get involved in duels of this sort; it got his adrenaline going and often built up into the kinds of punch-outs Brown had seen enough of down at the *finca* in Cuba.

He began to kick quite hard, and I stiffened abruptly a few times in my chair, jolted, my eyes widening in surprise, a reaction which Hemingway must have assumed was related to the power of his grip. He was encouraged. He increased his efforts. The table jiggled; ice cubes *chinked* in their glasses.

I do not know what this would have escalated to had not Joan, sitting on Hemingway's right, leaned over and said, "Say, what's going on?"

Hemingway turned his head. She was an uncommonly pretty girl, with blond hair that framed a wide Scandinavian-boned head with big intelligent eyes in it. She was looking at him with such genuine curiosity—as if puzzled by some sort of rite which she did not understand—that Hemingway responded.

His grip relaxed. "We're just horsing around," he said. He flexed his fingers. He went on. "We're pretending we're a pair of Norman Mailers."

"Oh," she said. She seemed perfectly satisfied. She turned back to Hotchner, or Ordoñez—whoever was on her right—and picked up where she had left off.

But the spell had been broken; Hemingway was affable enough after that. He talked of his admiration for Mailer, though he wasn't so sure about the parlor games. When I got a chance, I glanced at my hand under the table; there were purple half moons where his nails had gone in, deep enough to last for five days afterward. . . .

I looked at them from time to time. I mentioned them on occasion. I was having dinner with a girl I thought might be impressed. She was telling me about a ritzy weekend she had spent somewhere. "Everything there was *flambé*. My God, you'd come down for breakfast and there'd be this sizzling sound and sure enough, coming through the pantry door, the something being carried in on a flambé platter was a grapefruit, for Chrissakes."

"Have you ever read *The Sun Also Rises*?"

"What?"

"Take a look at this hand of mine. You see these marks here?"

"Where?"

"Right here. In the palm of my hand."

"Are you talking about your life line or something?"

"No, I mean these little half-moon things. Wait a minute. Let me hold them up to the light."

I could not see them myself. I turned my hand in the candlelight but they had vanished. The girl, after a puzzled look at me, had hastened on to talk about something else. I remember looking at my hand a few times afterward just to be sure, but the marks had truly gone.

Norman Mailer never met Hemingway. He had stayed by a phone most of the night Hemingway was in town, waiting for my call—both scared and excited (he told me afterward) and then both disappointed and even a bit relieved when the call never came through. He had an idea that it would have been like visiting a South American dictator—not that Hemingway behaved like one, but there would have been a considerable entourage: Ordoñez and George Brown and Ingrid Bergman and some other famous friends—and the meeting would have been unnerving and perhaps difficult. He had a feeling Hemingway would have been pretty mad at him. "I had been impertinent," he said.

I wondered. Hemingway always seemed very polite to people at first, especially those he had admiration for, however grudgingly.

"I would have gone anyway," Mailer said. "Of course, we know that he was a man of many moods. I would have been 'Mister Streak' to get up there. I was dying to meet him."

"What would you have talked about?" I asked.

"After a while I probably would have criticized him for not being in the country when we needed him—spending so much time out of it when we were slipping into totalitarianism. What seemed to concern him were insignificant private preoccupations that bored the hell out of us ... the feuds between his friends Leonard Lyons and Walter Winchell. I would have said, 'Stop perfuming your vanity, get your hands dirty; we're tired of you and your little hurts ...' The sort of criticisms I had made in *Advertisements for Myself.*"

" 'Perfuming his vanity.' Well, that would have been a hell of an evening," I remarked.

"Oh, I think so," Norman said.

20

Almost every day the ritual for the writers was to take the morning run up to N'Sele in the press bus to watch the workouts. The ride took a good three quarters of an hour—the first part of it in the heavy traffic of Kinshasa, the bus mired among the smooth car roofs of the Mercedes and the Fiats, everyone in his seat squinting his eyes in the bright sunlight reflected off the cars and off the white building facades—and then finally the bus was expelled from the traffic quite quickly, like a squeezed peach pit, and we moved freely on the highway past the stadium with the tall cranelike light standards at each corner, and we thought of the work on the ring going on in there and what was coming up the following week—the bus creaking in the quiet—and then finally there was the relief of the open country, the brown hills to the east and the warm African wind washing in the open windows.

A Chinese pagoda gate stood at the main entrance of N'Sele. The complex had been developed by the Chinese nationalists. It was an odd place—enormous, built for the pleasure of government officials—and it was comparatively deserted. Loudspeakers murmured—songs, and marches, occasionally, and often what I took to be political rhetoric. Subjected to this were the inhabitants of a small zoo. What was supposed to be the biggest swimming pool in Africa was at N'Sele, but I never saw anyone in it. Also, I was told, the continent's largest supermarket was in the complex somewhere. It had fifty check-out counters, and bore the grand, if somewhat ironic, name "Tembe na Tembe" (the Elephant of Elephants). But the customers were few and hesitant, perhaps because of the prices: a bottle of Belgian hair spray cost fifteen dollars.

The training ring was set up in the middle of a large bare-floored auditorium which was painted light green and had orange curtains at the windows. A number of blue-nosed fans, twenty-four of them to be exact, were installed high on the ceiling and trembled lightly as they revolved. There were chairs at ringside, and a raised stage at one end of the room for which the spectators, almost all Zairians, paid the equivalent of a dollar to occupy. The stage was invariably choked with people.

I sat down in front with Murray Goodman, who was in charge of keeping the press corps happy. He is a portly gentleman with not much of a neck, and around the fight crowd in the old days he was not only nicknamed Lou Costello but was often mistaken for the comedian. Once, in a Syracuse night club, Goodman gave away his necktie to someone who thought he *was* Costello and who wanted a keepsake, a gracious act Murray has regretted ever since. "I don't know what got into me," Goodman told me. "I had to be soused. I think of that tie a lot."

Up in the ring Ali was sparring with Bossman Jones. "A real fine pro," Goodman was saying. "But he's not got too much of the killer in him. Before the Foreman-Norton fight in Caracas I tried to get him a match with Pete 'Moleman' Williams for twenty-five hundred dollars to 'be on the underneath'—which is what we say for fighting a preliminary bout on the card. He wouldn't go for it at that price because he said Moleman was his friend. It would take at least five thousand for them to forget they were friends."

At the end of the round Bossman came and stood above us

against the ropes. He puffed his mouthpiece, a bright pink color, out on the shelf of his lower lip in order to breathe more easily; his dark eyes looked out over the audience. He rested his gloves on the top ropes. When time was called for the next round, his lips groped forward and gathered in his mouthpiece; his jaw muscles moved as he settled it back into his bite, and he turned and shuffled across the ring to where Ali was waiting for him on the ropes.

"That guy could have been the light-heavyweight champion of the world," Goodman said about him. "But he'd rather make a living being a sparring partner. In fifteen years he has not been marked once. Take a look."

When I pointed out some rather obvious scars (to me his visage seemed as crisscrossed as the brow of a sperm whale), Goodman admitted yes, the Bossman had a "couple of good marks," but they had nothing to do with boxing.

"Knives?" I asked.

"How he picked up those marks is his own personal business," Goodman said.

Up in the ring Bossman was working rather perfunctorily, leaning on Ali, who was relaxed against the ropes, and occasionally thumping his employer alongside his rib cage.

"How much does he get for that?" I asked.

"Sparring partners get paid from fifty to two hundred fifty dollars a day," Goodman said. "Back in the good old days they got five hundred, but of course the money situation was different then. Still, the Bossman up there has got a pretty cushy job. Ali doesn't pester his sparring partners. Most other camps they take a pounding. Joe Frazier beats up his people; Bob Foster'd break a guy's ribs in camp; Rocky Marciano murdered them, he truly did. Ali doesn't do that—he just toys with them. He doesn't even bother to tag them once in a while to show them they're fighters."

"The Bossman. That's an interesting name," I said.

"There've been some good ones," Goodman said. He mentioned a few: Danny "Bang Bang" Womber; Willie "The Worm" Munroe. I interrupted to say that I had met the Worm and had always wondered if he accepted his name gracefully. Some of the names got fixed before the owners could complain. I recalled that the so-called Dixie Kid, a turn-of-the-century welterweight, had been born in Missouri and was never quite sure himself why he had been given such a nickname. The Zulu Kid, who was the first U.S. flyweight champion, was not a black or from South Africa but was an Italian raised in New York.

"*He* might have been uncomfortable at times," Goodman said, "but I never heard the Worm complain. D'ja know that Ezzard Charles was called the Cincinnati Cobra?" he asked. "Well, that's so, but after a while he got slapped around some and he stopped being a 'cobra' and then he moved out of Cincinnati and that was the end of *that* moniker."

At Ali's workouts we often had to speak quite loudly over a background of thumping drums provided by a huge musician who looked as if he had stepped out of a football front four— Danny Big Black, he was called. He had prepared a special Ali war beat for his conga drums, a beat he told me he had adapted into a 6/8 structure from the war-chant rhythms of the Yurba tribe in Nigeria.

"Oh, yes," I had said, impressed.

"The tribes get into a very heavy consistent bag with their drums," Danny Big told me. "When they're getting themselves ready for warring, they play the drums for thirty days straight, all through the night, and even when they set down at the table to eat. Muhammad Ali was very impressed when I told him this, and we thought maybe I could call in some local people to help out and we'd slam away at the drums, day and night, right up to fight time, like we was a tribe going to war. But after four or five hours of those drums, particularly playing them in the villa, and during mealtimes, everybody got a little glazed in the eyes and the champion said it made him yawn a lot."

I mentioned this to Murray. Everybody gossiped about promotions—it was an inevitable topic at an Ali fight, since he was such an expert at it. "Ah, yes, war drums, but there were others in the promotion game made Ali take a backseat," somebody said. "You should've seen Tony Galento punch the light bag smoking a cigar. He brought out the guys. He boxed a kangaroo once. He boxed a bear."

"Didn't he box an octopus?" asked a writer.

"Of *course* he did. In a tank they moved outside a Seattle restaurant where they had the thing on display. Tony got in the tank and waded around, pushing at the octopus, who scared the crap out of him with a squirt of ink. Galento didn't know an octopus could do anything like that, and he clambered out and wouldn't get back in. He thought it was poison gas, like mustard gas in the war. The octopus died two days later, I got told, and they had it stuffed and put up on the wall in the restaurant. They got a sign under it, the same sign they had on the tank when the octopus was alive, except they got the LIVE scratched out. Now it just reads OCTOPUS. They should have put on the sign that it was kayoed by Galento in the first. Tony wading around in a tank would kayo anything in there with him, I'm guaranteeing you, put it right into a coma."

Another writer leaned forward. "You guys heard of Don Fraser? Talk about fighters and animals! He's a California fight publicist who once took a fighter named Lauro 'The Lion' Salus out to a jungle habitat and rented a goddamn lion for four hundred fifty dollars for Lauro to stand beside for some publicity photographs. Lauro put on his trunks and a pair of gloves. They guided him up next to the lion, who everybody thought was very docile and toothless, which turned out to be a big error, because the lion took a liking to the leathery smell of the boxing gloves and fastened a set of goddamn substantial teeth into one of them...." He told us that Lauro "The Lion" Salus had managed to skin his fist out, to leave the glove hanging from the lion's lip like a morsel of food.

When the workouts were over, some of the writers would wander over to the villas along the Zaire—Ali's was one of them—and drop in to chat with Ali or Goodman or Angelo Dundee and tell fight stories to pass the time.

One afternoon Budd Schulberg and I dropped in on Angelo and he showed us his kit bag—the medical supplies he took with him to the corner to patch up his fighter if things were going badly. Sometimes in the ring there were rough injuries—Angelo called them "magnificent beauties"—that truly taxed the corner men. The "nose split" was the most frightening to see. In the Ezzard Charles–Rocky Marciano fight, the second one, Marciano's nose had been belted so hard that the flesh came away from the bone; you could actually see it. Schulberg and I winced and looked at the floor. Aw, the nose was simple to work on, Angelo assured us. Plug it up if it was hemorrhaging; tell the kid to spit the blood out. No problem. Just tell the kid to breathe through his mouth.

"There must be some strange—"

"Well, sure," said Angelo. "Flores Fernández, who was a real belter, broke Gene Fullmer's *elbow* in the thirteenth round of their fight in Utah. Nothing to be done about that. So Gene backpedaled from him, ran for three rounds, and, my God, he saved his crown."

He opened up the medicine bag.

"Now here are the salves and the pastes and the pills: tincture of myrrh for the lips; ananese pills (two every four hours) for swelling; abisthement subgalate powder over here, which is an antibiotic powder for dusting cuts. Now here are my special homemade salves for cuts—the base is Hydro Wolffat, very tangy and just right for a combined cleanser and coagulant. It comes in two shades—light for the white and dark for the black fighter—so that the paste doesn't make a target for the other guy.

"Of course, here are the obvious things: an ice bag; a pair of surgical scissors; gauze pads for wiping blood off (never use a towel); an extra pair of shoelaces; an extra mouthpiece for the fighter in case his opponent knocks the original out into the tenth row and somebody steps on it; smelling salts, fifteen or twenty of them, which come in felt containers and I get them in bulk from funeral parlors where people do a lot of fainting.

"When I go into the ring I keep the gauze pads and the Q-tips in my left shirt pocket. Some guys keep the Q-tips behind an ear, which I consider a filthy habit. I keep a vial of smelling salts behind my right ear, but that's not the same as Q-tips which you dab in a guy's cut. The reserve smelling salts and the absorbents

I keep in my right shirt pocket; all the coagulant powders and extra gauze I keep in my left hip pocket, and the liquid coagulants on my right hip, along with a pair of surgical scissors. I look fat at ringside."

He talked about his equipment much as Rat did in *The Wind in the Willows,* preparing the weapons for the assault on Toad Hall—everything just right, functional, laid out in his kit bag where he can get at it.

"Very neat," Schulberg observed.

"I put the caps back on the tubes, and if there's any extra tape from finishing up with Muhammad's hands, why, I roll it up into a little ball and pop it into my mouth to chew on during the fight.

"I have all that equipment in there and I know how to use it; and yet this one time in Miami, my daughter fell off her bike and cut her legs in the bicycle spokes. Do you think I ran in and got my kit? Hell no. I called the doctor on the phone."

Angelo talked about himself not only as a "surgeon" but also as an engineer and a psychologist. He defined his special brand of psychology as trying to get his fighter in the proper state of mind at the stiffest moment of adversity. He once looked at one of his fighters collapsed achingly on a stool, complaining that he couldn't feel anything in his legs at all—they were *numb*—and Angelo said, "That's a *very* good sign; it means that you're getting your second wind."

"Oh yeah," Angelo said. "I drop ice down their pants. I slap them on the insides of the thighs. The pat I give them on the rear end has produced a pretty good backhand." He demonstrated. "Not bad, eh? Nice form?"

We got to talking about sex and the fighter. I said that Hemingway had once told me that sex was considered so debilitating that oldtime trainers would fit a "ring" over the fighter's privates at night, so that if he began to get an erection and was in danger of having a wet dream, the pain from the ring would wake him up and the trainer would rush in to throw a pail of cold water over him.

Angelo snorted, but Schulberg said he remembered from his

research for *The Harder They Fall* that Primo Carnera's handlers made him wear a rubber band at night for just that reason.

"Didn't do much good," Angelo remarked. "They could've put *eight* rubber bands on Carnera and he never would've been no fighter."

"How much time do you ask your fighters to lay off?" I asked.

"Ten days to two weeks," Angelo said cheerily. "It's not the act itself—natural things don't harm anyone—but it's the chasing it, and the wine, and the late hours. I tell them to do the right thing ... they're grown-up. It's really a question of getting them mentally ready ... just so they spend a good time concentrating on the fight bit."

Schulberg was saying that one of the theories was that deprivation of sex triggered up the fighter and made him more ferocious.

Angelo sighed. "Theories," he said. He remembered that Leonard Schecter, the writer, had told Willie Pastrano at the height of his career in Angelo's stable that he had it on good authority from long-distance runners that a lot of sexual activity made them "lighter" and improved their performance. To Angelo's despair, Pastrano accepted this notion just before his challenge of Jose Torres for the light-heavyweight championship, and fooled around with such savage enthusiasm right up until the fight that he got knocked out in the third round.

"So you think sex *was* responsible."

"Well, it didn't help," Angelo said.

I wondered aloud what Muhammad Ali was doing about the problem. There were rumors about a marital scrap. In Salt Lake City he had met a girl, Veronica, who had now come to Africa. Ali's wife, Belinda, had taken considerable exception to this and, being a karate expert, had supposedly chopped her husband up a bit; a small scratchlike cut had appeared on Ali's cheek. Not only that: Belinda was wearing a large George Foreman button.

Angelo said, "I don't mess with anyone's personal life. He's the one in the ring who's going to be taking the shots ... one guy against one guy, the moment of truth, and he's responsible for himself. Maybe you can fool around just before a fight, but you can't have any misgivings about it. That's what's so great about Muhammad. He doesn't let anything bother him. A guy like Pastrano'll shake his head in the ring and moan about what he's done the night before—kicking himself—but Muhammad doesn't do that. He has the greatest attitude of any fighter who ever lived."

"Lucky for you, Angelo" I said. "Otherwise, you'd have to bring out the bag of rubber bands."

Angelo laughed. "What are you doing to me here? It's terrible to think of a trainer as nothing but a penis holder."

Still on the subject of sex, he told us that afternoon about a boxer from his hometown of Miami who had turned small-time pimp. He was not very good at it, apparently, or especially enterprising, because he only had one girl in his stable, whom he supplied to a small circle of regulars. But then he fell in love with her, and he could not adjust to the idea of her having been with these men: he finally found the mental picture of her with them so devastating that he went systematically to each of his former clients, turning up at their doors and bursting in and roughing them up. The clients would answer the door, grinning, and then step forward with a hand outstretched—"Good to see you, Vince ... got something for me ... eh?" and all of a sudden *bop!* He was so furious at one of his victims that he told him he was coming back the next day to beat him up again. Sure enough, he turned up, but this time the guy was waiting for the fighter with a gun, and he shot him twice in the chest as he came through the door. The fighter languished for a few days in the hospital and then died.

Budd Schulberg was absorbed by Angelo's story. He asked me afterward, as we stood outside the villas, "I don't supp-upp-uppose"—he stammers slightly—"you would mind if I w-w-w-wrote up that story—the one A-A-A-Angelo told us about the p-p-p-pimp."

I said of course not, it was his, and later, as the evening was coming on, the steel flatness of the Zaire beginning to show streaks of orange as the sun dropped to the horizon, I saw Schulberg wandering toward me up the balustrade along the river bank, meandering from one side of the walk to the other, obviously lost in thought as he approached. I could see his lips moving. He started when he saw me, and blushed; he said that he had been working on Dundee's story in his mind: he saw the dying fighter in the hospital telling his roommate about his rampage of jealousy—a flashback technique—and I only had time to tell him it seemed an interesting way to do it when he ambled off into the dusk, murmuring, rocking from side to side, as punchy-looking in the throes of creation as an oldtime fighter.

Down the line some of Ali's people were betting on which hyacinth clump out on the river would cross an imaginary finish line first, the murmur of the voices rising from the balustrade walk—"Hey, man, you're switching clumps on me.... That's my clump with the branch ... yours is that flat mother"—but then the sun would begin to fall into the low hills of the Republic of the Congo, across the water, the voices would die away, and everyone would lean on the stone balustrade and watch the sheetmetal expanse of the great river reflect the sun's red disk just briefly before the gray of the evening settled down; it always came so quickly, and with it a small chill, not a wind, but a temperature drop, and then the lightning from the cloudheads that studded the horizon would begin to flicker more sharply.

21

We all poked around for stories. Norman Mailer went out running with Muhammad Ali one morning. He asked me to go with him, but I thought of the long ride to N'Sele in the darkness, and thumping along for five miles or so in the wake of the challenger, and besides, I had done that sort of thing before with Joe Frazier. So I begged off. I said I didn't have any equipment to run in.

We came in very late from the gambling casinos—around three in the morning—and Mailer was just coming through the lobby on his way out to his car. He had sneakers on, and long athletic socks rolled up over the legs of what was probably a track suit but of a woolly texture that made it look more like a union suit, so that as he came through the lobby Norman gave the appearance of a hotel guest forced to evacuate his room in his underwear because of fire: the impression was heightened by the fact that he was carrying a toilet kit.

Immediately, I was sorry I had not accepted his invitation. Why had I not jumped at the chance to go out there to run with these two men? Something would surely happen that would have made it worth my while.

That night Mailer and I had dinner and he told me what had happened. He had kept up with Ali for a couple of miles into the country upriver from the compound at N'Sele, but then he had begun to tire, and finally he stopped, his chest heaving, and he watched Ali disappear into the night with his sparring partners. In the east, over the hills, the African night was beginning to give way to the first streaks of dawn, but it was still very dark. Suddenly, and seemingly so close that it made him start, came the reverberating roar of a lion, an unmistakable coughing, grunting sound that seemed to come from all sides—just as one had read it did in Hemingway or Ruark—and Norman turned and set out for the distant lights of N'Sele at a hasty clip. He told me he had been instantly provided with a substantial "second wind" and he found himself moving along much quicker than during his outbound trip. He reached N'Sele safely, jogging by the dark compounds, exhilarated not only by his escape but by the irresistible thought of how highly dramatic it would have been if he hadn't made it.

I asked him what he was talking about, and he grinned shyly and began to admit that once he had got to the sanctuary of the compound he had been quite taken by the fancy of being finished off right there by the lion ... all in all not a bad way to go, if one *had* to go, certainly a dramatic death right up there with the more memorable of the litterateurs'—Saint-Exupéry's or Shelley's or Rupert Brooke's—and the thought crossed his mind what an enviable last line for the biographical notes in the big dun-colored high-school anthologies: that Norman Mailer had been killed by an African lion near the banks of the Zaire in his fifty-first year.

Well, his fancy had all come to dross, he went on, because Muhammad Ali had returned from his run, his villa crowded with his people, and Norman had not been able to resist revealing the incident of the lion. It was greeted first with silence, everybody looking at him, and then the laughter started, first giggles, then hard thigh-slapping whoops, because they had all heard the lion, too, and heard him just about every morning, because that lion was behind bars in the presidential compound, a zoo lion—there weren't any lions in the wild in West Africa anyway—and the thought of Norman's eyes staring into the darkness, and his legs pumping in his union-suit track clothes to get himself out of there ("Feets, do your stuff") was so rich that Bundini finally asked him to tell them about it all over again. "Nawmin, tell us 'bout the big *lion!*"

It was interesting listening to Norman talk about this—quite shyly and not without self-mockery, and yet with a curious wistfulness. He told me that the other fancy of this sort which he could remember involved a whale he had seen swimming through a regatta off Provincetown, Massachusetts—very impressive sight—and he thought *that* would not be a bad obituary note either: "Taken by a whale off Cape Cod in his fifty-first year." Hemingway? Melville? He couldn't make up his mind.

Later that evening, in the bar at the Inter-Continental, I found myself talking to an Englishwoman who described herself as a "free-lance poet." She was hitchhiking her way up the west coast of Africa. I thought of her standing in a dusty African road in the darkness of the early dawn, and I mentioned Mailer's fantasy. "Consumed by a lion? What on earth for?" she asked. "I can't imagine anything worse. The *breath!*" Her eyes widened, as if she had suddenly seen an image, and she said that *she* thought—if one had to "shuffle off"—it would be terrific to be electrocuted while playing a bass guitar in a rock group.

"Oh, yes," I said.

"I think it happens quite often," she told me. She had an idea that rock groups which flickered into vague prominence, with a hit record perhaps, and were not heard of again were actually victims of electrocution. "In Alabama in the summer, that's when it happens," she said. "In an open-air concert in a meadow outside of town where they've built a big stage of pine, and the quick summer storms come through, or the local electricians aren't the best, and all of a sudden *zip!*—the top guitarist of the Four Nuts, or the Wild Hens, or whatever, *glows* briefly up there on the stage, his hair standing up like an old-fashioned shaving brush, and he's gone."

"Zip?"

"Zip," she said. "I'm practically tone deaf and I can't play a *thing*, but that's how I'd like to shuffle off . . . all those faces out there in the darkness, and the rhythm just pounding all around . . ."

She suddenly asked me how I saw myself "shuffling off." I had an awkward time telling her, my standard fantasy coming from an innocent time when I thought of death as a very attractive *pose* people got into when they had performed a great heroic—brave soldiers lying in graceful attitudes in the poppy fields, their rifles beside them—and since at that time the most important deeds I thought to be associated with sports, I usually saw myself "shuffling off"—as she put it—in Yankee Stadium . . . sometimes as a batter beaned by a villainous man with a beard, occasionally as an outfielder running into the monuments that once stood in deep center field . . . a slight crumpled figure against the grass. The fantasy had not changed that much—still that thirteen-year-old whiz center fielder, *bong!* lying out there and the crowd rising. Quite unoriginal.

"You're right," the poet said. "Boring. I've changed my mind, incidentally, about mine," she went on. "I don't want to be electrocuted at all. What on earth could I have been thinking of?" She announced that she wanted to be raped to death by an ape.

I did not see her around the hotel after that. She had no interest in the fight at all, and though it was just a day or so away, she would not have stayed for it. But I made some notes about her death fantasies. And about Norman's, of course. As I did so, it occurred to me that writers traditionally *do* seem to come to dramatic ends themselves, as if they deserved the same ironic or bizarre conclusions they so often gave the characters in their books. The Russian writers were especially good at death: Tolstoy, packing his knapsack and setting off from home on that last strange journey of his that ended up at the railroad station at Astapovo, where he died in the stationmaster's room; or Gogol, with the leeches on his great nose, the bishops filing slowly by, as he lay thinking how he could destroy all extant copies of *Dead Souls;* or Chekhov, packed in a box labeled

OYSTERS, being transported back home on a bed of ice from the Black Forest, where he had died.

It was not only the manner in which certain writers died that was interesting; often they managed to push out a memorable last word or two which seemed too studied even to put into fiction: Goethe's "More light!" or Henry James' "Ah, it is here, that distinguished thing." Or Oscar Wilde: "I am dying beyond my means." Some of the words which one would like to have overheard were lost, of course. Aeschylus must have had a final comment on being conked by the turtle which an eagle, trying to break it on the rocks below for a meal, dropped on the dramatist's bald pate. In my notes I imagined Aeschylus regaining consciousness briefly:

"What happened?"

"Well, sire, you were hit on top of the head."

"By what? It felt awful."

"A turtle."

Then the memorable phrase must have come, just a faint, unheard murmur, before the dramatist's eyes clouded over.

When I got back to the U.S., I told some literary friends about Norman's lion. Most of them felt it was a very disagreeable conclusion. Kurt Vonnegut told me he thought Mailer must have been crazy to pick anything like that—the rip of claws, that huge cat breath. Then John Updike wrote me a letter in which he urged me to look up what Livingstone had written in his African memoirs about being attacked by a lion; he remembered that the experience had been quoted by Darwin "to mitigate his frightful thesis of universal and continual carnage, in which the explorer describes the curious numbness that overcame him when he found himself in the mouth of a lion (who let him drop, I forget why)."

I looked it up: The lion that caught Livingstone—as one might have expected—was one he had wounded. While he was ramming a pair of bullets down the barrels of his flintlock weapon the lion sprung out at him from behind a small bush and caught him by the shoulder. "Growling horribly close to my ear," Livingstone wrote, "he shook me as a terrier dog does a rat. The shock produced a stupor similar to that which seems to be felt by a mouse after the first shake of the cat. It caused a sort of dreaminess, in which there was no sense of pain nor feeling of terror, though I was quite conscious of all that was happening. It was like what patients partially under the influence of chloroform describe, who see all the operation, but feel not the knife. This singular condition was not the result of any mental process. The shake annihilated fear, and allowed no sense of horror in looking around at the beast. This peculiar state is probably produced in all animals killed by the carnivores, and, if so, is a merciful provision by our benevolent Creator for lessening the pain of death. Turning around to relieve myself of the weight, as he had one paw on the back of my head, I saw his eyes directed at Mebalwe, who was trying to shoot him at a distance of ten or fifteen yards. His gun, a flint one, missed fire in both barrels; the lion immediately left me and, attacking Mebalwe, bit his thigh. Another man, whose life I had saved before, after he had been tossed by a buffalo, attempted to spear the lion while he was biting Mebalwe. He left Mebalwe and caught this man by the shoulder, but at that moment the bullets he had received took effect, and he fell down dead. The whole was the work of a few moments."

The details—the peacefulness described—were reassuring. It was not such an awful finale for Mailer to have pictured after all. I sent him a copy of the Livingstone material along with a note. Certainly such an end weighed favorably against his other fancy—death by whale—which would have been dark, the sound of water sloshing about . . . abysmally foreign.

The subject stuck to my mind. I asked friends at dinner—"Ahem . . . I'm collecting deaths," I'd say, as if I were pinning moths to a collecting board. In the libraries I looked into the back stretches of biographies. My notes grew. What a variety! Robert Alan Aurthur, who wrote a very lively column for *Esquire* at the time, leaned across the wineglasses one night and said that the subject of death so often recalled for him a vignette at the assassination of Sitting Bull—that the old chief had a stallion named Gray Ghost which he rode in Bill Cody's Wild

West Show and which had been trained to rear up prettily at the sound of a gunshot and dance on his hind hooves, and that when Sitting Bull was gunned down by Indian police there was a great stirring in the yard, and they looked over to see the horse responding to his cue, his great height, and the front legs pawing at the air.

I told someone at another dinner about Sitting Bull's horse, and he said "oh, yes" in a very arch way, and mentioned Gérard de Nerval's raven. When I looked puzzled, he said, "Nerval, of course, was the nineteenth-century exotic—you'll remember him as the one who walked the lobster in the gardens of the Palais-Royal (he had it on a pale-blue ribbon leash) and when asked about this he said he preferred lobsters to dogs because they didn't bark and they knew the secrets of the deep."

"I remember about him," I said truthfully. "But I don't remember anything about his raven."

"Well, Nerval hanged himself on a winter night with an apron string he thought was the queen of Sheba's garter," my informant said. "He had taken to carrying it around with him in his meanderings through Paris; he tied it through the bars of a grating in a stone staircase near the Place du Châtelet. The police discovered him hanging from it, with a raven capering around him repeating the only words it had been taught by its owner: *'J'ai soif.'* 'I'm thirsty.' Terrific scene. *'J'ai soif.'* "

"Oh, yes," I said.

Other scenes were quieter, but no less appropriate. John Cheever told me about the death of E. E. Cummings. It was September, a very hot day, and Cummings was out cutting kindling in the backyard where he lived in New Hampshire. His wife, Marian, looked out the window and asked, "Cummings, isn't it frightfully hot to be chopping wood?" He said, "I'm going to stop now, but I'm going to sharpen the ax before I put it up, dear." I wrote the scene down on the back of an envelope. Cheever looked at me oddly, and I told him I was making a collection. "I see," he said. "Well, those were his last words." I told him how grateful I was.

I went after others. I worried vaguely about myself ... this steady preoccupation, but it did not seem to deter me. I called an editor at *Harper's* magazine whose name is Timothy Dickinson. He would have much to offer. One of his functions at the magazine is to be asked questions; he is a tremendous source of knowledge, a sort of living house encyclopedia. One can drop in at his office and ask him what he knows about Holstein's great work on the army ant, and it will be an hour before one is able to escape. I had first been astonished by him when he began telling me more about my forebears—in particular, a Civil War general named Adelbert Ames—than I knew myself. He speaks in quick explosions of verbiage, often shifting from one language to another, lacing himself on with "Think, Dickinson, *think!*" as he takes one back with him into fine labyrinthine areas of arcane knowledge. He looks like an overgrown schoolboy from the English public-school system—which indeed produced him—with his black morning coat and trousers (I have never seen him in anything else), a white boutonniere to brighten the ensemble, along with a watch-chain running across his vestcoat. He carries a silver-knobbed cane with him everywhere, even indoors, and when he stands and talks, he keeps it tucked away under one arm like a swagger stick. People behind him at cocktail parties get poked. He was great company, though I always came away from him keenly aware of the empty stretches in my brain, knowing that if his was a cluttered *bibliothèque*-like vaulted chamber with balconies, great banks of volumes rising up, mine suffered badly in comparison—a broom closet off a corridor, a can of paint up on a shelf.

But it was always worth the intimidation. When I reached Timothy to ask him if he could supply me with some interesting artistic persons' deaths or last words—such as Goethe's "More light!"—I heard him clear his throat delicately on the other end of the phone. "Well, Goethe *might* have said, 'More light!' Very likely indeed. But it was probably a penultimate request: his *very* last words were almost surely 'Little wife, give me your little paw.'"

"Oh, yes."

" '*Weibchen, gib' mir doch deine kleine Tatze.*' "

"Yes, of course."

"He kept hopping out of bed in his nightgown to assure himself that he was still alive. Quite undignified. Teddy Roosevelt said, 'Put *out* the light!' but I don't suppose he's literary enough for you. It's true, isn't it, that the literary find distinctive ends. Pushkin was killed in a duel. Ambrose Bierce simply vanished, didn't he? And so did Villon. So many of them drowned, of course ... they seemed to have a *thirst* for it ... Shelley, Virginia Woolf, Hart Crane, John Berryman. Then we have Verhaever—the Dutch poet who always wrote about railroad trains, and sure enough, he perished under one, fell under a locomotive in 1916."

"He's not a poet whose work ..." I started to admit.

Dickinson was hurrying on. "Naturally, we have Brune, the rather obscure French dramatist who became better known as a marshal in the military ... *lynched* he was, and at the end he had the presence to complain, 'To live through a hundred battles, and to die hanging from a lantern in Provence.' Let's see. Think, Dickinson, *think!* Well, Gibbon, of course, said, 'All is dark and doubtful.' And then we have those mysterious words of Thoreau: 'Moose! ... Indians!' Claudel's, of course: *'Docteur, croyez-vous que c'est le saucisson?'* Samuel Butler asked, 'Have you the checkbook, Alfred?'"

I thought to interrupt and ask who Alfred was, but I stopped myself, realizing that Timothy would probably know, and we would get sidetracked for a time.

"... Chesterfield, of course ... great gentleman to the end. A friend was invited into the bed chamber, and Chesterfield murmured with his final breath, 'Give Dayrell a chair....'"

I couldn't resist testing him. Who might Dayrell be?

"The Swiss scholar ... one of the great Geneva family of Dayrells." I could hear Timothy snap his fingers next. "I have some more. I have always liked Lope de Vega, the Spanish dramatist, who called in his friends around his bed. 'Am I really dying?' he asked. 'All right, then, I'll say it. Dante makes me *sick.*' Aubrey Beardsley hoped to leave with a clean house: 'I am imploring you,' he said. 'Burn all the indecent poems and drawings.' Lytton Strachey said, 'If this is dying, I don't think much of it.' There were other complainers. Oliver Goldsmith was asked, 'Is your mind at ease?' 'No, it is not,' he said quite briskly, and died. Jonathan Swift complained, 'I am dying like a poisoned rat in a hole.' Then, of course, there were those much more comfortable with the situation. Hazlitt exclaimed, 'Well, it's been a happy life'—such an astonishing sentiment considering what a miserable time he did have of it—domestic problems, temper tantrums, and the rest.... Let's see. Ellen Terry—not quite the right category, but she's irresistible: she leaned out of her bed and wrote in the dust on her bedside table the word 'happy.' "

Timothy paused. "A lot of them were hard at work at the time," he went on. "Setting a good example. Petrarch, a day before his seventieth birthday, was discovered with his head pillowed on a manuscript of Vergil's; Bede was dictating his translation of the Bible to the end. Rossetti wrote an excellent poem on his deathbed; it's the one that starts:

> Our mother rose from where she sat;
> Her needles, as she laid them down,
> Met lightly, and her silken gown
> Settled—no other noise than that.
> Glory unto the newly born! . . .

"What about women authors?" I interrupted desperately.

"Well, let's see. Think, Dickinson, *think*. Not especially sensational, but when friends came in to tell Mrs. Trollope, who was very ill indeed, that Anthony had arrived from America and was hurrying to be at her bedside, she asked, 'Who is Anthony, and pray tell where is America?'—an odd question since she lived for some years in Cincinnati and, of course, wrote *The Domestic Manners of the Americans.* "

Timothy paused at the other end of the phone.

"Do you know General Sedgwick's?"

"General—?"

"Oh, hardly a literary man, but you should know him anyway. He was in the Sixth Corps with your great-grandfather, Adelbert Ames. He died in the Wilderness. Oh, his is excellent! He said, 'Oh, they couldn't hit an elephant at this dist—.' "

"What?"

"Yes. Absolutely what happened. General Sedgwick put his head up over a parapet to look at the enemy lines. Somebody must have warned him, and that's what he said, in considerable scorn: 'Oh, they couldn't hit an elephant at this dist—.' Last words. Very nice."

Another excellent informant was Brendan Gill, of *The New Yorker*. I told him about Dickinson. "You did the right thing," Brendan said. "You asked an Englishman. For some reason, every Englishman keeps forty or fifty of these last words on tap. Let's see. Well, Pancho Villa is supposed to have said, just before they killed him, 'What I do wrong?' "

"Oh yes," I said. "Actually, I was looking more for literary types."

"I've always liked that—coming, as it does, from a bandit figure."

"It's very nice," I said.

"Well, now. Edith Sitwell said, not quite at the end, but well along toward it, 'I'm dying, but otherwise I'm in very good health.' Do you know O. Henry's?"

"No," I admitted.

"At the time of his death there was a popular song that was the rage, with the line, 'Don't turn out the light, I'm afraid to go home in the dark.' Those were his last words. A friend was visiting him and at the bedroom door as he was leaving he asked O. Henry if he wanted the light off. That was the the reply: 'Don't turn out the light. I'm afraid to go home in the dark.' Quite nice. Oscar Wilde, of course. He turned his head to the wall and said about the wallpaper pattern, 'Either you go, or I go.' "

I said that I had always understood Wilde had said, "I am dying beyond my means."

"Well, he said that *too,*" Brendan said blithely. "He probably had four or five of them. Of course, biographers are always throwing us off. We now know through Leon Edel that Henry James' 'Ah, it is here, that distinguished thing' were not his last words at all, but that he trailed off from that with some rather maudlin, incoherent, quite un-Jamesian gibberish."

I asked Brendan if by any chance he had thought up something to deliver himself—any final quip or punditry. He said he meant to . . . he hadn't decided yet. Certainly it was important to do so well ahead of time, since very often the person, however primed, was so heavily sedated that something quite unexpected emerged at the last . . . often prodded by the subliminal effect of television or radio. "Toothpaste commercials!" he snorted. He had been reminded of a *New Yorker* girl whose father, a man of distinguished mind, expired after asking—everyone at the bedside bending over to hear what his excellent man had to say—"I wonder where the yellow went."

With all this in mind, I could not resist writing a few contemporary artistic acquaintances and asking them if they would turn their minds to how they might see their own ends. William Styron. James Jones. Capote. Terry Southern. Gore Vidal. Jules Feiffer. Hunter Thompson! I could never bring myself to ask them in person . . . seeing them at some social function . . . perhaps because a topic never came up which invited me to lean in easily and inquire, "Oh, . . . wondered . . . death . . . if you might describe . . ."

So I wrote them a careful letter, rank with apology, remarking that I felt I was conducting the sort of assignment junior editors at *Harper's Bazaar,* fresh from Vassar, are required to undertake. I told them about Mailer and the lion. I gave them the example of Jean Borotra, the great French tennis star, who liked to think of himself succumbing just as he served an ace on center court at Wimbledon. The letter was typed. It asked for a scene, or a deathbed quip. The copies sat around on my desk. Then after a while I sent them out.

The replies were varied. Gore Vidal's was predictably apocalyptic, though he neglected to give the circumstances. "When I go, everyone goes with me," he wrote. "You are all figments of my waking dreams and I suggest that each and every one of you shapes up and prays that I live long." Art Buchwald, like Borotra, fancied himself dropping dead on the center court at Wimbledon during the men's final—at the age of ninety-three. He provided a long obituary which described a career (which started when he was forty-five and picked up a tennis racket in a friend's house. "What's that?" he had asked) of such heroics that until his demise bodyguards had had to escort him from the stadium to keep the fans in "Artie's Army" from ripping the LaCoste crocodile trademark off his tennis shirts. The obituary detailed such exemplary habits as sharing his prize money with opponents if he felt they had played particularly well . . . and the fact that a whole wing had to be built on the Tennis Hall of Fame to house his trophies. The obituary ended with the announcement from the White House that the nationwide mourning, with tennis nets everywhere lowered halfway, was over, and that the president (President Christopher Kennedy) had ordered the nets to go up and the game to be played again. "Art Buchwald would have wanted it that way," the president's remarks had concluded.

Woody Allen's was terrifyingly private in comparison, an echo of his film *Love and Death*, in which Death takes on a corporeal form: "I enter a house where I have been invited. It's dark. Two large, silhouetted figures emerge from hiding. Their voices are familiar, though I can't place them accurately. One says, 'It's him.' The other says, 'I hope so.' Suddenly one grabs me and pins my arms to my side while the other holds a small pillow across my face. At first, the pillow is not centered properly and it takes some effort for me to adjust it. . . . Just before I succumb I hear one of the figures say, 'We did this because it was important, though not absolutely necessary.' "

Jules Feiffer sent his reply with an illustration depicting what had happened to him. The caption read, "In my twenty-fifth year of psychoanalysis I come up with the key breakthrough, the *answer!* I leave the session flushed with triumph. Too overwhelmed to endure the tediousness of public transportation I stride up town, oblivious of charging traffic, gangs of kids, blacks, free at last of the axiom that has ruled my life since earliest childhood.... On passing the Empire State Building I am crushed by a falling ape."

In the accompanying drawing the ape, in the eminent cartoonist's frizzly style, is properly massive, the victim squashed under a foot that looks like a mitten. His glasses, a book and a single shoe lie nearby.

Charles Addams, the great *New Yorker* cartoonist whose lugubrious turn of mind suggested an important source for a death fantasy, wrote (without sending an illustration) as follows: "I am hoping to break into a thousand tiny pieces while attending a theremin concert in Malone, N.Y., in mid January."

I was very excited by this, but not knowing what a "theremin" was, I had to reach Mr. Addams on the phone to ask. I said I was embarrassed not to know; someone had assured me that a theremin was a kind of "Eastern" religion, and the "cracking into a thousand pieces" was the consequence of being peered at by a waiflike holy man enveloped in a white shroud.

"No, no, no," said Mr. Addams. "Heavens no. A theremin is a musical instrument ... a sort of electrical coil which gives off a humming sound."

"Oh."

"It works by the distance you hold your hand to it. The closer you put your hand," Mr. Addams went on, "the higher the tone, until right up close you can get a terrific vibrational shriek. It's a bona fide musical instrument and by making the proper hocus-pocus gestures you can get Beethoven's Fifth out of it, or anything else."

I said I was relieved to know that he didn't want to be extinguished by a guru's glance, and he said, "No, no, no, no," again. "A theremin. A theremin." He said that he had thoroughly enjoyed working out the problem. "A real challenge," he said.

Allen Ginsberg, who wrote that he was spending an increasing amount of time in the "Company of Buddhists," allowed that for him there was very little difference between death and the deeper levels of meditation; he made it sound like a form of relaxation. "...dying," he told me, "I do that every time I sit down on my Zafree [which turned out to be a meditation pillow, thank Heavens], abandon my mind, observe thought-form fading, and the gaps between thought-forms, and breathe out my preoccupations. At the moment, one ideal death would be sitting on a pillow with empty mind."

John Updike also rather liked the idea of suspension. "Thought on dying? I can't decide if I'd rather go after the thirteenth or the fourteenth line of a sonnet; the thirteenth would give you something to do in the afterlife. By the same reasoning, while the ball is in the air, off the face of a perfectly swung 5-iron, and yet has not hit the green where it is certain to fall."

The watery end which Timothy pointed out had beckoned to so many turned up in a number of cases. Dotson Rader told me that Tennessee Williams, who had asked him to see to his funeral arrangements in one of the many wills he seemed to draw up on impulse, requested that his remains be dropped off in the ocean as near as possible to where Hart Crane had disappeared off the stern of the *Orizaba,* in the Caribbean.

"Tennessee, what on earth for?"

"Well, I've always admired the gentleman," Tennessee had replied, "and I never had the opportunity to meet him."

Hart Crane's suicide certainly had its ironies. His father had invented Lifesaver peppermints, which were exactly the same shape as the old-fashioned life rings that passengers tossed off the stern when they saw the poet bobbing in the liner's wake, and which, though they surrounded him on the sea, he studiously ignored.

James Dickey also had a nautical setting. He wrote me he dreams of voyages—his house is full of sextants and other navigational aids—and that he wished to die of navigational ineptitude, finding himself in Fiji in the hurricane season. "I wish the wind to begin to blow and the waves to roar. I will leave the sails up, so that I can hear the mast go like a barrage from the long guns of the Storm King's fleet ... sit in the dark cabin listening to the nails squeak as the hull is pulled apart. I shall then go on deck and founder with the ship, backing slowly off from it under water, as the craft sails down. The sky shall be clear, now, and I would like to catch one last glance of the moon through the thickening film and then feel it dance invisibly over me as I inhale the whole ocean."

It was an appropriate end for a poet who would, as he has said, like to be reincarnated as a migratory seabird—a tern, perhaps, or an albatross. He had written that the notion of reincarnation appealed to him very much, and that he remembered the lines of Theodore Roethke talking about coming back after death as an animal of some sort, or, "with luck, as a lion."

Joseph Heller, on the other hand, wrote that he had never given any thought to the matter, and on receipt of my letter had not really given any serious consideration either. "I expect," he wrote, "I really don't care much how it will happen, and I don't think I will care much more when it does. 'What a pity!' is about all I think I'll think, if I'm able to think at all, and 'What a pity!' pretty much sums up the way I think about it now."

How awful, I thought, when I received the Heller reply—I've given him a rotten day. For him it was not a question of fancy at all. "I know you want the truth," he had concluded his letter.

Kurt Vonnegut also turned out to be more truthful than fanciful. "I will tell you a story I never told anybody else," he wrote me. "Years ago, when I put the *Cornell Daily Sun* to bed late at night, I used to walk the two miles home to my fraternity house alone, crossing deep gorges and encountering other spooky things. So, I had spooky thoughts—and one of these became obsessive: that I would be killed, not there but eventually by a *dog*. I believe this still, and dogs, mind you, have always been my closest friends. I have been unable to shake this belief, and have often been turned back from some cheerful errand by the sound of a barking dog. I will consider it approximately in scale with my accomplishments as a writer and lover if a rabid Chihuahua does me in."

Donald Hall, the poet (who dies at ninety-three "forceful and gross ... too hot to handle down on the farm"), was one of the

few to speak of his "return." "At the Peabody House I grumble
... run my wheelchair into bannisters and nurses, and crawl
through dark corridors at midnight in search of cold stew or
listeners' praise. I die when the furnace freezes in the March
blizzard, and they find me white and stiff, stuck face-first to a
long mirror.

"Furious I return, crazy incontinent ghost, leaking ectoplasm
over the back chamber at Eagle Pond Farm, spelling my name
on the grass in dingy smoke, which pulses purple and indecent
upon the approach of the Committee for Psychic Research."

One of the writers I asked for a death fantasy was Alden
Whitman, who had been in charge of the obituary page of the
New York *Times* for a decade and wrote the longer pieces on the
great dignitaries. I had an idea that anyone absorbed in the
subject professionally would have an extraordinary fantasy to
offer—for some reason I thought Alden Whitman's expiring in a
Chinese *tong* war was refreshing, and I almost called him up to
suggest it—but he turned out to provide nothing of the sort at all.
"I suppose I should have formed some sort of apocalypse for
myself. But the awful truth is that I haven't." He went on to
suggest an empathetic relationship with the great majority of
those he wrote about who died peacefully in their hospital beds,
and he didn't see why that wasn't appropriate enough for him.
He was very apologetic.

Some of my literary friends, of course, did not reply, or said
that such thoughts were not evocative. I was not deterred in the
slightest. I even began to think up death fancies for such
friends—as I had wanted to do for Whitman. I asked Peter
Matthiessen if he would contribute a fantasy; just a day or so
after my request he told me that he'd had a dream which he
thought had been brought on by thinking about what I'd asked
him. In the dream the two of us were in Greece, he thought,
standing above the Aegean Sea. Apparently, on the other side of
the sea, on the African continent, the animals had all been
forced off the land by some sort of human encroachment ...
driven off into the water ... an environment in which they had
been able to adapt themselves so that they moved across the
ocean floor much as they had across the plains—a giraffe's head

just a couple of yards below the surface, and then deeper down the lions waited in the overhangs of the coral. Their manes were puffed out in the water, like the flow of a sea anemone, and when they came out to hunt, the gazelles moved from them in long slow leaps in which they had learned to tuck their legs back so they soared streamlined like seals. Peter and I were standing on the steps of a sort of Grecian amphitheater that fell away to the sea, with the steps leading underwater to the bottom, fathoms down, which stretched away, great white ponds of sand, quite visible in that crystal water so that we could stand and watch the animals far below. From deep down a lion began coming up the steps, moving slowly, and Peter said that he would have to step short of the surface because he couldn't get along in the air. But he kept coming up, his head breaking out of the surface of the sea, the water streaming off him as he came up the steps toward us, his mane wet-cat flat against his body.... We turned away from him.

Peter continued on about how the lion had walked down the corridors of a small Grecian temple behind us, his paws leaving wet marks on the marble.

"It is very pretty, but it doesn't have anything to do with death," I said.

"Well, that's what I dreamed," he said. "Quit fooling around with it. What do you want to know such things for? I thought you were writing a book about boxing."

"I am," I replied. "But a lot of other stuff seems to creep in. It's mostly about people taking matters into their own hands—gangsters, mercenaries, jealous lovers, outraged writers. I've developed a near-vigilante, antibureaucratic attitude I don't like at all. Maybe it has to do with how ineffectual we were with Ali when he had his title removed—those feeble efforts we made, as custodians, to press for his rights."

"And what does that have to do with death fancies?" Peter asked.

"Nothing," I admitted. "But I like your lion coming up out of the sea."

Predictably, sex turned up in some of the fantasies. Both Irwin Shaw and James Jones suggested that a bottle of white wine and a girl were essential props for their ends. But their replies were sketchy, just hinting at the scene. Jones' was outdoors. He had a tree in his.

William Styron's, on the other hand, was splendidly explicit: "I am almost certain that by now you have received a number of answers from respondents (I am thinking of the likes of Terry Southern) who, like myself, members of the non-sporting fraternity, have associated death in their fantasies with Eros rather than anything so preposterous as an encounter with a lion or serving an ace in tennis. Or any other *machismo*.

"However, my own death-fantasy does have a sporting overtone. Even though it is basically erotic.

"The single sport with which, over the years, I have ever felt any affinity is *water-polo*. It seems to me to be the perfect nonspectator sport, and marvelously dumb from a lot of other aspects, therefore it fulfills a lot of my antipathies towards sports in general. Anyway, in my fantasy I am captain of an all-male water polo team playing against an all-female team captained by Lee Remick. One of the necessary components here is the fact I am now *dans le cinquantième an de mon âge* (oh so true!) and that after an hour of fantastic slippery seal-like underwater combat with all this incredible pussy, put in the penalty box three times for crotch fouls, and so on, I find myself in the throes of a *cardiac arrest*.

"The game is halted. I am moved tenderly up on a water mattress. Grand, tender, bulging desires pass through me. Though terminal, I am enormously rampant. 'I am dying, Lee, dying,' I hear myself murmur. And the last earthly thing I know is the vision of the *captain of the other team,* Lee Remick, bending down to perform that little yummy touch of oral delight without which any passage into the Beyond is not complete."

Terry Southern's contribution of a "sports death-fantasy" was also sexual (just as Styron had prophesied), not surprising from the author of *Candy,* but one which in its complexity even Southern found a bit "odd."

His lengthy fantasy seemed to stem from "early visits with Gore Vidal and Larry Rivers to *China*—not your mainland China, mind, but your tiny off-land China"—to cover (for a quality slick magazine named *Pubes)* the "highly touted Great Ice Ping-Pong Tournament." Southern continued:

"As sports buffs will recall, the sport did not differ from ordinary ping pong so much *en principe* as in the actual mechanics of the game—making use as they did of rounded ice-cubes instead of the conventional hollow plastic balls, and using foam-rubber padding on both table and paddle surfaces to afford the necessary resilience for the bouncing cubes.

"I was attending the 'Young Ladies Finals' when the incident in question occurred. The contestants, ages 15 to 21, were clad ostensibly to give them 'the maximum in freedom of movement,' in what can only be termed the 'scantiest attire.' In fact there was a thinly veiled aura of *pure sexuality* surrounding the entire proceedings, so it did not come as a total surprise when I was approached by one of the 'Officials,' a Mr. 'Wong Dong,' if one may believe him, who, with a broad grin and a great deal of ceremonious bowing and scraping, asked if I would care to meet one of the competitors. 'Very interesting,' he insisted, 'a top contender.'

"I agreed, and soon found myself in an open alcove with 'Kim.' A most attractive girl of 18 or so—attractive except for what I first thought of as 'rather puffy cheeks.' I soon learned however that the puffiness was caused merely by the presence and pressure of an ice-cube in each cheek—this being the technique of preparing the ice-balls *('la préparation des boules')* for play, holding the cubes in the cheeks until they melted slightly to a roundness.

"The girl seemed extremely friendly, and Mr. D. now asked to examine the cubes. 'Ah,' he said, beaming, when she produced them—two glittering golf ball size pieces of ice—one in each upturned hand. 'We have arrived at a propitious moment,' he continued, turning to me again, 'the *boules* are now of ideal proportion for . . . *la grande extase des boules de glace.*'

"Not entirely devoid of a certain worldliness, I had heard of the infamous 'ice cube job' as it was commonly known—the damnable practice in my view of *fellatio interruptus,* or according to other sources, *'fellatio prolongata'*—whereby at the moment of climax, the party rendering fellatio, with an ice cube in each cheek, presses them vigorously against the member, producing a dramatic counter-effect to the ejaculation in progress. As I say, I was aware of the so-called *'extase des boules de glace,'* but had never experienced it—nor, and I would be less than candid if I did not say so, was I particularly keen—though, of course, I did not wish to offend my host—who then spoke to the girl in Chinese, before turning to me.

" 'It is arranged,' he exclaimed happily. 'Allow her to grasp and caress your genitalia.' And returning the cubes to her mouth, she extended her hand in a manner at once both coy and compelling, and with a grace charming to behold. Even so, I was not prepared to respond to this gesture without first working up a bit of heft.

"I adroitly stepped just beyond her reach, though quite without ostentation so as not to offend. 'Perhaps we should, uh wait,' I said, glancing about the room as though wanting more privacy.

" 'Ah,' observed Mr. D., with a most perceptive smile, 'you shall be quite comfortable here, I assure you.' And so saying, he drew closed a beaded curtain, and then stepped through it, bowing graciously as he departed.

"Alone with Miss Kim, I felt immediately more secure, and a slight unobtrusive squeeze assured me that a fairly respectable tumess was near at hand.

" 'Very well, Miss Kim,' I told her, 'you may, uh, proceed . . .' which she did, with, I can assure you, the utmost art and ardor. We had been thus engaged for several moments, and I was just approaching a tremendous crescendo—indeed was actually into it, when the beaded veil was burst asunder and in rushed the two madcaps, Vidal and Rivers!

" 'Get cracking, you oafish rake!' shrieked Vidal with a cackle of glee and inserted two large amyl nitrate ampules, one in each of my nostrils and then popped them in double quick order. Simultaneous to this, Miss Kim pressed with great vigor the two ice cubes against my pulsating member, and the diabolic Rivers injected a heady potion of Amphetamine laced with Spanish Fly into my templer vein. The confluence and outrageous conflict, of these various stimuli, threw my senses into such monstrous turmoil that I was sent reeling backwards as from the impact of an electric shock, torn from the avid embrace of the fabulous Miss Kim, who bounded after me in hotly voracious pursuit, screaming: *'Wait! L'extase des boules de glace COMMENCE!'* I now lay supine as she swooped down to resume her carnivorous devastation, while around us, obviously themselves in the crazed throes of sense-derangement, Vidal and Rivers pranced and cavorted as though obsessed by some mad dervish or tarantella of the Damned! Thus my monumental and unleashed orgasm, prolonged (throughout eternity it seemed!) by the pressure of the *boules,* and intensified beyond endurance by *drogues variées,* caused me to expire, in a shuddering spasm of delirium and delight. Ecstasy beyond all bearing! Death beyond all caring! 'I die!' I shouted (as I still do when I relive the experience) ... 'FULFILLED!!!' "

Southern went on to say in a postscript that of course he did not actually succumb ("Oh no, Vidal and Rivers had other plans") and that just in time "A newly arrived member of our party, the near-legendary 'Dr. Benway' (who later gained certain prominence as an author using the name William S. Burroughs) administered certain so-called 'remedial elixirs' (the exact nature of which I have never ascertained) and brought me around. In any event," Southern concluded, "I continue to re-live (almost nightly, in fact) the sensations of that most memorable experience."

I have on occasion tried to explain Southern's death fantasy to friends ... but have bogged down almost immediately, quite sorry I ever got started.

"What sort of a game? ..."

"Well, *Ice* Ping-Pong it's called ... and they get the ice balls just to the right shape and consistency by revolving them in the cheeks."

"Oh yes."

"Machines won't do the job right," I said.

"No, of course not. [*Pause*] Well, go on. What happens then?"

"[*Pause*] Well, what happens then is ... did I tell you Jules Feiffer's death fantasy? I did. Well, what about hearing it again? ..."

22

found myself getting very edgy and nervous about the fight coming up—not only because it was a deadline assignment (which was nerve-racking enough: as usual, *Sports Illustrated* had a backup writer and editor, Bob Ottum, on hand in Africa, in case I fell to pieces on the job) but because I knew that if Ali did not win, the chances he would ever regain the crown would be remote. I had nothing against Foreman, but if he knocked out his opponent it would emphasize once again the inadequacies of our little committees' trying to get Ali reinstated when the boxing commissions barred him from fighting. At least, back then, if we had been successful and if Ali's title were destined to be lost, it would have been lost in the ring, which was proper. So there was a strong emotional bias in his favor, a feeling which turned out to be shared by most of the writers in Kinshasa. Murray Goodman had organized a poll among them which showed Ali a three-to-one favorite, though the heavy odds announced on Foreman suggested that they were being much more hard-headed in the copy they sent home. Dave Anderson, of the New York *Times,* prophesied a first-round knockout of Ali, but it would not have surprised me if in the private poll he had cast a sentimental vote for the challenger.

Of course, the thought of Ali's winning the title back on his own was exhilarating. Indeed, it must have been a strong motivating force for Ali himself—that he was trying to get something back which truly belonged to him. I had heard him say about the title, "I started missing it. I heard about Frazier sitting in a restaurant and everybody standing up to see the champion. And then I heard about Foreman checking into a hotel with his dog and everybody crowding around the lobby. I began to see the value of it. I had took it for granted. . . . I want it," he added succinctly.

Motivation for a fighter can be the simplest of exercises. Sonny Liston once said that all he had to do was imagine that what stood between him and a night with Lena Horne was his opponent, which in the case of Floyd Patterson, who could not last through the first round of either of their fights, was a very successful device indeed.

As for Patterson, he once told me that his best fight was one in which he was *over*motivated—the second Johansson fight, for which he prepared by thinking of no one else for months, a near-venomous concentration on the Swede who had upset and humiliated him in their first fight. Patterson thought about him with what he called a "terrible and lonely intensity" which in the Yankee Stadium vented itself in an awesome hook that put Johanssen on his back, completely out, one foot sticking up and trembling like a frog's on a dissecting table when a nerve is touched, and Patterson, looking down in horror, suddenly realized that perhaps he had killed his opponent; he vowed never again to occupy his mind in such a way . . . which though it may have been a comfort to his state of well-being turned out to lower considerably his abilities as a prizefighter.

In Africa, Bundini told me something more about Ali's motivation, something I had not known. It was not only a matter of his trying to get back what belonged to him: always part of Ali's impetus to regain the championship was his relationship with the Black Muslims and the assumption that when he finished fighting he would become a minister. He could be fully reinstated in the movement only after he gave up prizefighting, because in his religion no sports are allowed. The laws and directives of the movement are tough: no dancing or moviego-ing, no dating or alcohol or tobacco, no gambling, no sleep "more than is necessary to health," no quarreling or discourtesy (especially toward women) or insubordination to civil authority (except on grounds of religious obligation—this last tenet the one which Muhammad Ali felt allowed him to refuse induction into the armed services). Because of the sports ban, Ali lived in a sort of benevolent exile with his manager, Herbert Muhammad, but was not officially a minister. "I have a dream," Ali said, "in which I put on my suit and get my briefcase ready, and my suitcase packed, and I'm going to see what the Leader say my mission is going to be. The championship strengthens my reputation as a prophet. No more am I the onliest lil' voice crying in the wilderness. The stage is set."

Bundini told me he played on these aspirations when Ali came back to the corner in his fights. "He want the championship so he can fish for Allah; so he can keep his mouth open and talk for the Muslims. Ali's a 'stop-look.' "

"What's that, Bundini?" I asked.

"That's a cat who's good enough to make you stop and listen to him," Bundini said. "But Ali's not the only one. There're other bright people, thousands of them, just like him; why, I heard a guy talk on a ladder back up there on 'Hundred Twenty-fifth Street, shabby suit, lived in a little room, and he could go on so you stan' there listenin' for four *hours*. But he was no champion. He was no Messenger.

"So that's what I remind Ali of sometimes in the corner—when Angelo has taken the stool down and the bell's just about to ring to start the round: I pat him on the trunks and I tell him that the other fellow is trying to *close his mouth,* take that thing away that make people listen, his championship, and I feel his body harden."

Actually, with the fight at hand, Ali looked sleek as an otter, and powerful. He told us he was ready. Ali always speaks of his body as if it were a separate entity, rather like a man speaking of his house and the possessions he would like to buy for it. Just before he left for Africa he discovered he was suffering from a diet deficiency of sugar, so he had begun eating apple turnovers and pies, long banished from his diet, and chocolate cakes, and he sat in his villa and talked about food, his eyes glazed, listing pies and cakes and ice creams and puddings in a loving litany.

"There's a fat man just aching to get in that body," Dave Anderson of the *Times* observed.

Ali had trained long for the fight—much of it back in the U.S. in a complex of cabins built on the side of a hill in the Poconos of Pennsylvania which Ali calls Fighter's Heaven. The grounds of the camp are set about with huge boulders which Ali had trucked in, each bearing the name of a famous prizefighter—a landscaping device obviously borrowed from Archie Moore's San Diego training grounds. On the boulders the prizefighters' names are all spelled correctly, but most of the signs around the place display an orthographic quaintness which turns out to be Cassius Clay, Sr.'s, who is a sign painter by profession. One of his notices read ALI A SLEEP DO NOT DIS TERV. Another, in a list of rules posted in the kitchen, proclaims, IF YOU MUST PINCHE SOMETHINGE IN THIS KYTCHEN PINCHIE THE COOKE.

Ali designed the camp himself ... very proud of its decor, which might be described as "Spartan rustic." Set in a corner of the main cabin was an indoor outhouse—which may seem a contradiction in terms, but I can't think of another way of describing it: a cupboardlike structure, the usual outhouse dimensions (indeed it lacked only the half moon on the door), standing as solid in the room as a grandfather clock.

Ali slept in the smallest of the bunkhouses, which he referred to as "My Uncle Tom's Cabin"—In it a narrow bed, a table with a Big Ben clock, a coal stove, and a table made from a tree trunk.

There was almost nothing to do at the camp. It was as easy to do heavy roadwork (on a country lane ironically named Pleasant Run) or chop trees as anything else. Even Ali spoke of his time there as "suffering," picking the place because it allowed him to "stay away from temptation." "Look at the kind of things that happen in the city," he said. "A pretty girl comes by and says we're having a party. She's just down the hall in two-fifteen. You're in two-ten across the hall. You're trying to sleep and you hear the music going *bum-de-bum bum bumbum*. So you get up and you say, 'Well, okay, just for a while.' But nothing like that can happen at the camp. Nothing around there but Pennsylvania Dutch and coal miners."

Once I went poking around his carport at the camp and counted two Rolls-Royces, a Volkswagen, a station wagon, a jeep, a nine-passenger Chevrolet van, a Mercedes 300, a "Blue-bird" mobile home, and a huge Greyhound fitted out with a shower and a kitchen and roomy enough for twenty people. As Ali has said, he has more cars than suits. He drives them himself, even the Greyhound bus. The destination panel of the Greyhound reads FOOLIN AROUND, and I wondered how many car passengers out on the highway, looking out the rear window, have seen the huge bus gaining on them, idly wondering if it's barreling along for Pittsburgh or Harrisburg or wherever, and have been startled not only at the odd destination but the sight of the familiar face up behind the big horizontal steering wheel.

Ali has a number of chauffeurs, but since he ends up doing the driving himself, the chauffeurs, one of whom is white, sit in the backseat of the limousines. At the toll booths on the turnpikes the collectors recognize the fighter and they lean down and ask how things are going. Ali tells them that times are so rough that he's taking on a little part-time work as a chauffeur. "I got the white boss in the back," and he motions over the seat with his thumb.

Nighttime is when Ali enjoys driving the best—just lazying through the Poconos in one of his machines, chatting with the truckers out on the highways on his citizens'-band radio. Users of the CB radios all have monikers, of course—River Rat, Wino Bill, the Cherokee Kid, and so forth; Muhammad Ali's is the Big Bopper.

Conversation on the citizens' band is supposed to be relegated to shop talk—road conditions, where the police radar traps are hidden—but since the identity of the Big Bopper is generally known among the trucking fraternity, someone will break in, unable to resist, and ask, "Big Bopper . . . you really fixin' on beating Foreman?"

"You ask a crazy thing like that when you talking to the Big Bopper?" The famous voice, incredulous, drifts over the airways. He produces a poem:

> I done wrassled with an alligator
> I done tussled with a whale . . .
> Only last week I murdered a rock
> Injured a stone, hospitalized a brick
> I'm so mean I make medicine sick

Cars were such an essential apparatus for him—bearing him away from responsibility, perhaps, but more likely because he is nomadlike and simply likes to stay on the move. His houses were always in the process of construction, renovation, crates in the yard either being packed or unpacked, and inside, the bare floors always had a phone sitting squatlike there, perhaps the first item installed, as if a ring, a conversation, and it would be time for everybody to get into the fleet of cars out back and move on to the next place.

I remember Bundini once describing the house Ali had moved into in Philadelphia. "The champ's home," he said, "has twenty-two phones."

"Twenty-two phones?"

"That's what I said. Every room's got two phones. There's two phones out in the garage. He carries a phone with him in a suitcase when he goes out. He's got four phones in the bathroom. There's two phones over there by the toilet bowl and two phones settin' by the bathtub. That bathtub is a swimming pool. You could set a dozen ducks in there and they could live just fine. There's a big rug in the bathroom and one of those Greek couches like you see queens, young queens, lounging on, eating grapes. And he's got a big color TV set sittin' in there right near the bathtub." Bundini began to laugh. "If that set falls in the bathtub, the champ's goin' out in living color!"

When Bundini got himself under control, I asked him about the bedroom.

"He's got a big round bed in there. The champ says 'bout

lying in that bed, 'I'm six feet three and no nothing hang off.'
Big bed. It sets in the middle of the room. The tables hang from
the ceiling on chains, and there's a gold bird cage hanging there
too. There's nothing on legs in the room 'cept the bed and a
lounging chair. It's the champ's house," Bundini said. "It's the
finest house a champ has ever lived in—why, there's a carpet on
the floor out in the garage."

"In the garage?"

"That's right. The carpet's there for the cars, a *brown* carpet,
as I recall, at least in the brown family. The garage has framed
pictures of cars hanging around the wall. When the champ gets
into one of his cars he's got a phone in the front and a phone in
the back and he always has got that phone with him in a black
suitcase. That is so he can stay in touch."

Ali had sold the Philadelphia house and moved on. Once, he
showed me through a great hulk of a mansion he had purchased
on Chicago's South Side, just a few houses down the street from
Elijah Muhammad's compound. The place was in the process of
being renovated. The interior had been gutted out. Water
dripped everywhere. A vast excavation in the cellar was to
contain the machinery for a large elevator—something of a
luxury, especially for a great athlete, since the building only had
three floors.

The bedrooms were enormous—thirty by fifty feet. One of
them had two fireplaces. The furniture for them was stored in a
warehouse—whole bedroom sets he had bought in Lebanon. "All
the bedrooms will be different," Ali told me. "One will have a
round bed. One will have a diamond-shaped bed. One room will
be Japanese with the bed flat on the floor. One room will be
Egyptian with camels on the wall, and the desert stars and the
moon. One room will be Indian with tepees to climb into, real
tepees made from real Indian material. . . ."

We spent most of our time in the kitchen, which was even
larger than the bedrooms. He pointed out where the stove was
going to be, and the refrigerators (two of them, so there'd be
plenty of room to "store things"), and the larders, and the racks
on the wall where the big forks for turning the steaks would

hang along with the ladles for spooning the gravy over the roast chickens, and he showed me the hooks for the big pots for the bean soup.

He looked out the window at a mansion of considerable size across the way. The rain glistened on its dull-red bricks. Just opposite, a woman was sitting by the window in an armchair, holding either a small dog or a cat—it was difficult to tell through the rain streaks on the glass.

"I'm buying that house and tearing it down," the champion was saying. "I'll put up a wall there, and there'll be a garden for the children to run in."

He stood briefly and stared at the house. I was mildly surprised that the woman in the chair didn't start up and glance nervously out the window, or that the animal, whatever it was, didn't jump down from her lap and scoot. The two of them were briefly in the champion's force field—he was seeing that mansion gone, and in its place the lawn, and some apple trees, and his daughters playing. It must have had some effect, some chill, on them.

I believed in that. No sport existed in which one's attention was so directly focused on the opposition for such a long time—except perhaps chess—so that the matter of psychological pressures was certainly in effect. No one was better at bringing them to bear than Ali. Many people thought that Sonny Liston's ineptitude in their two fights was probably caused by this—the constant, nagging awareness that his opponent's strange looney thought process was absorbed by Liston, Ali's image being carried around like a concept of a voodoo doll in a madman's brain, which must have been truly debilitating. Not long before he fought Liston, Ali drove his bus into Liston's front yard out in Denver, Colorado, at three in the morning, and called for Liston to come out; he was going to thrash him right there; lights began to go on up and down the street; police were called; Liston appeared at his front door, dressed in his underwear. I remember how Ali described it: "Three in the morning. He chased me down the street and I took off, jumping over bushes, and I could look back and see him coming after me through the moonlight—it was like a cartoon with the mummy coming through the trees. I was too fast for him, leaping over hedges, and I could hear him calling out, '... crazy ... crazy ... you must be crazy!' "

I myself had got a small sense of what it was like to be in a Muhammad Ali force field. In 1974 he and I had arranged the same sort of boxing bout I had had with Archie Moore; it was to be part of a documentary on boxing I had been asked to do by the BBC. Everything was arranged. He and I were going to meet in the ring in Louisville, Kentucky, where he was going back to be honored—it's his hometown, of course—on the eve of the Kentucky Derby. Everyone in the audience was to be in black tie—like the crowd at the Sporting Club in London.

Ali had agreed, somewhat sulkily, to the exhibition. When it was arranged, he said, sort of annoyed, "I mean, what am I supposed to *do* with you?"

I understood his annoyance. I said, "Oh, well, I'll train very hard. I'll really work at it."

He shrugged and then he asked, "You mean I'm supposed to *hit* you?"

I told him about my experience with Archie Moore.

"He *hit* you?"

"My nose went," I said. "Not the whole thing. Just the tip."

"Oh, yeah," he said vaguely.

But then the idea sort of got to him. We'd meet somewhere and he'd grin and announce that he was going to beat me up and knock me flat on my back and he was going to stand on my stomach there in the ring and do the Ali shuffle—he'd never thought of that before, sliding his gym shoes back and forth on a man's belly—and he thought I was just the person to practice on: besides, he saw me as a symbol of all the trouble he'd had from writers; he was going to beat me real bad so that my fingers couldn't work the typewriter keys. He'd motion me into the backseat of his car. "Let the Writer in there so he can stretch out and relax. We want him all cool and nice and sassy for the fight. Close the 'frigerator do' on him."

So, I began to sense what it must be like to be scheduled to fight him, to be the object of his attention. He settled you in some compartment in his head—like a toy in a trunk to be taken out on occasion and examined and pushed around on the floor. One became a possession of his, available for whatever fanciful manipulation came to mind. The phone would ring ... and the high voice, near a giggle, would say without introduction, "You is goin' to fall the *quickest*. You is goin' to fall during the ring instructions..." and then I could hear Bundini's voice in the background saying, "Don't scare him like that, Champ; he'll take to drinking cocktails," and the phone would click dead.

Once, he spotted me in the lobby of the Sheraton Hotel across from Madison Square Garden. I was heading for the elevator banks, and he guessed, quite correctly, that I was going to a party on the fourteenth floor—boxing writers, some such group where he had just been. Without my spotting him, he hopped into the elevator and went on back up. He beat me to the fourteenth floor. My elevator was crowded. We had made a number of stops. I moved to the front of the elevator as we came to the fourteenth floor, and as the door slid open, there he was, immediately in front of us, poised in a fighter's stance, with his chin tucked down, and he was glowering at me. If one ignored the fact that he was dressed in a brown business suit, he looked precisely as if he had stepped off a life-sized fight poster. I stared at him. I remember the sound of a short snuffled nasal snort—the kind he makes in the ring when he throws a punch—and he shot out a left-hand jab, thrusting it into the elevator, and stopping his fist just an inch or so short of my nose and then withdrawing it, all of it was swift as the flicker of a bullwhip. His presence, just there in front of us, was awesome, and behind me I heard a woman yell, and the crash of her bracelets as she caught a hand to her throat. We all continued to stare at him. Nobody moved to step out of the elevator—all of us stunned—and then abruptly the automatic doors began to slide silently shut, closing out the apparition, and the elevator shuddered slightly and began to move up.

The odd thing was that no one mentioned it. Nobody said, "What the hell was that?" The elevator stopped a few floors above, and a woman carrying a large shopping bag pressed to the front and began to get off, though perhaps a bit apprehensively, as if the thought had crossed her mind that the phantom fighter might be waiting for *her* down the corridor.

So he kept me thinking about him. I began to do some strenuous training. I remember I called up Bundini and asked him if he would refresh my mind as to how best to fight Ali. He and Ali once had a violent set-to and falling out (supposedly because Bundini refused to join the Muslims) after which he had gone out to Las Vegas to try to advise Floyd Patterson; it had been essentially an act of revenge against his old employer. But Patterson had been suspicious of Bundini; his entourage kept Bundini even beyond voice range. They bulled him out of the training sessions. He had been so firmly identified with Ali over the years that they could only think of him as a spy for Ali's camp. At one point he thought of disguising himself as a washerwoman and creeping down a hotel corridor with a mop and a broom in the hope of getting past Patterson's security, where he could leap out at him with his instructions. He *did* finally get to him—in the parking lot of the church where Patterson had gone for services the night before the fight and where the two men talked for a few moments, Floyd edging away. What Bundini told him had no effect. The fight was a dreadful mismatch, Ali at his meanest, taunting Patterson throughout—"white nigger"—and most every time Ali hit him in the face he punctuated the blows (there were a sickening amount of them) by calling out "boop! boop!"—an odd childlike steamboat-whistle sound. The other cry I remember was Bundini's "Cook, Floyd, cook!"—a plea which became more ironic as his choice began to fade.

"Bundini," I asked, "what did you tell Floyd there in the parking lot the time we went out to Las Vegas?"

"The way to fight Ali. I told him to put his tongue in the side of his mouth and pretend he's a nut. That's to begin with. There's no blueprint. He shouldn't try to think. A *street* fighter. That's what I would do if I was a manager fighting the champ—turn loose a street fighter."

I asked Bundini what he thought would happen down in Louisville and I could hear him giggling at the other end of the line, "Lawdy me! You in *trouble.*"

I remembered that Bundini had been cuffed around, too. Ali

would say to him, "You ain't so bad," and then *bop!* I never
could understand it.

"You don't understan' nothin'," Bundini said when I mentioned it. "Body got to hit somebody sometime."

"But you never hit back," I said.

Bundini laughed. "You 'spect I'm looking to hit back at the
champion of the *world.* Lawdy!" He shook his head. "I did hit
back once," he said. "Me and him fought in the bus once. I was
drinking in the back—and we fought back there for half an hour.
Everybody else—all the cooks and people—was too scared to
separate us. He hit me in the mouth—a lot of blood—but he
never close his hand to make a fist. I ain't tried nothing like that
again. No suh. You go right ahead, Gawge, and try to street-
fight him. You just go right ahead and put your tongue in the
side of your mouth. . . ."

I ran into Roger Donoghue, my ex-fighter friend, who was
very savvy about boxing. I said, "Bundini says I should street-
fight him—just go crazy in there." I asked Donoghue if he ever
remembered a fighter who fought berserk.

"It'd be idiotic," he said. "There were guys who fought savage,
but never mad. Ike Williams was savage. They said that he hated
white guys, but the one thing wrong with that was that he hated
black guys more. There were cruel guys—Jake LaMotta, who'd
carry a guy and torture him, keep him around for a while. But
that isn't the same as fighting crazy," he said. "Besides, what are
you going to get mad for?"

"Well, from being hit."

Donoghue laughed and said that he remembered an Italian
guy, Joey Scarlatta, in a fight for the featherweight championship of the Bronx, up in an arena off Jerome Avenue in the old
Yankee Stadium parking lot with ten thousand people watching,
and more hanging off the girders of the elevated, in which
Scarlatta's opponent suddenly hooked him in the groin and
knocked him down. "So Scarlatta got up and hooked him right
back—right in the balls. That might have been fighting berserk."

Wasn't the protective cup a pretty good shield? I wanted to
know.

"Straight on, maybe, but not from a hook," Donoghue said.

"Holy smacks," I said.

"Well, that just about says it," Donoghue observed.

The exhibition fight with Ali in Louisville never came off. A couple of months before it was scheduled Ali got his jaw broken in his San Diego fight against Ken Norton. He had missed most of the final week of training because of a sprained ankle ... suffered while trying to revolutionize the game of golf by trotting up and socking the ball on the run. He said that he had been hitting it three hundred yards by *walking* up to the ball. "I figured I'm going to do even better by giving it a running start." He hit a divot the first time, and on the next attempt lost his balance, swung all the way around, his club whistling in the arc of his turn, and he twisted his ankle badly.

So he lost the fight.... His mouth was wired shut for three months and he took sustenance through a straw. I happened to see the end of that fight on a television set in the corner of a passenger lounge at O'Hare Airport, in Chicago. I gave a loud groan when the verdict was announced, because preparations were well along for our exhibition. I had been training hard, running in the park, and I was getting ready to call up George Brown. It was going to be like old times. When I groaned in despair, a few people looked around; they must have supposed that I had lost a bet on the outcome. It struck me that among those waiting there—bored, out of sorts (it was storming outside, and with plane delays the lounge was crowded)—if it were possible to get everyone to divulge *exactly* what was on his mind, I'd certainly win a prize for what was on mine. There could have been someone in the lounge with embezzled funds in his briefcase, scared stiff about it; or someone else who had bet and lost the family car trying fill an inside straight, and had his wife to tell; or a man who had locked up his house to leave on a vacation and was now fairly sure he had left the kitchen range on.... But it was unlikely anyone could match the odd mental disturbance of the passenger bemoaning, and kicking at the red lounge carpet, that he was probably not going to get a chance to fight the heavyweight champion of the world ... and not quite sure whether he was sorry or relieved.

23

The day before the Foreman fight I ran into Hunter Thompson in the lobby of the Inter-Continental. He was exultant with misfortune. "Nothing's gone right," he told me. "I've rented a car in which you have to dim the lights to get the steering wheel to turn. I haven't got my credentials for the fight. I don't know anything about what's going on around here ... except that I think they're closing in." He leaned forward alarmingly. "Don't you think they're closing in?"

"Well, I don't know," I said. "Who do you think—?"

"Who what?"

"*Who* do you think is closing in?"

"Well, that's what *I'm* trying to find out," he said. "I went looking for Bill Cardoza—he's the guy from *New Times*—at four A.M. last night to ask him if *he* felt they were closing in. I found him, but then I felt we should have some preliminary drinks and before I could ask him I lost him somewhere in Kinshasa. I couldn't remember the number of his room in the Memling Hotel. That's probably where he had gone. I believe in kicking in a door if you really want to find somebody—especially in a good police-state hotel like the Memling. So I got up into the corridors and I gave a couple of doors one of my Kung Fu sneaker shots; the people inside really got tightened up. 'Who is it? Who is it?'

"This place is heavy with agents," Thompson said abruptly. "Did you see the guy running after George Foreman with a tennis racket?"

"When?" I craned to see. The lobby was jammed.

"Yesterday," he said.

"Maybe it was a guy who'd just finished a tennis game and wanted an autograph," I suggested.

Thompson raised an eyebrow at my innocence.

"Maybe it was just someone asking for a game..."

"The disguise was too perfect," Thompson was saying.

I told Thompson that there was a Swedish correspondent staying in the hotel who played tennis. Maybe he was the one. Indeed he and I had played on the one court in Kinshasa—an ancient shadow-shrouded clay court with a fine sheen of lichen covering most of it where we had been supplied with a thin-limbed gawky ballboy with the disconcerting habit of working the tennis balls up his leg with his bare toes so that he could grasp them without bending down. I had the feeling, halfway through my description, that Thompson was going to tell me *he* was an agent, and of course he did. "You were under The Eye," he said. "We are all under The Eye."

Thompson suddenly pointed across the lobby at a dudish black gentleman in a red velvet jumpsuit with portholes down the side of his pant leg. "I understand that's Baby Cassius, a failed lightweight."

"I don't think so," I said. "I've been told he's a San Francisco jeweler."

Thompson shrugged. "Well, that shows you how reliable my sources of information are."

"Did you ever find Cardoza?" I asked.

Thompson shook his head. He went on to say that he had not found Cardoza, but there had been an excellent problem with the Memling management's being summoned by people alarmed at having the slats in their doors kicked at. "I blamed Cardoza," Thompson said. "I told them he was a high police official from a foreign police state and that when he'd had a few drinks, it was his natural impulse to kick at a few doors—keeping his feet in, so to speak."

"Cardoza must have been pleased."

"Cardoza does great things for me too," Thompson continued. "He introduces me around the bars in Kinshasa as George Foreman's doctor. I say, 'Yes, yes,' and I say the champ is in great shape except that his lymph glands are falling out."

"Have you had a chance to talk to either of the fighters?" I asked.

"Oh my God, no," Thompson exclaimed. "Just the other day I saw Muhammad Ali going by and it was a chance to shove him into a doorway so's I could get to work on him. But there wasn't any way I could get him alone. It was in the ivory market downtown, or some damn place without anyplace to get him off to myself!"

He swayed back and forth like a circus bear. He moaned and told me that he was just about ready to give up on his assignment entirely. "I don't know anything, that's the trouble," he admitted. "I don't know who to ask and I don't know what to ask. But then I don't *want* to know anything. Except," he added mysteriously, "I *do* know what is going to happen tomorrow night at the fight."

"What's going to happen?" I asked.

"Why should I tell you?"

"Well, you said that you've given up on your assignment."

"I'll *bet* you, that's what. I'll bet you five hundred dollars."

"You'll bet me five hundred dollars that *what*?"

"That something very strange is going to happen."

"What's going to happen?"

"I'm not going to tell you. But I'll bet you five hundred dollars."

He suddenly asked me to do him a favor, and when I nodded somewhat tentatively, he said that he had figured out his angle for his *Rolling Stone* story. He was going to watch the fight with President Mobutu Sese Seko *himself*—there in the presidential palace—because it had been in the newspapers that the president was not going to the fight in person but would be watching it on television. "That's *the* place to be," Thompson said. "Hobnobbing with his nibs, and the generals all standing around, scraping, and mixing drinks and so forth, and the president and I rocking to and fro on our heels and looking at the TV set and conversing about things in general."

"Maybe you can tell him about the huge torpedo that the Republic of Congo people are going to fire across the river at Kinshasa."

"What huge torpedo?" he asked. "So what I need to do," he went on without a pause, "is to get into the palace. You got to help me get in."

That was my Thompson assignment. I did something about it, too. I went to see Jacques, the manager of the Inter-Continental, and asked him what he could suggest. He was puzzled, and I had to repeat a few times what Thompson wanted. Jacques nodded and said that the president did not live in the palace but rather in somewhat frugal circumstances in the middle of a paratroop complex, four battalions of soldiers around him, and the only way he could imagine getting in to see him would be to brazen ahead and very glibly keep telling the guards that the president expected him—this distinguished American journalist—and perhaps the president would hear about it and invite him in. He thought the chances were a thousand to one.

Hunter was delighted when I told him. "A thousand to one! Fine," he said.

"You could get shot," I told him.

"Steadman will be interested in all this," Thompson went on. "It smells just right."

I wished him luck. I envied him, really—thinking up these strange approaches. His *Rolling Stone* readership required very little of the event he was sent to cover, except, perhaps, that everything go *wrong* ... to the degree that the original purpose of his assignment was finally submerged by personal misfortune and misadventure. His superb *Fear and Loathing in Las Vegas* started as an assignment (indeed, from my own magazine, *Sports Illustrated*) to cover the Mint-500 off-road dune-buggy race in

Las Vegas. But there is only the most fleeting reference to the event in the copy. He was like a man stepping onto the wrong train, or boat, without a dime to bring him back, or even to communicate from where he was delivered, and not too anxious about it either—as if wishing to feast on the excitement of chance and ruin.

Sports Illustrated required a more prosaic approach. Mine (I decided) was to try to set my story against the background of mumbo jumbo. After all, West Africa was the locale of incantations and voodoolike spells and witch doctors—they were called *féticheurs*—and even President Mobutu did not make an important move without checking with his witch doctor, and an astrologer or two.

Jacques had told me of an odd rumor: that the word around the Kinshasa betting circles was that Muhammad Ali had been to see the best *féticheur* in Kinshasa—indeed, the same pygmy that President Mobutu himself used—and that a considerable sum had been paid for the *féticheur* to cook up a hex against George Foreman. The odds were three to one against Ali at the time, and it seemed a judicious if last-ditch sort of step to take. The spell was supposed to manifest itself in the form of a beautiful girl "with slightly trembling hands"—Jacques himself described her as being "fevered up" with vibrations—who would clasp Foreman's hand in some chance meeting—like Blind Pew passing the Black Spot in *Treasure Island*—and the strength would slowly drain from him.

I asked Bundini. Had Ali been to see a *féticheur?* "What are you talking about?" he cried. "There ain't but one witch doctor in Africa, and that one is Bundini. What is you talking 'bout? They ain't *room* in Africa for more than one witch doctor when that witch doctor is Bundini."

Bundini to the contrary, I was told that the *féticheurs* were common enough, especially at sporting events, where they turned up on behalf of clients to try to influence the outcome. Even a soccer club had its own *féticheur,* who was considered as indispensable to the team as a star fullback. I asked Jacques if a

féticheur was fired if the team did badly. Very rarely, apparently.
He told me that the *féticheur* always kept on the offensive
whatever happened: if the team was beaten badly it was because
the players did not *trust* him properly, or they'd had the wrong
sort of *thoughts,* all of which had gone to counteract his
efficiency. The *féticheurs* got very huffy if their teams lost; they
stomped around.

Of course, the fans also had their *féticheurs*—hired largely to
advise, and to protect large bets placed on a game. They
performed voodoolike ceremonies to influence the outcome. At
the events, they could be seen in their seats surrounded by their
clients, distinguished, Jacques said, by a slightly different form of
dress, many amulets, and a curious stilted walk when they
moved around, like someone with a stone in his shoe; they kept
up a sustained humming sound up in the stands, which increased
in volume if things were going awkwardly down on the field.

Jacques said that he had heard that the betting was heavy on
the Ali-Foreman fight, the *féticheurs* working long hours to keep
up with the demands made on them. I asked what a *féticheur*'s
ceremony was like; Jacques said he had never been to one, but
he understood that a fire was built under a casserole in which
were put parts of animals, keepsakes, small carved representa-
tions, various herbs and stones—a not untypical rat's nest of a
witch's brew—and after a number of incantations the contents of
the pot were dried out and put in a small pouch, which
contained the "hex." The closer the *féticheur* could get these
pouches to the object of one's proclaimed support (or ire), the
more efficacious their power, and I was told that at the soccer
matches the pouches were thick in the grass around the goal
posts, and often out on the field itself, where a player would step
on one and feel a dried antelope bone crack underfoot, and gulp
as he wondered against whose fortunes the hex had been
directed.

Considering the amount of betting on the Ali-Foreman championship, Jacques suspected that under the ring at fight time
there'd be dozens of hex pouches placed down there by the
féticheurs.

I asked Jacques if he could arrange a *féticheur* ceremony for me—it seemed appropriate to my story—and he nodded but said that the best *féticheurs* (the pygmies like Mobutu's were the most highly regarded) were expensive and that even a low-grade ceremony would cost upwards of five hundred dollars.

I winced. Wouldn't it be possible to get a second- or third-echelon *féticheur* ... or perhaps one who might come out of retirement just this once? Five hundred dollars for a hex pouch was not an item I could imagine explaining (I saw myself as translating *féticheur* as "wizard") on a *Sports Illustrated* expense voucher.

"Well, what do you want the *féticheur* to do? What do you want of him?" Jacques asked. "A win for Ali?"

"Well ..." And then I felt awkward, sensing it was the wrong way to resolve things after all these years: have it on my conscience that if Ali *did* indeed win, I would always associate it with an incantation and the steam drifting out of a witch doctor's pot. "No, I think that would be unethical—for me, at least," I said rather pompously, surprised at myself considering my hopes for Ali. "I would like him to cast up a spell that would assure that I ... *um* ... would write a fine story."

"But you *are* a writer," Jacques said.

"Yes, Jacques, but things go wrong. Some of us need help."

Jacques said he was going to have a lot of trouble explaining this to his contact who would be arranging for the *féticheur*. Quite out of the ordinary. These people dealt in very straightforward things—their spells killed off someone's brother, or produced a winning goal for a football team, or made an enemy's cow come down with rickets, that sort of thing—and working on smoothing out a man's literary style, well, that was probably going to *tax* them: what were they going to put in the pot to simmer? My typewriter keys? Wasn't there something else I could ask of him?

Well, yes, if he couldn't get a *féticheur*, I did have another idea. I described it. Everywhere in Kinshasa, at the ends of the avenues or in the center of the traffic circles or in front of the government buildings, I had noticed great bare stone pedestals, flat on top, with weeds springing up through the cracks, on which, I was told, had once stood the statues of Belgian colonial rule. They had been toppled off during the shift of power—even the famous statue of Stanley himself peering up the Congo from under the palm of his hand like an Indian chief. But they had not been destroyed or melted down, as one might have thought. I had learned they had been thrown helter-skelter into a giant shed near the National Museum, where they lay in a clutter of cast-iron horses and kings. A strange sight they must have presented—symbolic of the temporary nature of power and the shifts of fortunes, not unrepresentative of the character of the heavyweight crown—and perhaps I could get Ali, or Foreman, in there for a *Sports Illustrated* photograph, leaning nonchalantly against the iron flanks of a great horse on his side—the copper-eyed kings and emperors standing or collapsed at odd angles around the shadowy and cluttered room—and perhaps it would work even better than the mumbo-jumbo stuff with the *féticheurs*. I explained this to Jacques. "You wish to get in this shed?" he sighed. "*Very* difficult," he said. "They are very sensitive about that place." He shook his head. "Writing must be very difficult," he said. I think he was beginning to sense that I truly *did* need a *féticheur* at my craft.

As it turned out, Jacques was not able to arrange either for a *féticheur* or for a visit to the shed near the National Museum. He saw me wince, especially at the bad news about the *féticheur*. He explained he had been unable to track one down at such short notice—after all, the fight was only hours away—and they were all "Booked," as he put it, by clients wishing to influence the outcome; there simply weren't enough *féticheurs* to go around.

I stalked about. To me it seemed a considerable blow—the loss of a peg on which I had relied. "I wish I could help you with your story," Jacques said. "You'll just have to go to the fight and *look.*"

24

It was after midnight when Norman Mailer and I drove out to N'Sele to join the entourage for the fight, which was scheduled for four A.M. to suit the closed-circuit television viewers in the U.S. Deprived of a *féticheur* ceremony, we had arranged with Angelo Dundee to stick with Ali's camp right up until fight time. Ali never seemed to mind writers' watching him at a time when most people in his profession shunned outsiders.

We found his handlers standing on the esplanade overlooking the Zaire. The moon was directly above, and there was almost no conversation—the group looking out over the great river with the hyacinth drifting by in dark clumps, the mood that of men getting ready for a patrol. We waited. I remembered an old African legend about the moon: that two tortoises were called upon to carry a moon and a dead man across a river. The tortoise that carried the dead man had short legs and it drowned. The other tortoise had long legs and managed to get the moon across to the other bank—which is why, according to the myth, a dead moon always reappears and a dead man, fortunately, does not.

Ali appeared. He was dressed in a black shirt, black trousers, and the heavy workman's boots he considers the trademark of his profession. I remembered how scornful he had been of Foreman for wearing a pair of patent-leather shoes in Salt Lake City during a promotion there for the Africa fight, almost as if he had let down the side to be seen in such things—"fly-fly shoes," Ali had snorted.

Ali's mood was somber out there in the African night and during the bus trip into the stadium. His dressing room was a white-tiled morguelike place with white pillars and fans revolving slowly in the ceiling—Mailer whispered that it made him imagine a comfort station in a Moscow subway. Ali came in blinking, squinting his eyes open and shut. He looked at some of the long faces around him and asked, "What's wrong around here? Everybody scared?"

He told us that he had watched a film earlier that evening called *Baron of Blood,* and *that* had scared him, kept him right on the edge of his seat, but he wasn't at all frightened about what was coming. "No, sir!" We stared at him in awe. "This ain't nothing but another day in the dramatic life of Muhammad Ali," he said. "I am used to dramatic things, but when I think of our leader—for forty-two years predicting the doom of America and the weight of this on his shoulders—why it makes *this*"—gesturing out toward the ring—"look like a child's kindergarten. When I walk out, it's easy. I am fighting for a man who is the Messenger of the Lord. *Scared?* A little thing like this? Do I look scared?" He grinned and put on a mock face of fear, his eyes rolling. "Nothing much scares me. Horror films. They scare me. Mummies scare me. I also fear Allah, thunderstorms, and bad plane rides. But this is like another day in the gym."

Someone reached for his hand and said, "Good luck!"

"Luck!" he repeated in derision. "No, man, *skill!*"

He sat Norman and me down next to him on the rubbing table, and, opening up a fight program, he began comparing the records of the two principals much as a handicapper works the *Racing Form.* He ran his finger down Foreman's column of victories, an awesome list of KOs. "Look at this," he said blithely. "Foreman's only had three rounds in 1973." It seemed not to concern him that the three rounds had taken place in *two* fights, a statistic which truly suggested a devastating slugger. "Now look over here at me ... all this experience ... I had fought *all* these names." He began reading them off.

When he was done, he hopped off the dressing table and undressed. He drew on a long white ceremonial robe with black trim designed for his ring entrance. He turned in front of a full-length mirror. "It's a Rolls-Royce robe. Look how long and beautiful it is. It's African and everybody can look at it and tell it's African." Usually Ali wears a robe designed by Bundini, who now stood by looking uncomfortable.

"Where's your robe, Bundini?" he asked.

Bundini brought his forward. It was also white, trimmed with green and red stitching, the Zairian colors, and it had a map of the country designed above the heart. Bundini wore a matching jacket. The Everlast firm had made the pair from a design Bundini had worked up himself.

"Look how much better *this* one looks." Ali spun like a dress model in front of the mirror. "It's African. Bundini, look in the mirror, and see how pretty."

Bundini refused. With his robe draped over his arm, he stared fixedly at the fighter.

Ali slapped him, the sound quite sharp in the dressing room. "You look when I tell you!" He slapped him again. Bundini stood with his feet together, swaying slightly, still holding his robe and looking at Ali. He kept refusing to look in the mirror.

I was stunned. I had seen it happen before, and while I had some vague notion that any outburst with that huge drama so close at hand was acceptable (Mailer did not seem surprised at all), it seemed so gratuitous, and shaming, with everyone standing around, that I loathed Ali suddenly. Bundini seemed such an odd target—his concern and love for his fighter was almost pathological. In the ring he never took his eyes from him—a singleness of interest like a parent's staring at a three-year-old—and sometimes he cried seeing Ali hit by a sparring partner's punch. In Ali's villa I remember the painter Leroy Neiman, a day or so before showing his wash drawing of the fighter down on the canvas in the first Frazier fight, mentioning that his pose, lying on his side, was exactly that of Michelangelo's *Dying Gladiator.* "Everything you do," he had said to Ali, "you do classically, even getting knocked down." Ali had looked at him. "What do you mean 'classically'? You mean going down 'pretty'?" Neiman had nodded, and Ali looked quite pleased with himself. But Bundini, I remember, could not stand this sort of conversation, or the picture, and he ran from the room. It seemed so contrary that this sort of affection should merit the concussive slap that Ali gave him in the dressing room.

No one seemed to take much notice. It was perhaps quieter, the hum of the fans turning, and then Ali shrugged and went over and sat on the edge of the training table. In a low singsong voice he began a soft litany of verses and musings, some of which stretched back exactly ten years, to the night in Miami when he had won the championship from Sonny Liston: "Float like a butterfly, sting like a bee . . . you can't hit what you can't see . . . I been broke . . . I been down . . . but not knocked out . . . it must be dark when you get knocked out . . . it's strange getting stopped . . ." concluding the little review of his career with the cry very much discouraged by the Zairian officials but one he could not resist and which brought him clear up to the present: "Now let's rumble in the jungle!"

He hopped off the table and tried on a number of white boxing trunks with black stripes down the side, turning from side to side to judge them in the mirror, slapping fretfully at the bulge made by the fighter's protective cup.

Then abruptly he set about making Bundini feel better about the incident over the robe.

"Bundini, we gonna dance?" he called. Silence.

"Ain't we gonna dance, Bundini? You know I can't dance without you." Silence.

"Hey, Bundini."

"You turned down my robe," Bundini said moodily.

Ali shrugged his shoulders. He said that a champion ought to be able to make *some* decisions on his own—what to eat, when to sleep, what to wear—and he did it so beguilingly that finally Bundini, despite himself, had a smile working at his lips.

"Are we going to dance?"

"Aw, hell, Champ," Bundini said resignedly, "all night long," drawing the line out like a response at a prayer meeting. The atmosphere in the place brightened considerably.

Someone called out, "Ten minutes."

Angelo Dundee began to tape Ali's hands. Doc Broadus, Foreman's representative, stood by to watch. Ali looked at him. "Tell your man to be ready for the dance," he said.

Broadus said, barely audibly, "He can't dance."

"What's he say?"

"George Foreman's man says he can't dance."

"He can't *dance!*" Ali made a face of disbelief. "He can't dance! But what we goin' to *do* if he can't dance?" Around the room his people began to smile, most of them sheepishly, as if high spirits were not at all appropriate to what was coming up just minutes away.

Ferdie Pacheco, Ali's physician, came back from watching Foreman's hands' being taped. "Man, is it tense in there," he said. "Not a sound. They got Foreman's face covered in towels so you can just see his eyes looking out."

"He's getting warmed up for the Big Dance," Ali said. "Are we going to dance with him?" he called out.

"All night long," Bundini replied.

With five minutes to go, Herbert Muhammad took Ali into the only area of privacy in the dressing rooms—which was a toilet stall—and I heard him reading the official words of exhortation from the Muslim hierarchy in Chicago, his voice rising, and I thought of the two of them jammed in there over the toilet bowl, a very tight squeeze, with Ali as big as he is and Herbert quite squat, so that there must have been barely room to hold out the paper to read from.

I preceded Ali out to the ring. The night was soft. The giant illuminated portrait of President Mobutu glowed above the rim of the stadium. As I walked through the infield toward the ring, I wondered how Hunter Thompson's plans were coming along. He would be out on the boulevards somewhere in his strange car that only steered when he jiggled the light dimmer. The crowd was huge and noisy. I wanted to check quickly under the ring to see if I could find any little fetish bags. I imagined dozens of them under there, their necks tied with thongs to keep the chicken claws and the clay figurines and whatever else was in them from spilling out. The photographers were packed in and around, arranging their equipment; their legs set up a formidable picket barrier.

"Can I get through, please?"

"Where are you going, man?"

"Under. I'd like to get under ..."

I don't recall that any of them were startled; perhaps they thought that I was an electrician of some kind. Underneath, I crouched below a crisscross of wooden beams. The earth was soft and cool to the touch. What an odd place from which to cover a fight, I thought—to try to gauge from the shuffle of feet, the thump of a body, what was going on up above on the canvas. I put my fingertips up and I could feel the tremor of feet against the drumhead surface. Officials were up there, walking around. Under, it was dark. No sign of the pouches. I ran my hand across the grass, feeling for them. Then I had the sense that someone was down there with me ... the glint of a hand, perhaps the shine of a robe. A witch doctor on the other side of the beam? perhaps two of them?

One would not want to be discovered fooling around with fetish bags, trespassing among them, and the enormity of trying in the surreal darkness to reason with an aggrieved witch doctor crossed my mind.

"Coming out, please."

I pressed forward against the photographer's legs, appearing from between them like an animal emerging from its burrow, just as the roar went up from the crowd's greeting one of the fighters coming out of the tunnel leading back to the dressing rooms.

I sat next to Norman. He was fine and valuable company because so often he caught a mood up there in the ring that he would share; he paid tremendous attention; it was disconcerting, too, because when a fight began and settled into its course, he would begin to sway, and the rhythm and motion of the fighter seemed to activate him like puppet strings, so that he bobbed and weaved and ducked, just as they did, occasionally snuffling like a fighter clearing his nostrils. I suppose the ultimate of this would be if his head snapped back at a good left hook and he fell backward over his press-section chair. Well, it wasn't as sympathetic as that, but he did seem plugged in to the fighters. Only after the round was done would he reach up and adjust his school-marm spectacles; he would scrawl some notes in a fold-back notebook, and chat until the bell sounded for the next round, when he would stiffen slightly, as if a master puppeteer up above the ring had picked up his sticks.

But certainly neither of us—nor anyone else in that huge crowd—expected to see what happened in the first round. The mental image of Ali *dancing* was what everyone expected. He had kept telling us that in the locker room. Not one person except for Ali himself had the slightest suspicion that at the sound of the opening bell he would take a few flatfooted steps toward the center of the ring and then back himself into a corner—with Foreman, scarcely believing his eyes, coming in after him.

For one sickening moment it looked as if a fix were on, that it had been arranged for the challenger to succumb in the first round and that it would be best if he went quickly and mutely to a corner so that Foreman could get to work on him. It was either that or Ali was going through the odd penitential rite he seems to insist on for each fight, letting himself suffer the best his opponent has to offer. In either case, the consequences were appalling to consider. We all stood. I shouted at Norman, "Oh, Christ, it's a fix,"—an echo of the fifth round of the Liston fight ten years before—hardly hearing myself in a great uproar of sound. Ali's corner men, in the shrieks reserved for warning someone walking blindly toward the edge of a cliff, urged their man to stop doing whatever he was up to and start *dancing*.

Far from obliging, Ali moved from the corner to the *ropes*— traditionally a sort of halfway house to the canvas for the exhausted fighter who hopes perhaps the referee will take pity on him and stop things. Here was Ali in the same spot, his feet square to his opponent, stretched back out over the seats at the angle of a man leaning out of a bedroom window to see if there's a cat on his roof, his eyes popping wide as if at the temerity of what he was doing, while Foreman stood in front of him and began to punch—huge, heavy blows thrown from down around the hips, street-fighter style, telegraphed, obvious, so that we watched Ali slip and block them with his elbows and arms, but it seemed inevitable that one of them would penetrate and collapse him.

With the bell coming up for the end of the round, Ali suddenly came off the ropes. While Foreman's arms were down in punching position, Ali hit him with a series of quick, smart punches in the face, the best of them a right-hand lead that knocked the sweat flying off Foreman's head in a halo. But compared to the fusillade Ali had been undergoing, it seemed the mildest sort of retribution: the crowd roared, but I suspect there were few who sensed they were not in for a night of lunacy after all. When Ali came back to his corner, I could hear his men storm at him as he sat on his stool: "What you doin'?" "Why don' you dance?" "You *got* to dance." "Stay off the ropes."

The second and third rounds were carbon copies of the first—hugely exciting, though very few of the ingredients of scientific boxing were involved. No countering, no feinting, no moving; simply the terrifying and unique process, as it turned out, of seeing a man slowly drained of his energies and resources by an opponent swaying on the ropes, giving him—as Angelo Dundee was to say later—"a lot of nothing."

In the third round, in the midst of tremendous pressure from Foreman, Ali lurched up off the ropes and hit him some concussive shots, staggering the champion, and suddenly everyone except Foreman seemed not only to understand the plan but to see that it was working almost inexorably. Ali's corner men looked at him with eyes wide with delight—I described them on my pad as a trio of Professor Higginses looking at their Eliza and realizing they might pull it off.

In the fourth round Ali began to talk to Foreman. It is not easy to speak through a boxer's mouthpiece, but Ali began to do a lot of it, more as the rounds progressed, as if it would quicken the matter of Foreman's destruction—"Is that the best you can do?... You can't punch.... Show me something!... That's a sissy punch!"—until Ali finally came around to what must have been a devastating thing for Foreman to hear: "Give it *back* to me! It's mine! Now it's my turn!"

There was no change in Foreman's tactics. He kept it up, this useless exhaustion of energy; he threw his punches in immense parabolas—one almost heard him sigh with futility as he began them—the punches coming slower and more ponderously, until, rising off his stool after the bell and coming across the ring to deliver them, he seemed as pathetic in the singlemindedness of his attack plan as the mummies of Ali's beloved horror films, lurching through the mists after the life-giving draughts of tana leaves. Indeed, it occurred to me as I watched transfixed that "the Mummy," one of the inspired appellatives Ali finds for his opponents ("the Washerwoman" for George Chuvalo, "the Bear" for Liston, "the Rabbit" for Floyd Patterson), had been Ali's name for Foreman, and nothing could have been more descriptive of Foreman's groping for him in the last rounds. "I am going to be the Mummy's Curse," Ali had said a few days before the fight.

By the eighth round nothing was left inside Foreman. He seemed to wobble off the stool, swayed by the shattering roar of the crowd as he advanced on Ali; he seemed a man getting off a sickbed. I yelled at Norman, "The girl with the slightly trembling hands! She's *got* to him! The succubus!" He looked over, alarmed. It occurred to me that he could not have had the slightest idea what I was talking about.

With Foreman helpless, Ali did not toy with him any more than a mongoose fools with a prey exhausted from striking. He tagged him. In the sad business of dispatching a hulk, he did it quickly and crisply. Foreman staggered, and I heard Bundini shout, "Oh my Lawdy, he on Queer Street!"—the last sound the fighter must have heard before the bruising sock that put him away, collapsing him to the canvas on his back.

Archie Moore, his face round and benign under his wool cap, came up onto the ring apron; he moved along the ropes, trying to attract Foreman's attention with arm motions, signaling him to turn on his stomach and get a knee under him to push himself up. The count went to nine. Then I saw Archie give a small wince of despair as the referee swept his arms briskly back and forth over Foreman, as if he were safe at home in a baseball game.

George Foreman's dressing room was a huge chartreuse emporiumlike parlor—like a Las Vegas anteroom. He came back into it under his own steam, but with his handlers close at his shoulders. He was wearing a red and blue robe with WORLD CHAMPION embroidered on the back in schoolboy script. Did they pack these things away, I wondered, these deposed champions? "Where's my dog?" he asked. He touched Dago on the head; the dog's tail swept back and forth. Foreman was guided to the rubbing table; he lay back on it, gold lamé towels draped over his shoulders, ice packs applied to his face. He asked Dick Sadler if he had been knocked out cold. Then, like a hand flexing a leg that had gone to sleep, he began testing his senses, counting slowly, backward from 100, and then calling out the names of everyone he could think of in his camp—the cooks, the guards, even Bill Caplan—a doleful call of more than twenty names. Caplan's name stuck in his mind. "I have a statement to make," he said. "I found true friendship tonight. I found a true friend in Bill Caplan." Caplan could not have been more surprised; he wondered if there had been neurological damage. "The Ping-Pong games. All those games." Foreman *did* seem in the grip of a euphoria. "With this fight I have found serenity in myself," he was saying. "I felt secure until my corner jumped into the ring." Everyone stared at him astonished. "I was not tired. I truly felt like I was in control of the fight. It was a privilege to fight in my ancestors' land. We have built a bridge that never will be broken again." The fists were pounding on the dressing-room door, from people outside trying to get in. "I'm still my own man. He won," he said unsurely, "but I cannot admit that he beat me. It's never been said that I have been knocked out."

He continued: "When Ali dies, he should have only the words on his headstone: 'Heavyweight Champion of the World.' Nothing else."

Then he began to repeat, at times so slowly that it seemed as if he were stumbling through a written text, what he had so often said in dressing-room statements following his victories: "When the competition is tough, there is never a loser. No fighter should be a winner. Both should be applauded."

Everyone stood around uncomfortably, knowing that it would finally sink in that for the first time in his career his generous words for a loser referred to himself.

I ran into Bundini in a corridor outside. He was subdued—perhaps by the incident with the robe. "Ali gets into trouble when he don't listen to me," he told me. "He wasn't wearing my robe for the fight when Ken Norton opened up and busted his jaw. He cursed me in Lake Tahoe and Bob Foster cut his eye. He is crazy to do that to a witch doctor like Bundini."

"What a fight tonight, though, Beau."

"Yeah," he said. "We took the butterfly and slowed him down, put wet on his wings, and more sting in his bee."

I asked him if he had given Ali any special instructions during the fight. "I told him to stop playing," he said. "The tank was empty. He had nothing in front of him."

"What a fight, though, Bundini," I said again. I knew that I was wearing an idiotic grin. "Oh, my, Bundini."

I wanted to get in to see Ali, but the press of people in his dressing room was so thick that I went out through the corridors to take one last look at the infield and the ring there. It was full of celebrants now—cheerful black faces, many of them tall young men with bare legs and knobby knees, miming what had happened there earlier, the stumbling collapse of Foreman, imitating it by tumbling down on their backs, and then leaping up and doing it again; but of course there were many more Alis, hands up and lolling back on the ropes. Small bonfires burned on the stone steps of the stadium. People did not seem anxious to leave—staring down into the ring as if the mock shows going on there, clumsy and Chaplinesque as they were, would give them at least a sense of what had so excited them. The thought crossed my mind that kids who for years in the backyards and the dirty streets had emulated the more flamboyant style of their idol, the butterfly who floats, yet stings like a bee, or practicing their version of the Ali shuffle, would now have to add to their repertoire his innovation of leaning against the ropes, peeking out over his gloves.

I rode back out to N'Sele sitting next to Angelo Dundee in the camp bus. Ali and Belinda were up ahead of us in the backseat of a Citroën. We could see its twin rear red lights ahead in the gray dawn. At every village and crossing the crowds that had heard the news were out along the road, often whole rows leaping in exultation, so that the passing of our small caravan—headed by a police car with an orange beacon revolving on its roof, then the Citroën, and the two camp buses with his people—seemed like the passage of a military column through a liberated territory.

Angelo was wearing a Los Angeles Rams souvenir cap which he had "defused" (as he described it) by writing on it with a felt pen "can't win." Angelo is a rabid Miami Dolphins fan.

"Look at those lines of people!" I said. "Thousands. Leapers. It's like a Kennedy campaign."

"He can howl tonight," Angelo said. "He did it all himself. I was a spectator like everyone else. You never know what he's going to do. He like to kill us with fright in that first round, lying back like that and getting hit. But he told me after the third round that Foreman's punches were acceptable. 'They're not that bad,' he tells me, like he's been tasting things out of a box of candy."

He took off his hat and began turning it in his hand.

I suddenly said that I thought it was one of the . . . oh, I think I said *titanic* moments in sports, saying it in such heat that Angelo looked over surprised. It had all been sweetened by being such a surprise, I went on to say: Ali wasn't supposed to win, truly, and for many of his supporters it was going to be a question of trying to accept that he too would fail, just as we—in trying to write one pathetic letter to some senators—had failed in trying to right something wrong, and he would be getting himself *smashed* in the bargain, as if to punctuate our ineptitude. But it had not turned out that way at all. He had *prevailed;* he had got back his title himself, which was the purest way that unhappy business could have been straightened out.

Well, wasn't that the satisfaction of watching sports? Angelo wanted to know.

I ventured that sports didn't usually have that ingredient of redress. The great moments people wrote about and remembered about sports were a nice combination of dramatic timing and skill—Bobby Thomson's home run, or Aaron's 715th, Venturi winning the Congressional, or Jerry Kramer's block for the Packers, Spitz' seventh medal at Munich, Havlicek's last-second shot against Philadelphia in '67 ... none of these moments, however fine, were involved with an issue such as retribution. I tried an example: "If Yepremian of the Dolphins kicked a seventy-yard field goal to win the Super Bowl ..."

Angelo brightened. "Wait a minute. That involves a big issue—my happiness. Talk about *titanic!*" he said, laughing.

"Well, maybe for him," I said. "And for you."

"Damn right," Angelo said. "If he misses, he kills me."

I agreed that my sense of well-being had been greatly bolstered by what had happened that night, mostly, I thought, not because I preferred Ali to Foreman but because another issue had been resolved at the same time.

"You're telling me you're happy."

"Sure."

"You did this once, didn't you?" Angelo asked.

"Box? Archie Moore hit me in the nose. Some guy said, 'That's the start of the education.' "

"I hope he told you that it's better to pop the guy than being popped."

"He didn't say how it worked," I said.

"Did it scare you?" Angelo asked.

"I guess so," I said. "But there was something so inevitable about it. I mean, once I had committed myself, there was nothing I could do to stop it. It wasn't as frightening as I thought it was going to be."

"Well, you wouldn't catch me doing a thing like that," Angelo said. "My favorite stance in the ring is when I have my right foot outside the second rope and I'm climbing out."

We rode along for a while and something came to mind I had not thought of in years. "Hey, Angelo, I think the most frightened I ever was at the fights was once sitting at ringside, just on the aisle, with the back of the press section across the way, and down the aisle came Frank Costello, the biggest New York gangster there was. He had a bunch of his henchmen with him. Everybody was watching him come, nudging one another, jaws dropped.... God, he looked just like a hood *should,* wide-brimmed fedora, and a white tie, very trim man in a long overcoat, coming along not looking to one side or the other, very lordly he was, leading this little group ... and I ... oh, I suppose it was to impress the girl I was with, or I'd had a beer too many, or maybe even—and I hope this is so—I truly wanted to express my feelings about this guy putting himself on display like a great baseball player coming down to take his place at ringside ... I let out a long, quite audible hiss ... *s-s-s-s-s-s-s* ... which died away somewhat prematurely, because Costello heard it and as he came opposite he stopped. He turned slightly and faced me, looking down at me sitting there—a grim pale face, with these narrowed eyes—just the way they're supposed to look. His group stopped around him, also looking down ... a very tight situation ... and my heart began to crash in my chest ... petrified."

"What did you do?" Angelo asked. "For Chrissakes."

"Well, there was this strained sort of confrontation, just for a second or so, and then I heard a voice coming out of my mouth. 'Down in front!' it said. It came out more a squawk than I meant it to. But the great thing was that suddenly someone in back of me said, 'Down in front,' and then the person next to him said the same, and my girl called 'Down in front,' and so did the person on the other side of her, and suddenly we had a whole chorus of people shouting 'Down in front!' louder and louder ... very intense ... and of course it was directed at *him* because there was absolutely nothing going on in the ring behind him at all. Well, the hoods backed down. What else could they do, all these people yelling at them? Costello moved off. He looked a little surprised when all this shouting began—his face smoothed out and he looked like someone had poked him in the rear. Off he went. My girl turned out not to know who he was. 'Who was that?' 'C-c-c-ostello,' I said. 'Fr-r-r . . .'

" 'Well, who's *that?*' And she damn near died when I told her."

Angelo laughed. "An awkward situation. I wonder if you enjoyed the fight."

"I can't remember. Probably not. But I remember the Costello thing. It was a very rich feeling," I said. "Part of it was being scared. The other part was that everybody stood up against him. We never truly did that for Ali when he got faced down."

We looked out the windows, the crowds thinning out as we got out into the countryside, but knots of people were still standing by the road, leaping when they saw the Citroën and who was in it.

"What a ride for him," I said. "What do you suppose he's thinking up there?"

"I guess you'll be asking him," Angelo said.

The first drops of rain began to fall. Heavy low clouds scudded on the hills ahead. Angelo and I reminisced. It had rained furiously in Miami after Ali had won the championship from Liston. Now the rain drummed on the bus roof. The big wipers worked futilely against the sheen of water on the windshield. "Listen to that rain," Bundini called from the back of the bus. "Bullfrogs is falling out of the sky." For the last miles to the compound we crept along . . . through the first true downpour of the rainy season. In a quirk of luck that finally graced the fight, the storm had held off just long enough. We heard later that as it came down the river toward Kinshasa it knocked out the huge signal-sending facilities to the satellite, so that the millions who watched the fight on closed circuit or on television would have seen their picture fade and go blank if the storm had come through an hour or so sooner. When the storm reached the stadium, the water drained down the seats on to the grass and toward the center of the field, as if the ring stood above a giant sluice. Under the stadium stands, the water stood a foot deep in Foreman's chartreuse dressing room. In the city it thrashed the flame trees and sent the bright blossoms swirling down the boulevards. I thought of the great tin shed near the National Museum with its jumble of cast-iron horses and kings ... and how in the dawn—on this day when the heavyweight crown had shifted hands—the sound of the rain on the roof must have been deafening.

had a number of people to see the next day. I dropped in to see Hunter Thompson.

I found him in his room. "I got everything stashed behind the pipes," he said, after he had peeked out a crack in the door to make sure who I was. "The authorities could search the room and unless they had one of those sniffing dogs this place'd check out clean." He prowled around, three steps taking him the room's length; he turned and bumped into the bed. He was wearing his aviator glasses. I perched upon a chair to keep out of the way. "This is a bad town for the drug scene," he was saying. "In Nevada you can shoot anything into your body you want. You can get stark naked and lie in the backseat of a Pontiac with the accelerator wired down, and touch the steering wheel from time to time with a toe, and if you lose control at a hundred twenty m.p.h. going along Route Ninety-nine, all that happens is that you spin out into the desert and kill a lizard. But Kinshasa . . . it's a bad scene."

I asked him about the fight.

"What fight? Oh, I didn't go to the fight. I stayed in the hotel swimming pool. I lay on my back looking at the moon coming up and the only person in the hotel came and stared at me a long time before he went away. Maybe he thought I was a corpse. I floated there naked. I'd thrown a pound and a half of marijuana into the pool—it was what I had left and I am not trying to smuggle it out of this country—and it stuck together there in a sort of clot, and then it began to spread out in a green slick. It was very luxurious floating naked in that stuff, though it's not the best way to obtain a high."

"No," I said.

"But a very luxurious feeling nonetheless."

Thompson began mixing himself a drink. "I don't know the time, but it feels like the evening—cocktail hour, isn't it? Do you know what I paid for these two bottles of bottled water? Five-twenty! Every day here I get this hideous whipping. I need human contact . . . preferably nine nipples."

I blinked and asked him how he had found out about the result of the fight.

"I went to bed after my swim," Thompson said. "So I got the news this morning. Somebody slipped the hotel newspaper under the door."

"So you didn't try to see the fight with President Mobutu."

"Who?"

"The president. You said you had some idea about being with him and watching the fight on TV."

"On TV? Frankly, I've had my mind on something else. My big concern is how to get these two enormous elephant tusks I bought in the ivory market out of the country." They stood in the corner, reaching halfway to the ceiling.

He told me that the day before, bringing the elephant tusks back to the Inter-Continental, he had almost been thrown into a Kinshasa jail.

"Are the tusks illegal?" I asked. I'd given up asking him about the fight.

"Frankly, I don't know. I bought the tusks off a street person—probably an informer of some sort—but they are in some sort of raw state which attracted a great deal of attention. I mean, the elephant wasn't still attached to them, but he might just as well have been." Hunter went on to tell me that riding around Kinshasa with those tusks was like running through an airport with two large plastic bags of heroin, or perhaps a bazooka under each arm. But apparently the problem was not only the tusks but that he had been going a hundred miles an hour in that strange automobile of his around a traffic circle. The car had "got away" from him. He had been flagged down by a military car and a soldier carrying a machine gun had climbed in alongside him and the tusks in the front seat. Hunter sensed that the soldier was trying to get him to drive to the jail down by the river waterfront but yelling at the soldier that he didn't under-stand—"Quien sabe? Quien sabe?"—he started heading for the Hotel Inter-Continental at a rattling speed, the soldier hanging on, the gun barrel waving back and forth by Thompson's ear, as he finally made the ramp and roared up to the entrance. He stepped out and told the concierge to explain to the soldier that Bill Cardoza, down in the Memling Hotel, was the person to see if there was any complaint to be lodged—an important foreign police chief—and with that he turned and sailed into the lobby with his tusks. He had a feeling that the soldier had impounded his car, but there was a certain amount of smug satisfaction in knowing what sort of a monster car—all those weird electrical connections—the authorities had a hold of. "Unless they know how to work that dimmer," Thompson said, "a lot of innocent people are going to get killed out in the streets of Kinshasa."

I remarked that he certainly lived right on the edge. Hunter nodded and said that he'd feel himself lucky if he got back into the U.S. alive. As he paced up and down, turning like a caged mink, I was reminded of Norman Mailer's death fantasy—being taken by an African lion—and Thompson laughed when I described it and he said that such a thing wouldn't be bad for Norman at all, would it, and he wished him luck.

I couldn't resist asking him what his would be.

"Well, vehicular, of course—something in a very fine car." He sat on the edge of the bed and with surprising calm went on to say, "Back in the U.S. there was a mountain I used to drive over

in the sixties on the way down from Louisville past Birmingham
to the Elgin Air Force Base—Iron Mountain, I guess they call it:
a lot of big houses upon it and rich people from Birmingham
and the road is sort of scenic, with big entranceways and fine
views, and there's one place where you come around a sharp
curve to the left, and straight ahead, down beyond the cliff, is
the city, acres of steel mills and Bessemer furnaces and smelting
yards below—and my concept of death for a long time was to
come down that mountain road at a hundred twenty and just
keep going straight right there, burst out through the barrier and
hang out above all that in ... well, it was important that it was
the right sort of car, the Jaguar XK120, though later on I began
to connect the XK140 with the fantasy, painted white, though
sometimes I vacillated between white and British racing green,
which is very nice too, and it had to be a convertible, of course,
because you'd want to feel the air against you ... and there I'd
be, sitting in the front seat, stark naked, with a case of whiskey
next to me, and a case of dynamite in the trunk, or *boot*, it
would be in a Jaguar, honking the horn, and the lights on, and
just sit out there in space for an instant, a human bomb, and
then fall on down into that mess of steel mills. It'd be a
tremendous goddamn explosion. No pain. No one would get
hurt. I'm pretty sure, unless they've changed the highway, that
launching place is still there. As soon as I get home, I ought to
take the drive and just check it out."

I finally left Thompson puttering around in his room and went
to look for someone more knowledgeable about the fight the
night before—an expert with a less quixotic turn of mind. I
found Archie Moore downstairs in the lobby. I said I had some
questions.
    "I had a friend in St. Louis who could sleep with his eyes
open," he said. "I have often wondered if he could do it through
an interview."
    "Probably."
    We sat down and had some coffee. "Well, it was a big
surprise," he said. He told me that just before leaving the locker

room for the ring the Foreman boxing trust—himself, Foreman, Sandy Saddler, and Dick Sadler—had joined in a ritual of prayer the four have practiced since Foreman became champion in Jamaica with his win over Frazier. They had done it in Caracas, Venezuela, before the Ken Norton fight, in which Foreman knocked out his opponent in the second round, and now, in Zaire, they held hands again, and Archie, his head bowed, found himself struck by the thought that he should pray for Muhammad Ali's safety. "In fact," he said, "I found myself praying, and in great sincerity, that George wouldn't *kill* Ali. I really felt that was a possibility—George truly doesn't know his own strength."

"Well, what happened?" I asked. "George had him on the ropes."

"Ah, but George did not really have Ali on the ropes," Moore said. "Ali put himself there, which is quite different, and so you can say that he was following the tradition of the great rope fighters. . . ."

"Rope fighters?"

"Like Young Jack Thompson, a good welterweight champion back in the twenties, who I hear tell used the ropes like a spider, skittering along them."

Moore cleared his throat. I knew from experience that he had an analogy to offer.

"Ali swayed so far back on the ropes that it was like he was sitting in an old convertible Cadillac. The 'fifty-four model," he added, being very accurate about such things. "Now, George tried to enter from the side doors. But they were *shut*. So George began to bang at them, hitting at Ali's arms that had the elbows protecting his hips, on up to the gloves protecting the lower mandible. On occasion George struck Ali some tremendous blows on the upper cranium, causing Ali no little discomfiture. But Ali weathered that, and he cunningly convinced George that he could not punch, and other nonsensical things, until George began to behave like he actually believed it, until this tremendous puncher lost his power from punching at that Cadillac's doors and he turned from an atomic force into a firecracker. In short," said the great ex-fighter, "as they say in the idiom of Brooklyn, he blew his cool."

"What would you have had him do?" I asked.

"I wanted him to do two things," Moore said after a sip of his coffee. "I wanted him to utilize his left hand in the form of a jab. In the fifth round he jabbed Ali four times and shook him up, and I thought, well, he's found the key. But he jabbed him back into those ropes, and when he saw him there he went back to those long swipes.

"Then, second, I wanted him to keep his hands up. We had all talked to him about that. I told him, 'George, Ali can punch, too. He can't punch near as hard as you can, but he can hurt you. Please go out with your hands up—and keep them up at all times.' "

He leaned across the table. "But it was an excellent spectacle. One of the all-time-great fights. George should not feel bad about it. He gave all that he could muster—in his own way, of course. If he had been more scientific, he would have won."

Moore got ready to leave. "One more thing," he said. "The psychic values can move a fighter far beyond his expectations, or retard him below his ability. The latter is what happened to George. Pandemonium got into his mind. Something else was in Ali's. He thought the title belonged to him."

"That's right," I said.

"There is big psychic value in that," Moore said.

Dick Sadler was in the lobby, perched upon his favorite table, his legs swinging back and forth like a sulky schoolboy's. He looked confused, as if a friend had turned and lashed at him. Indeed, every time I ran into members of the Foreman entourage that day (except Moore, with his wise, unflappable mien) I saw that same bewildered look—what had happened was so unexpected that black magic *must* have been involved, as if the girl from the *féticheur* with her "slightly trembling hand" had indeed got to Foreman to drain the strength from him.

"I don't understand," Sadler was saying. "Everything we planned to do—cutting the ring, overpowering Ali, going after him—was designed to put him on the ropes. And there he was. Just exactly where we wanted him." His voice was high-pitched with frustration. "The bird's nest was on the ground. It was time to sit down to eat the feast. You tuck your napkin under your chin. I didn't figure anything could go wrong." He winced and gave a high strange squeak of despair. "Anything George hits, he hurts. He hit a man, Perralta, the Argentinean heavyweight champion, on the arm, and he broke it. He put Perralta in bed for four days."

I left Sadler mourning in the lobby and went out to N'Sele to see the new champion. He was just up—having slept most of the day—sleepy, wandering around his villa, yawning, but rolling his shoulders, and flexing his muscles to keep loose as if he had another contest to worry about that evening. He was trying out his title. "Heavyweight champion of the world," he said, drawing out the words. "It's going to take some time to sink in."

I suddenly remembered the scene ten years before in his training quarters in the little corner house in North Miami— when I had wandered into his room and discovered his mattress covered with HEAVYWEIGHT CHAMPION OF THE WORLD, scrawled dozens of times across it with his name alongside, just to see how the two linked together would look if he won. Now it was his once more. I told him that his winning it meant a lot to others of us, too.

He did not seem especially interested. He kept up his limbering exercises, jerking his chin over his shoulder to stretch his neck muscles. I asked him what moment he would remember about the victory—what I had wondered the night before with Angelo Dundee. Could he tell me what he had been thinking about in the Citroën, driving down those lanes of exulting Africans jumping in delight? He stopped his exercising and thought for a moment. Yes, he could remember very exactly— that as he and Belinda lounged in the backseat of the car, they began talking about how odd it seemed to be coming out of a fight into the light of day. Usually, fighters arrive at the arenas in the late afternoon or the early evening, and after the night's work they come out into the darkness and the neon lights flicking and the bright lights shining in the windows of the bars across the street. But this time they had come into the dawn. He did not suggest there was any symbolic value to what he recalled; he just stated it as a matter of fact.

"And what about you?" he asked.

"You mean, what I remember?" It was one of the first questions I had remembered Ali asking me in the years I had known him.

He nodded, and I said, "Well..." And then I was not really able to oblige him ... such a welter of possibilities that I was barely able to muster anything. I finally said, "What I remember is that it made me so unbelievably content."

His expression did not change. I thought for an instant he looked vaguely miffed, as if for giving me his memory I owed him something more in return than what I had said.

Reporters began to drift in. They had finished their fight stories and columns, most of them anguished reappraisals of their predictions: Maury Allen, of the New York *Post,* started off his column with "He *is* the greatest" and he compared his "passion and dedication" to that which helped "Washington at Valley Forge, Lincoln survive a nation split, and Lindbergh survive an angry ocean crossing," and he called for "parades and a call from the White House." Lester Bromberg, also of the *Post,* commenced, "Can I stand in front of the class and cop a *mea culpa?*" and he proceeded to do so in extravagant terms. The stories were not untypical. None of the copy I saw seemed bitter, however wrong the author might have been with his prognostications. Indeed, one of the prevailing sentiments in the stories was that rarely had red faces been so easy to bear, and that never had so many large bets been handed over so cheerfully to their winners. That is not to say there was not *some* sensitivity. Dave Anderson, who had predicted Ali would be knocked out in the first round, caught me looking at him, and before I could say "Ahem" he called across the room, "Okay, but I got Oakland in five!"—this indeed an accurate assessment he had made in print a month before of how the World Series was going to come out.

I kept a few notes. Ali seemed vaguely distracted, as if the exhilarations of the fight were drifting away. He sat on a sofa, hugging a pillow to his middle. I heard him say that he would like to do something for the president of the U.S. "Perhaps he could send me somewhere for my country. I am known everywhere," he said wistfully. "I could enlighten countries about ours. I would do anything if it didn't interfere with my religion or Islamic beliefs."

No one seemed especially interested in this. Pencils remained poised over pads or worked on little inconclusive designs on the paper. The questions began to come about the fight. He started off, rather wearily, "I trained according to what might happen ... trained on the ropes, getting used to the idea of seeing punches coming ... I might have to go there if he tagged me ... or if he cut the ring so's I couldn't dance ... he was too fast, cutting the ring ... on the ropes he came for me like a pot of honey was out ... flies and bees come to honey ... he is in trouble with me on the ropes ... because boxing is like running a long race ... Foreman is a puffer ... he don' pace himself ... I'd have danced in the eighth round if he'd gotten up...." The pencils worked busily. His voice was stronger now.

I wandered out onto the esplanade. The sound of band music drifted from distant amplifiers. The river swept by. The great thunderheads were building up beyond the low hills of the Congo. It was getting difficult to remember the exhilarations. So often, even after the most inspired of athletic performances, the joy of having been a witness seems to slip away with infuriating ease, however one tried to hang on to it, so that driving back in the traffic from those ballparks, or arenas, everyone quiet in the car, one's mind full of what had been seen, the image flowed away, like a sink's emptying, so that one was left with just the vaguest sense of evidence.

"What was great about it?"

"Oh, ma, you should have seen it ..." But finally just a mood remained. "Content." That *had* been an odd word to offer the champion: "content." "Hey, tell us about Africa!" "Well, I was content, very *content*." The euphoria I had felt was too difficult an emotion to remember, much less to explain, and as I stood on the esplanade I wondered what image, or feeling, would prevail when afterward, the story done, I thought back on Zaire and what had happened there.

What surprised me was what finally did. It turned out to be something quite else. It had nothing to do with the fight. Ali would have been puzzled. It was something I remembered about the airports up on the Uganda border, where I had gone during the postponement of the fight. At these back-country airfields, while I sat on a piece of luggage waiting for a flight to appear—the air services worked on no discernible schedule—I noticed that down at the end of the runway, when a plane turned to take off, scores of village children would appear at the edge of the Tarmac, their black heads just showing above the tall elephant grass. They would position themselves behind the plane, and as the prop wash or the jet thrust would increase, bending the elephant grass flat around them in quicksilver waves, they would lean forward precipitously, arms akimbo for balance, into the hot wind sweeping back, until finally, especially if the engines were jet, revving up to full throttle before the pilot let the brakes go, they would be picked up in that awesome blast and tumbled across the flattened grass, their shouts of laughter lost in that maniacal roar. I went down to watch when there was a plane. It seemed a game for them—to see who of them could keep to his feet, the wind whipping his face silly, the clothes flat against his lean body, without being flung away, so that once in a while the plane would move off down the runway, taking its rattling power with it, and someone would survive, the elephant grass rising slowly up around him as if the earth were now in support of him, and I could see friends running toward him, shouting at him gaily, congratulating him apparently, and as the grass came back up to its full height I could see them surround him, and their dark heads as they jumped like dogs above the grass to see if anything else to test them was coming out their way.

INDEX